Boston's Back Bay

BOSTON'S BACK BAY

The Story of America's Greatest
Nineteenth-Century Landfill Project

William A. Newman and Wilfred E. Holton

Northeastern University Press   Boston

PUBLISHED BY UNIVERSITY PRESS OF NEW ENGLAND
HANOVER AND LONDON

NORTHEASTERN UNIVERSITY PRESS

Published by University Press of New England,

One Court Street, Lebanon, NH 03766

www.upne.com

© 2006 by Northeastern University Press

Printed in the United States of America

5   4   3   2   1

The authors gratefully acknowledge permission to print the photograph of the locomotive
"N. C. Munson" on the title page. Photograph courtesy of the Needham Historical Society, Inc.,
Needham, MA.

Library of Congress Cataloging-in-Publication Data
Newman, William A.
    Boston's Back Bay : the story of America's greatest nineteenth-century landfill project /
William A. Newman and Wilfred E. Holton. — 1st ed.
      p. cm.
    Includes bibliographical references and index.
    ISBN-13: 978-1-55553-651-0 (cloth : alk. paper)
    ISBN-10: 1-55553-651-4 (cloth : alk. paper)
      1. Sanitary landfills—Massachusetts—Boston—History—19th century.
    2. Back Bay (Boston, Mass.)—History—19th century.   I. Holton, Wilfred E.   II. Title.
    TD795.7.N545   2006
    627'.5490974461—dc22   2005035371

Contents

Preface

Boston's Back Bay neighborhood is well known today for its upscale housing, large, high-rise office buildings, expensive specialty stores, fine hotels, and excellent restaurants. What is now called the Back Bay extends from Arlington Street to Massachusetts Avenue, and from the Charles River to the Amtrak and MBTA tracks. Area residents and tourists alike are familiar with highlights of the neighborhood, including Commonwealth Avenue, Newbury Street, Boylston Street, the John Hancock and Prudential towers, Copley Square, and the Charles River Esplanade. Many of Boston's most expensive condominiums and apartments are in elegant Victorian brick and stone town houses on the Back Bay's tree-lined streets, with their brick sidewalks and nineteenth-century-style gas lamps. Thousands work in the area's offices and retail establishments. The Back Bay today contributes heavily to Boston's image as a prosperous, modern city with a rich historical legacy.

Many people today puzzle over the strange name of the Back Bay and know very little about the Back Bay's creation in the second half of the nineteenth century. In fact, before about 1820 the region was a tidal marsh that appeared to early settlers to be a large bay behind the town when it filled with water at high tide twice each day. Only one road, now Washington Street, extending across a narrow peninsula, or "neck," connected Boston to the mainland. The Back Bay was part of the Charles River Estuary, which filled a wide area between Boston and Cambridge. The estuary included extensive marshes on the Cambridge side that covered most of the territory now occupied by the Massachusetts Institute of Technology and the industrial area behind it. The Charles River was quite narrow above today's Kenmore Square, but it carried tidal water inland to Watertown, a distance of about seven miles.

Fig. P.1 shows a map of the Back Bay and Fenway neighborhoods, which now occupy the area of the original Back Bay tidal marsh, which covered about 850 acres south of Beacon Street. This wetland area extended from today's Charles Street at the foot of Boston Common westward to Kenmore Square and southward into the present South End neighborhood

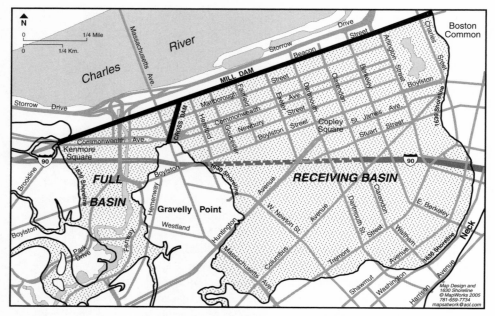

FIGURE P.1. Map of the Back Bay with present streets, the 1630 shoreline, and the dams that separated the former tidal marsh into the full basin and the receiving basin. The Mill Dam and the Cross Dam are shown separating the Back Bay from the Charles River Estuary and creating the Full Basin and Receiving Basin for the purpose of generating tidal power. The dams were completed in 1821. *(© MapWorks 2005.)*

near Washington Street. The tidal marsh filled with a mixture of fresh and salt water at high tide, and it was an important habitat for fish and other marine life. At low tide the Back Bay marsh was mostly covered with salt marsh cordgrass and other marsh plants between deep channels that drained the Muddy River and Stony Brook through the marsh. A low peninsula, Gravelly Point, jutted into the tidal marsh near the present line of Massachusetts Avenue.

In the early nineteenth century Boston expanded by filling in some shallow areas around the edges of the Back Bay. Around 1805 filling along Charles Street was aided by the use of a "gravity railroad" that carried sand and gravel down Beacon Hill from near today's Louisburg Square. Two dams for generating power from the tides, shown on the map as solid black lines, were completed in 1821; they cut off the former tidal marsh from the Charles River, dividing it into two basins: the "Full Basin" and the "Receiving Basin."

The one-and-a-half-mile-long "Mill Dam" closed off the wide, north-facing mouth of the Back Bay. This dam was built along the line of the present-day Beacon Street to Kenmore Square, and much of it is still buried under the street. The much shorter "Cross Dam" connected the end of Gravelly Point with the Mill Dam roughly where Massachusetts Avenue runs today from Boylston Street to Beacon Street. The Full Basin lay west of the Cross Dam.

The water in the Full Basin, the smaller basin west of Gravelly Point in today's Fenway neighborhood, was maintained at a high level. This basin collected the drainages from Stony Brook and the Muddy River, which flowed from Hyde Park, West Roxbury, Jamaica Plain, Roxbury, and Brookline. To augment the water held by the Full Basin, high-tide water was let in from the Charles River Estuary twice a day. The water from this Full Basin ran through millraces twenty-four hours a day to power mills located on Gravelly Point.

The larger basin, the Receiving Basin, included all of the area that is now considered to be in the Back Bay neighborhood. This area lay between today's Charles Street and Massachusetts Avenue from east to west, and between the Charles River and close to Washington Street from north to south. The Receiving Basin, so called because water flowed into it after passing through mills on Gravelly Point, was kept as empty as possible by draining water into the Charles River at every low tide. This maximized the fall of water through waterwheels in the mills. The nearly empty Receiving Basin became polluted very quickly because sewers continued to drain into the area and tides no longer washed it out twice daily.

The tidal power generated by the massive mill project in the Back Bay never met expectations. The promoters of the Boston and Roxbury Mill Corporation foresaw eighty-one mills, which would have made Gravelly Point a major industrial district, but no more than four mills ever operated there at one time. Not enough water was available from the Full Basin to keep a large number of mill wheels running efficiently twenty-four hours a day. The Full Basin had too small a holding capacity to prevent it from being drawn down quickly when the mills were running at full power. The corporation was never able to meet its expenses and pay out profits to its investors.

In the 1830s two railroad lines were built across the Back Bay on low embankments and trestle bridges that extended over the mudflat. These railroad lines, intersecting in the middle of the Receiving Basin, further reduced water flow in that basin, contributing to the failure of the mills

and increasing pollution in the smaller basin areas that remained between the railroads and the shore.

This book focuses on the filling of the Receiving Basin, the former
tidal marsh's largest section and the part that is now known as the Back
Bay. (The story of filling the western part of the former tidal marsh, in
today's Fenway area, has been told elsewhere).[1]

By the 1850s three factors combined to motivate the filling of the former tidal marsh with sand and gravel. The Back Bay was horribly polluted because sewage emptying into the former tidal marsh, along with
dumped refuse, was no longer cleansed by twice-daily high tides. Boston
was severely overcrowded, with over a hundred thousand people living
on a peninsula that totaled about one thousand acres. A rapid increase
in the poor, and often destitute, immigrant population provided social
motivations and led city and state leaders to seek ways of keeping
wealthy Protestant families in Boston by creating a new, elegant neighborhood.

Although pressing reasons for filling the Back Bay came into focus,
stiff challenges had to be met to carry out the massive engineering project. Bold new solutions were required in planning, financing, and innovative technologies. A three-man State Commission, appointed in 1852,
determined the master plan and coordinated the entire project. In 1856
the commission divided the ownership limits and responsibilities of
three entities: the Commonwealth (State) of Massachusetts, the Boston
Water Power Company, and the City of Boston. The Boston Water Power
Company was an offshoot of the Boston and Roxbury Mill Corporation,
which had completed the tidal power mills in 1821. By 1850 it had long
been clear that the mills would never be profitable. The Boston Water
Power Company could recoup its losses and pay off its stockholders only
by filling and selling land in the Receiving Basin and Full Basin.

The State Commission took on full responsibility for planning the
new Back Bay neighborhood and reserved the most desirable hundred
acres of the area to be filled by the State. The lion's share of the filling was
to be carried out by the Boston Water Power Company, and the City of
Boston was given only a narrow triangle of land that enlarged the Public Garden. A number of options were considered for the Back Bay, including a series of proposals for putting a lake near the middle of the
planned neighborhood. The State Commission settled on a design with
rectangular blocks and a very wide Commonwealth Avenue to provide
an elegant centerpiece. The State's plan was carried out for the entire

Back Bay, and strict zoning regulations were enforced to preserve the exclusive nature of the neighborhood.

The term *landfill* as applied to the Back Bay refers to the sand and gravel that filled the former tidal marsh and created a' new and elevated land surface. The filling of the Back Bay in the second half of the nineteenth century was a huge engineering feat that moved sand and gravel from glacially formed hills and deposited that material on the Back Bay mudflats. The Back Bay landfill work began in 1858 and ended by 1890.

Accessible sources of sand and gravel on Boston's original peninsula had been exhausted earlier in the nineteenth century for smaller landfill projects. Therefore, filling materials had to be transported eight or more miles from several towns west and south of Boston, among them Needham, Canton, Newton, and Hyde Park.

George Goss and Norman Munson, New England natives who had been railroad contractors in the Middle Atlantic states, won the contracts to fill new land for the State and the Boston Water Power Company. In the beginning, Goss and Munson obtained gravel rights on land in Needham in exchange for paying off a Charles River Branch Railroad mortgage. Then they brought together the new kinds of machinery needed to do the work and built a new track parallel to the Boston and Worcester Railroad tracks to carry the heavy gravel trains on part of their route. Although George Goss left the partnership in mysterious circumstances after about two years, Norman Munson continued for many years to complete most of the Back Bay landfill work, while he also took on railroad construction contracts and invested heavily in other projects.

Important, relatively new technologies were required to move heavy loads. Steam locomotives, newly improved steam shovels, and side-dumping gravel cars made it possible to move massive amounts of sand and gravel from pits in large glacial deposits to appropriate sites in the Back Bay. Even with the technology in place, a steadfast State Commission and bold contractors had to cooperate to get the work done as fast as possible. Remarkably, the filling went forward steadily in spite of the Civil War, a deep national economic depression, and the sudden departure of one of the two contractors.

The State Commission obtained cash for startup costs needed by the contractors by selling most of a valuable block before it was filled. At first, both the State and the Boston Water Power Company paid the contractors in land rather than in cash. These arrangements made it possible for the commission to continue the work without drawing on the

State treasury. The contractors began selling their land at the best prices they could get, but the State held out for higher prices in hopes of attracting only wealthy families. The ensuing competition was seen as unfair to the State. The Boston Water Power Company started in the same way, and within two years the contractors were being paid in cash by both the company and the State. About half the land was sold at auction. The last State land was sold in 1886, although some of the other new land was vacant and unsold for several more decades. In the end, after all expenses were covered and contributions were made to educational and cultural organizations, the state treasury was enriched by more than $3.4 million as a result of the Back Bay landfill project.

The Commonwealth of Massachusetts completed filling its hundred acres by about 1866, with over four hundred carloads of sand and gravel delivered to the Back Bay every twenty-four hours until 1863. The Boston Water Power Company continued to fill a larger area into the 1880s. This is the largest landfill project ever undertaken in the United States for residential and commercial purposes.

When sections of new land were completely filled, effective technologies were required to construct substantial buildings on very soft ground and to handle sewage in the growing neighborhood. About 200 to 300 wooden piles made from full-size trees, topped with specially carved granite foundation stones, supported each Back Bay town house. These wooden piles are very sensitive to changes in the water table, since alternating wetting and drying lead to pile decay and a loss of foundation support, a problem that continues to this day. Sewers in the low-lying neighborhood had to be near the level of low tide, a challenge that was not solved until a few decades after the project began.

The Back Bay today has both brick and stone residential structures from the Victorian period and modern, high-rise office buildings and residential towers. The older buildings, supported by wooden pilings, are susceptible to crumbling foundations if the water table drops. The brick and stone buildings could also fall if a large earthquake strikes near Boston. The newer, tall buildings have steel and concrete pilings that go down to bedrock more than a hundred feet below the surface, making them much safer in the event of an earthquake.

We mined many unpublished sources of information during our ten years of research for this book. It was like detective work because information was often hard to find and new questions repeatedly arose that had to be answered through more research. This long process led us to State and City reports and records, archives with materials on railroads and corporations, nineteenth-century plans and maps and credit-rating information, photograph collections, and more.

Special thanks go to dedicated staff members at many libraries, archives, and other organizations: Andrea Still and Christine Gebhard in the Special Collections Department of the Massachusetts State House Library; the Massachusetts State Archives; Peter Drummey at the Massachusetts Historical Society; Nancy Richard and Chris Carden at the Bostonian Society Library; the Baker Library Archives at Harvard University; Laura Katz Smith at the Archives and Special Collections of the Thomas J. Dodd Research Center at the University of Connecticut; Sally Pierce and Stephen Nonack at the Boston Athenaeum; Lorna Condon at the Society for the Preservation of New England Antiquities (now Historic New England); Henry Hicks and Lou Crumbaker of the Needham Historical Society; Henry Scanlon at the Boston Public Library; Theodora Eaton, Needham Town Clerk; Sandra Waxman at the Dedham Historical Society; Susan Abele at the Jackson Homestead of the Newton Historical Society; James A. Roache of the Canton Historical Society; Ralph Buonopane of the Westwood Historical Society; Constance Cooper at the Historical Society of Delaware; Lou Ekberg of the Needham Department of Public Works; Clayton T. Ruan, Jr., of the Norfolk County Engineering Department; the Hyde Park Historical Society; the City of Boston Archive; Joseph Gaffney in the Probate Office at the Suffolk County Courthouse; Dr. William Marchione of the Brighton Historical Society. We also thank Delecia Hill, Family History Consultant at Brigham Young University; Nancy Seasholes, independent scholar; Professor Terence J. Hughes in the Climate Change Institute, University of Maine at Orono; David Fletcher of the Walker Transportation Museum; David Woodhouse at Quest Environmental Sciences; Professor Richard Scranton, Associate Dean of Engineering, Northeastern University; Alan Saiz, College of Criminal Justice, Northeastern University; and Meredith Marcinikewicz of the Shirley (Massachusetts) Historical Society. Special assistance with technical editing was provided by: Professor John E. Ebel, Director of the Weston Observatory of Boston College; Professor Richard H. Bailey in the Department of Earth and Environmental Studies at Northeastern University; and Professor David M. Mickelson in the Department of Geology and Geophysics, University of Wisconsin at Madison.

Professor Thomas Koenig, Chair of the Department of Sociology and Anthropology, provided valuable advice and support. Kirsten Lindquist designed and produced many of the illustrations. Bruce Hamilton, Technical Director of the Department of Photography at Northeastern University, took excellent photos for the book.

We thank our wives, Anna M. Newman and Susan C. Holton, for their prodding and patience during the long process of research and writing. Anna M. Newman also carried out nineteenth-century newspaper research in the Boston Public Library. Several colleagues at Northeastern University in the Geology and the Sociology and Anthropology departments provided support and suggestions. Professor Emeritus Thomas O'Connor of Boston College and Maureen O'Rourke, a state planner, read several chapters. Staff members at the University Press of New England were very helpful and professional in bringing our work to a successful conclusion, especially Executive Editor Phyllis Deutsch and Managing Editor Mary Crittendon, who guided our progress at every stage.

W.A.N. and W.E.H.

Boston's Back Bay

CHAPTER 1

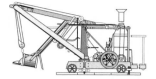

Prehistory of the Back Bay

The Beginnings of Boston's Landscape

The context for filling Boston's Back Bay in the nineteenth century must be understood in terms of over 800 million years of geological history. Although much of the evidence is missing, the broad outline of the story can be pieced together quite well. The oldest rock that is buried deep beneath the Boston area is thought to have originated on an exotic fragment of Africa or South America, perhaps the size of California and from 60 to 150 miles thick, during an episode of volcanism, faulting, and earthquake activity about 700 to 800 million years ago.[1] This exotic fragment of a non–North American continent is named the Boston Avalon terrane.[2]

Following the rifting of the Boston Avalon terrane from its mother continent and its subsequent deposition, violent episodes of earthquake and volcanic activity were associated with a sequence of igneous intrusions and cataclysmic volcanic eruptions. Molten rock, expanding superheated steam, and volatile gases breached the earth's surface, producing a series of violently erupting volcanoes.

These catastrophic events, far more powerful than the Mount Saint Helens eruption in 1980, blasted apart and pulverized entire volcanic cones into volcanic ash and angular blocks that were mixed with occasional lava flows. Other volcanic episodes followed a few million years later, with similar results. The ancient volcanic landscapes have long since disappeared following millions of years of deep erosion in New England. The partially molten rock material below the earth's surface, which produced the early volcanic eruptions, slowly cooled and solidified into granitic rocks about 600 million years ago.[3]

Millions of years of erosion stripped away the overlying softer rocks, allowing the harder volcanic and granitic rocks to become mountainous uplands to the south and west of present-day Boston. These uplands were eroded by vigorous mountain streams and possibly by alpine glaciers that transported the eroded material to the coast, where it formed the sand and gravel that probably accumulated on a large delta in an ancient sea close to the edge of a continental slope. Periodically, portions of the delta collapsed, sending some of the sand and gravel sliding into deeper water to form submarine slump deposits.[4] The finer silt and clay drifted farther out into the deep water basin, where it settled gently on the sea floor (generally to the north and west of present-day Boston, including East Boston to Beverly and Cambridge to Somerville) (see fig. 1.1). These mud deposits became rock after being subjected to heat and pressure for an extended period, eventually reaching an aggregate thickness of over seventeen thousand feet.[5] Today, the gravelly shelf and slump deposits of conglomerate, or "puddingstone," are known as the Roxbury Formation, and the deeper-water mudstones are the Cambridge Formation.

Generally, the rocks directly under Boston and the Back Bay are the mudstones of the Cambridge Formation, and the rolling hills a short distance to the south and west are the conglomerate rocks of the Roxbury Formation, which contains stream-rounded stones of varying sizes. The Cambridge mudstone is much weaker and softer than the Roxbury conglomerate, which explains why it has been eroded and lies as much as 150 to 200 feet beneath the Back Bay today.

The exotic terrane containing the Boston area rocks, sliding on a deeply buried, partly molten zone, collided with the North American terrane around 380 million years ago and became permanently attached to the continent. This collision squeezed the rocks together, producing broad folds and thrust faults that forced one rock layer over another. The forces involved with this mountain-building event deformed rocks throughout New England. The collision uplifted the deep-seated granite-like rocks to the north and south of the city, above the level of the Cambridge mudstone and Roxbury conglomerate, to form the Boston Basin.[6]

Nearly all evidence of the early geologic history of the Boston area following the creation of the Boston Basin is missing, having been long since removed by thousands of feet of erosion. For millions of years, rivers flowed out of the hard granitic uplands to the north and south and across

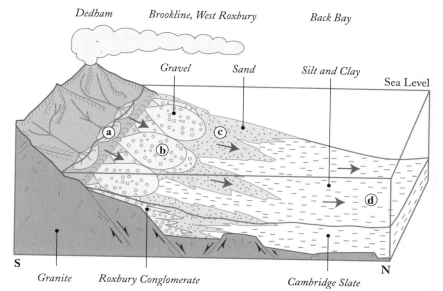

FIGURE 1.1. Model illustrating the origin of the Roxbury and Cambridge Formations in a deep-sea basin approximately 580 million years ago. This model of the Boston area suggests a landscape with a topography and geology similar to the present islands of New Zealand. Volcanoes erupting to the south toward today's Dedham and beyond formed extensive chains of volcanoes. To the north the granitic rock that underlay the continental shelf and ocean basin underwent extensive faulting as indicated by the direction of the arrows on either side of the fault zone.

Weathered and eroded sediment is deposited along a narrow continental slope by rapidly flowing mountain streams. These deposits form deltas or alluvial fans (a) that periodically collapse and flow down the continental slope as submarine debris flows. The gravel portion of the flow rapidly settles near the shore and forms fans on the upper slope (b). Later, the loose gravel is fused together into a solid mass forming the Roxbury Conglomerate or the Roxbury "Puddingstone." The lighter sand portion settles further out into the deep sea basin (c) to eventually form sandstone, and extremely fine particles of fine-grained silt and clay slowly settle on the deep sea floor (d) to eventually become the Cambridge mudstone. *(Drawn by Kirsten Lindquist from information provided by William A. Newman.)*

the softer mudstones of the Boston Basin. These ancient rivers, swinging from side to side, cut deep channels and scoured out broad valleys. Some of these abandoned and buried river channels, cut into the Cambridge mudstone, are filled with more recent glacial deposits.[7]

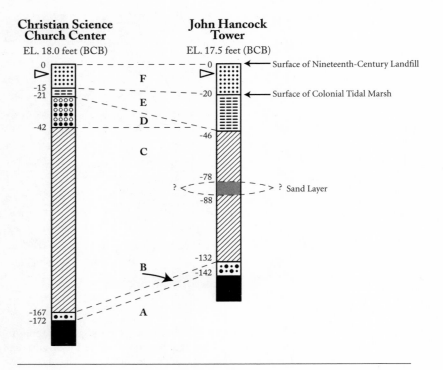

Christian Science Church Center
EL. 18.0 feet (BCB)

John Hancock Tower
EL. 17.5 feet (BCB)

← Surface of Nineteenth-Century Landfill

← Surface of Colonial Tidal Marsh

? < Sand Layer

Explanation:

Surface elevations measured in feet above the Boston City Base (BCB; footnote 54, p. 206) Depth to soil boundaries in each profile is expressed in feet below the ground surface.

▷ Groundwater level

F. Sand and gravel fill.

E. Silt interbedded occasionally with layers of peat.

D. Interbedded layers of sand and gravel deposited during the last glacial advance into the Boston Basin. Note that the outwash deposits beneath the Christian Science Center do not extend to the John Hancock Tower.

C. The Boston blue clay containing occasional thin sand layers or lenses. Note the discontinuous sand layer between -78 and -88 feet (BCB) below ground level under the John Hancock Tower.

B. Probably early Wisconsin glacial drift comprising of material deposited directly from the glacier and meltwater streams.

A. Cambridge Formation consisting of Cambridge mudstone with some interbedded sandstone beds.

FIGURE 1.2. Back Bay soil profiles beneath the Christian Science Church Center and the John Hancock Tower, located approximately half a mile apart. *(Modified from figure 3, H. P. Aldrich, Jr. "Back Bay Boston, Part I," Journal of the Boston Society of Civil Engineers Section/ASCE 57, no. 1 [January 1970]. Reprinted with permission of the Boston Society of Civil Engineers Section/ASCE, Civil Engineering Practice, Journal of BSCES. Created by Kirsten Lindquist.)*

Glaciation Shapes the Boston Landscape

Global cooling began about 65 million years ago; about 20 million years ago the cooling rate increased, and glaciers appeared in the higher latitudes of the northern and southern hemispheres. About 2 million years ago glaciers coalesced into a large ice sheet. As the expanding ice sheet received more and more nourishment in the form of snow, it became much thicker and began to flow in all directions. Part flowed southward and southeastward into the present day United States. At least two, but almost certainly more, of these invading ice sheets flowed across eastern Massachusetts, scouring and shaping the topography.

The last major episode of glaciation, the late Wisconsin glaciation[8] of the Laurentide ice sheet,[9] took place sometime before 23,000 years ago and lasted in New England until about 11,500 years ago.[10] The rapid buildup of the continental ice sheets was accompanied by a rapid drop in worldwide sea level, which preceded the arrival of the ice sheets in eastern Massachusetts. Rivers that flowed southward, away from the advancing ice margin, were larger than they are today because they carried glacial meltwater during the summer. As sea level fell, rivers in front of the advancing ice sheet had a steep gradient and began to deepen their channels into the underlying sediments and rock. This may have happened each time an ice sheet advanced into southern New England, not just during the last glaciation. These deep valleys were then filled with glacial, stream, and marine deposits as the glacier receded; thus, today they are mostly filled with sediment and are therefore known as "buried valleys."

The Back Bay district is located on the eastern slope of one such buried valley.[11] This valley may have been partly eroded in preglacial time, but ice sheets and glacial meltwater certainly deepened and modified it. The ancient valley is cut into the Cambridge Formation some one hundred to two hundred feet below the present surface of the Back Bay. For example, the surface of the Cambridge mudstone (see fig. 1.2) is 142 feet deep beneath the John Hancock Tower and 172 feet deep beneath the Christian Science Church Complex.

Sometime before 28,000 radiocarbon years ago,[12] thick blankets of sand, gravel, and boulders were released by one or more ice sheets advancing and retreating across eastern Massachusetts. This glacial sediment, or drift, (see fig. 1.2) was later resculpted and added to by the late Wisconsin Laurentide ice sheet that invaded the United States sometime before 23,000 radiocarbon years ago.[13] This last ice sheet to invade New

England was probably about 1,200 feet thick over the Boston area.[14] The ice sheet probably exerted a weight of over 67,000 pounds per square foot on the underlying Cambridge Formation when it reached its maximum extent off the southern New England coast (see fig. 1.3), around 21,000 radiocarbon years ago.[15] The extremely heavy weight of the ice depressed the ground beneath it by several hundred feet in the Boston area, and the worldwide sea level was also much lower, perhaps as much as four hundred feet lower than at present.[16]

To interpret the late glacial and postglacial history of Boston and the Back Bay area, we must understand relative sea level. What we know as sea level is not constant and can change either by a fluctuation in worldwide sea level or a change in land level, both of which occur independently and at different rates. Because there is no independent way of measuring these, we refer to relative sea-level change as the sea-level change that would be observed relative to some fixed point on land. At times in the past, a point that is now at sea level was under water and at times well above sea level. If we plot relative sea-level change against time, we would see a relative sea level curve that shows the history of the Back Bay as it was affected by these changes in sea level.

As climate warming began about 18,000 radiocarbon years ago, the forward advance of the late Wisconsin ice margin came to a stop, the glacier started to thin, and the position of the ice margin began to recede.[17] The retreating glacier was oriented more or less east-west across eastern Massachusetts.[18] The combination of glacier thinning and ice margin retreat reduced the weight of the ice on the underlying land, and the land surface rebounded in response. Global sea level was also rising. Glacial drift, released from the melting ice, was deposited on the underlying bedrock and on older glacial drift (see "B" in fig.1.2).[19] This drift, which now overlies the Cambridge Formation, ranges from two to thirty feet thick under today's Back Bay. About 14,000 radiocarbon years ago the ice margin had retreated just to the north and east of Boston,[20] and relative sea level was greater than sixty feet above the present sea level.[21]

Numerous streams, discharging all along the ice margin, dumped enormous quantities of sand, gravel, and mud into the adjacent seawater. The sand and gravel remained close to the ice margin where it was dropped, while the mud, formed from very finely ground rock particles called rock flour, rapidly dispersed and slowly settled on the seafloor in deep water to become Boston "blue clay." Although it is called blue clay, its color tends to be greenish gray, and it contains silt and interbedded fine

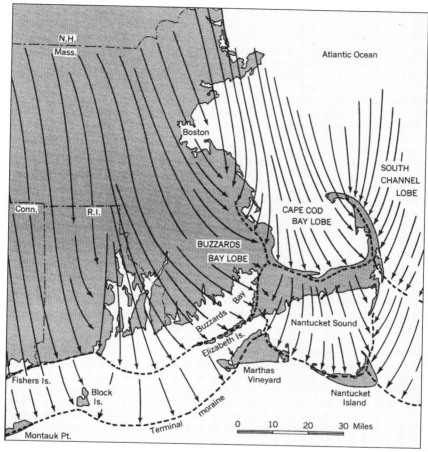

FIGURE 1.3. Maximum extent of the Laurentide ice sheet during the late Wisconsin advance. The late Wisconsin ice sheet reached its southernmost position in New England at various times and in different places between 21,000 and 15,000 years ago in southern New England. *(From A GEOLOGIST'S VIEW OF CAPE COD by Arthur N. Strahler, copyright © 1966 by Arthur N. Strahler. Used by permission of Doubleday, a division of Random House, Inc.)*

sand.[22] Most of the drift older than 14,000 years at low elevations in the Boston Basin is covered by blue clay. In areas west of Copley Square (see "C" in fig. 1.2) the blue clay is thicker than one hundred feet.

The late Wisconsin ice sheet, having retreated from the Boston Basin, staged a late and brief readvance into the basin from about 12,200 to 11,600 radiocarbon years ago (see "D" in fig. 1.2). The source of the ice for this readvance is thought to have been residual ice from the uplands surrounding the Boston Basin.[23] The Back Bay ice lobe probably joined other ice lobes advancing southward from the Malden area and advancing eastward along the Charles River Valley.[24] The Back Bay lobe appears to have pushed across the previously deposited Boston blue clays to squeeze up a low clay ridge at its southeastern margin, partially forming the Boston Neck,[25] the narrow, clayey isthmus that formed the southeast side of the Back Bay at the time of European settlement.

Glacial Landforms that Provided Sand and Gravel Fill

It was during the recession of the late Wisconsin ice sheet along the Charles and Neponset River Valleys that the sand and gravel that eventually supplied the needed fill for the Back Bay project was deposited.

As the ice sheet was retreating from eastern Massachusetts, large meltwater streams formed and descended the sloping ice surface. The channels of these streams were often intercepted by crevasses that caused the streams to plunge deep down fractures and continue along tunnels within or at the base of the glacier. Streams flowing in ice tunnels deposited sand and gravel up to sixty to seventy feet thick. As gravel was deposited along the bed of the subglacial stream, the roof of the tunnel melted upward to accommodate the large amount of flowing water. Once the surrounding ice had melted, these deposits appeared as long, narrow, sinuous ridges called eskers; in many places they extend over a mile in length.

Streams also flowed on top of the glacier or between the edge of the glacier and valley walls on the land surface. They carried gravel and sand, which was rapidly deposited where stream velocity decreased. Where the rivers entered ponds on the ice surface, they deposited sand and gravel in deltas that slowly increased in size. Later the ice beneath the gravel melted, leaving behind irregularly shaped sand and gravel hills on the landscape, called kames (see fig. 1.4).

As the glacier continued to thin, high spots on the land slowly began to project up through the ice, transforming the continuous ice sheet into a number of smaller isolated ice masses that occupied the river valleys. Meltwater streams flowed off the ice and then eastward between the ice and the valley sides. These ice-marginal streams deposited sand and gravel in their channels, and in places they formed extensive terraces along one or both sides of river valleys in eastern Massachusetts. These

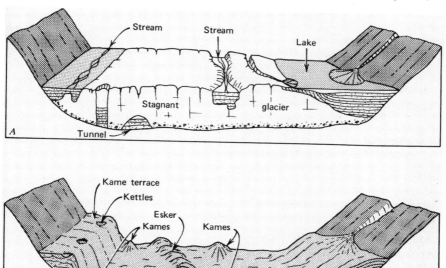

FIGURE 1.4. Origin of sand and gravel sources for filling Boston's Back Bay in the nineteenth century. *A.* Valley ridges projected through the Wisconsin ice sheet, as it thinned and receded, breaking it up into smaller valley glaciers. Sediment-loaded meltwater streams deposited enormous quantities of sand and gravel on, within, and around the glacier, which were held in place by ice walls. Streams often flowed into ponds or small lakes on the ice surface to form deltas. Other streams cascaded down crevasses and deposited the sand and gravel in ice tunnels beneath the glacier. Streams flowing along the edge of the ice filled the space between the ice margin and the valley slope with sand and gravel. *B.* All these deposits lost their support and eventually collapsed after the ice melted. The sand and gravel in the ice tunnels became long, sinuous ridges called eskers. The lake or pond deposits, lowered to the ground surface, became irregularly shaped hills called kames. The extensive sand and gravel deposits between the ice margin and the valley slope, known as kame terraces, are often characterized by pitted surfaces. These depressions, called kettles, were caused when buried ice blocks melted, collapsing the overlying sediments. *(Figure 8–4, Richard Foster Flint, Glacial and Quaternary Geology, Copyright © 1971 by John Wiley & Sons, Inc. Reprinted with permission of John Wiley & Sons Inc.)*

extensive sand and gravel deposits along the valley sides are called kame terraces, and they occur along the Charles River Valley in Needham and along the Neponset River in Canton, Westwood, and Hyde Park. Many eskers also were present in the same areas, providing ideal sources of sand and gravel for the Back Bay landfill project (see fig. 1.4).

Postglacial Evolution of the Boston Landscape

By about 11,650 radiocarbon years ago, the glacier was gone from the Boston area.[26] Following the glacier's final retreat from eastern Massachusetts, relative sea level in the Boston Basin continued to drop, until it reached a low point of seventy feet or more below today's sea level about 10,000 radiocarbon years ago, which exposed the blue clay throughout much of the Boston Basin ("C" in fig. 1.2). The top three to ten feet of the clay is generally oxidized and eroded because of atmospheric weathering and erosion that took place after 12,600 radiocarbon years ago, when relative sea level fell below present sea level.[27] This weathering and erosion gave the clay a yellow weathered and gullied surface a few feet thick, which behaves as a stiff crust. This crust would be important in supporting the spruce piles used later for building foundations in the nineteenth-century Back Bay.

A poorly drained grassland developed on the emerged Boston blue clay. This Back Bay meadowland had scattered ponds that formed in closed depressions and a higher and dryer central terrace that is now beneath the Prudential Center and Massachusetts Avenue. Later, the grass was replaced by trees.[28] The rising landscape gave the streams new vigor, and they began to entrench their channels into the Boston blue clay. All of today's Boston Harbor was dry land. The new channel of the Charles River at this time flowed across the Boston blue clay and followed a northerly course around the northwest side of present Boston, much as it does today, and then eastward, cutting a channel one hundred feet below present sea level.[29] "About 8,500 radiocarbon years ago, after an interval of relative sea-level stability that lasted approximately 2,000 radiocarbon years, sea level began a slow rise to its present position."[30]

The last marine invasion of Boston Harbor began about 6,000 radiocarbon years ago as the riverside land of the Back Bay sank slowly under the spreading estuary. Its forests were killed and buried beneath the advancing estuary muds, and the oxidized Boston blue clay that had been above the high-tide level once again became submerged.[31] The marine estuary extended up the Charles River Valley as far west as Watertown. Boston Harbor was again submerged and the Back Bay was a tidal estuary. Silt and fine sand carried by the Charles River, Muddy River, and Stony Brook were deposited continuously throughout the Charles River Estuary, especially during periods of flooding.

The pre-Colonial marshes were open, muddy bays. By about 3,000

years ago, the rate of rise of sea level had decreased enough so that mudflats could accumulate to the mid-tide level. Shortly afterward, salt marsh
grass spread across the mud flats leading to the formation of salt marsh
peat that covered much of the Back Bay prior to landfill activities.[32]

There may have been a partial closing of the Back Bay by waves and
currents that built higher and higher sandbars on the shallow, submerged
Boston Neck.[33] As sea level continued to rise and drown the land, the
fine-grained clays that were being deposited by streams in their channels
or on the adjacent river banks were now deposited by waves and currents
on the floor of the tidal estuary. Freshwater peat was overlain by up to
forty feet of silt, including some saltwater peat. Sea level continued to
rise rapidly in the Boston Basin until about 3,000 years ago, when the
Back Bay became an intertidal mudflat covering about 850 acres.[34] Twice
a day, ten-foot tides flowed in and out across two miles of these flats, as
they did until the construction of the Mill and Cross Dams in the early
nineteenth century. The salt marshes that flourished along the margins
of the spreading Back Bay were dissected by dendritic channels in which
was deposited black silt that contained decaying organic matter smelling
of hydrogen sulfide, the odor of rotten eggs.[35]

During low tides, the Charles River, Muddy River, and Stony Brook
flowed across the exposed Back Bay mudflat in broad, shallow channels
cut one to eight feet below the surface of the mudflat. On occasion, during winter thaws, ice jams developed in these stream channels, often
causing abrupt changes in flow patterns. For thousands of years the river
and smaller streams wandered back and forth across the Back Bay mudflats, carving channels and later abandoning them for other channels.

The Boylston Street Fish Weir

In 1913, while excavating a section of the subway tunnel beneath Boylston Street (see fig. 1.5), the workmen discovered a number of partly decayed vertical wooden stakes that were crudely sharpened, surrounded by
bunches of horizontal branches. These structures, thought at the time to
be the remains of an ancient fish trap known as a weir, were discovered
thirty feet below the ground surface, in the silt under Boylston Street between Clarendon and Berkeley Streets.[36] It is not known how many stakes
were discovered at that time, and probably many were destroyed during
excavation before the significance of the discovery was recognized.[37]

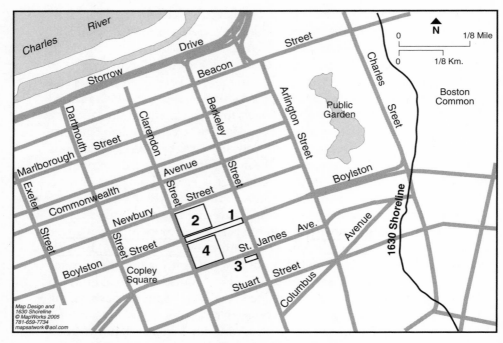

FIGURE 1.5. Location map of the major Boylston Street fish weir sites: (1) the Boylston Street Subway tunnel discovery site; (2) New England Financial Building foundation site; (3) John Hancock Tower foundation site; and (4) 500 Boylston Street foundation site. The fish weir site is located just to the west of the Eastern Channel (see fig. 3.5), which drained the mudflats in Colonial time. *(Street map of the Back Bay with the 1630 shoreline © MapWorks 2005 from information provided by William A. Newman.)*

Each hardwood stake was about four feet long and two inches or less in diameter. The sticks were pointed at the smaller end and had been driven down through the silt into a firmer layer of the Boston blue clay. Although they maintained their shape, the stakes were wet and very soft when found.[38] Some of the sticks were birch and even retained some of the bark.[39]

Many more stakes were discovered in 1939, during the deep excavation for what is now the 501 Boylston Street Building. The excavation exposed some 65,000 additional stakes and interspersed layers of brush that had been laid horizontally around the stakes. Eighty percent of the stakes were made from young sassafras, beech, alder, and oak saplings, one to four inches in diameter.[40]

The New England Financial Building excavation revealed dense concentrations of stakes that appeared to form six linear wall-like structures; they varied in width from two to ten feet and lay about twelve to fourteen feet below the present sea level.[41] Very little fish weir material was found during the excavations of foundations for neighboring buildings. Other than the fish weir stakes and brush, no tools or other artifacts were recovered relating to the people who built and used the structures.[42] After 1951 the radiocarbon dating technique permitted the dating of the wooden stakes and brush of the weirs as ranging from 4,900 to 3,700 years old, which led to a more sophisticated understanding of their evolution.[43] It appears that the "archaeological features represent a series of fish weirs that were constructed, repaired, and reconstructed over a time span of 1,200 years."[44]

The fish weirs were set just below low-tide level in shallow and relatively quiet water. Long lines and bands of upright stakes were driven roughly parallel to the contours of the sloping shore. As the sea level rose, new fish weirs were built closer to the shore at higher levels.[45] Bundles of branches were pushed down among them to create low walls of brush about three feet high that extended above the water surface at low tide. It was clear that branches had been bundled at their bases, even tied as "wooden bouquets," before being forced down among the uprights. The traps did not create big impoundments but, rather, artificial tidal pools contained by fish weirs. They were very effective only for trapping the multitude of small fish that would come in with the tide, swimming easily over the barriers of brush. When the tide fell, the fish would be held in the shallow water between the shore and the fish weir so people could gather them in baskets. Apparently, a combination of rising sea level and the rapid accumulation of silt made the fish weir impractical 3,500 years ago.[46]

Boston, the Back Bay Tidal Marsh, and Early Settlers

The Town of Boston was founded in 1630 on the tiny Shawmut Peninsula, which faced a sheltered harbor with deep channels. The earliest detailed description of Boston, Boston Neck, and the Back Bay was published by William Wood, an Englishman who visited New England in 1634.[47] In his book he describes the peninsula of Boston as being nearly square and connected to Roxbury by a narrow neck that is less than an eighth of a mile wide. He further mentions the hills on the peninsula that played a very important role in the defense of Boston. He described a "mountain" called Tramont with three small hills on top of it. The highest, central hill was called Sentry Hill and, later, Beacon Hill, because a lookout was posted there who could light a warning fire if an enemy threat was spotted from any direction. Two smaller hills near the harbor shore provided ideal places for defensive forts: Fort Hill, just south of the primary wharves near present-day Rowes Wharf (at the southern end of Batterymarch Street in the Financial District), and Copp's Hill, in the North End. At the entrance to the inner harbor, over two miles east of the town, Castle Island near the shipping lane was fortified and garrisoned in 1641 to guard against attack from the sea.[48]

William Wood also provided the earliest description of the Back Bay: "Up higher [upstream from Boston] it is a broad bay, being above two miles between the shores, in which run Stony-river and Muddy-river. Towards the southwest in the midst of this bay, is a great oyster bank." He also mentions the deepwater navigation problems associated with the Charles River because of the oyster banks, which must have been large.[49]

The defense of the town was aided also by the very narrow strip of land, the Neck, connecting Boston to the mainland. It was only about 120 feet wide at normal high tide and flanked on both sides by soft mud at low tide, making it impossible to enter the town by land except on one road. The single road, now Washington Street, passed through today's South End; the Neck's narrowest point lay where East Berkeley Street now crosses Washington Street. In 1631 a wall and gate were built across the town's only access road to keep out unwanted people and animals. It was replaced in 1714 and strengthened in the 1770s during the British occupation.[50] Because of the protection offered by these geographical advantages, Boston has never been invaded by attacking forces. (Occupation by the British Army during the 1760s and 1770s came gradually rather than by force.)

Plentiful freshwater springs and wells on the Shawmut Peninsula played a role in the Puritans' decision to move the colony's new seat of government across the mouth of the Charles River from their initial settlement in Charlestown. Boston's "Great Spring" was located near the corner of today's Washington and Water Streets, and its importance is shown by the fact that Governor Winthrop built his second house beside it. Another large spring lay on the slopes of Beacon Hill above Beacon Street, and shallow wells could be dug by hand in the soft, sandy soil near almost any home.

The earliest known detailed map of the Shawmut Peninsula is the John Bonner map, published in 1722, nearly one hundred years after the settlement of the peninsula by the Puritans (see fig. 1.6). More recent interpretations of Boston's Colonial and pre-Colonial geography are based on engineering studies of soil borings and building excavations as well as other historical maps and records. Pre-Colonial Boston, excluding Boston Neck, consisted of two islands separated by a tidal marsh that extended along today's Central Tunnel.[51] The smaller island, the North End, contained the Copp's Hill drumlin. Extending eastward across the northern portion of the larger island was a streamlined ridge on which there were three distinct smaller hills, Pemberton Hill, Beacon Hill, and Mount Vernon, so the ridge was called Trimountain (Wood's "Tramont") in 1630. The summit of Beacon Hill, removed in the early nineteenth century, rose about 138 feet above sea level.[52] The peak to the east, Pemberton Hill, rose some 80 feet above the present Pemberton Square. Mount Vernon, called Mount Hoardam or Whoredom by the British during the American Revolution, was located between today's Mount Vernon and Pinckney Streets, just above Louisburg Square.[53] Fifty-foot-high Fort Hill lay to the southeast, just northeast of today's South Station.

Justin Winsor, noting Wood's description, wrote in the late nineteenth century that Boston was connected to Roxbury by a "long narrow strip of land properly called 'The Neck' which, beginning to narrow just south of Eliot Street, stretched away like a ribbon of varying width to the mainland."[54] The road along the Neck crossed low-lying sections of the tidal mudflat that were "impassable in the spring, when horses were forced to wade knee-deep in surging water at full tides."[55] The Back Bay tidal marsh lay northwest of the Neck.

At the time the Puritan settlers arrived on the Boston peninsula in 1630, the landscape closely resembled that depicted on Bonner's map (see fig. 1.6). By 1722 several wharves had been built into the harbor for the docking of ships. Maps drawn by Sir Thomas Hyde Page and Captain Montresor of His Majesty's Corps of Engineers and published in 1778 (see fig. 1.7) show Boston to be essentially an elongate, irregularly shaped island of about 750 acres. Boston was about two miles long north to south and had a maximum width of about a mile and a half. During Colonial time the irregular relief that characterized the mudflat's surface in the Back Bay varied by several feet.

The marshes and bay lying to the southwest of the Shawmut Peninsula were variously named, until the region became known as the Back Bay because at high tide it looked like a bay in back of the town of Boston. The extent of the Back Bay and Charles River Estuary has been indicated on numerous early maps and nautical charts, particularly those of the British Admiralty. One of the reasons for the many fortifications around the Back

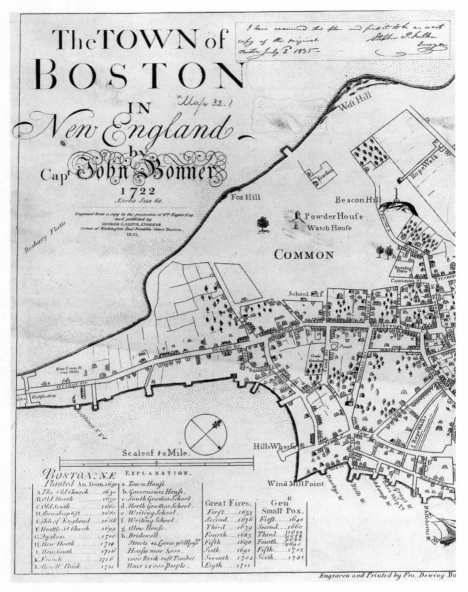

FIGURE 1.6. Captain John Bonner's 1722 map: "The Town of Boston in New England." The Bonner map is the earliest accurate map of the town of Boston. It shows the town less than one hundred years after its initial settlement. The shoreline has been changed only along the waterfront to the east and north of the town center, where many wharves extend out into the harbor. To the west, the Back Bay tidal marsh borders Boston Common and the base of Beacon Hill. Boston already shows hints of becoming crowded in the future, with a population of just under 10,000 at the time. (*Courtesy of The Bostonian Society/Old State House.*)

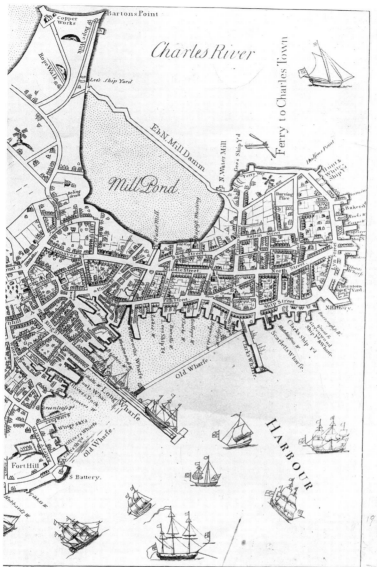

Copper Works
Bartons Point

Charles River

Lee's Ship Yard

Ferry to Charles Town

E b N. Mill Damm

Rope Walk

N. Water Mill

Mill Pond.

Boling Green

Burying Place

Salem Street

Middle Street

N. Battery

Ship Street

Long Wharfe

Old Wharfe

Old Wharfe

HARBOUR

Fort Hill

S. Battery.

193

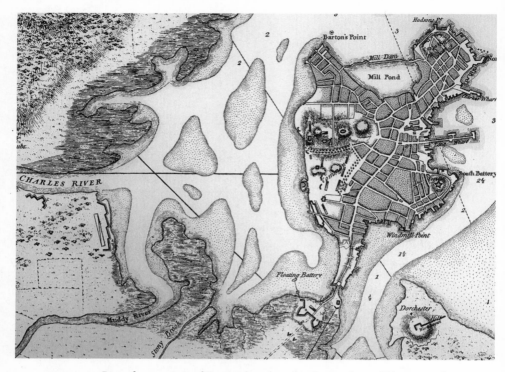

FIGURE 1.7. Part of a 1775 map of Boston, based on the observations of Lieutenant Page of his Majesty's Corps of Engineers and from the plans of Captain Montresor. One of the earliest maps to show the braided networks of channels in the Charles River Estuary, including the Back Bay tidal marsh, also shows Stony Brook entering the Charles River Estuary on the northeast side of Gravelly Point, the peninsula between Muddy River and Stony Brook. Fox Hill, a small drumlin along the shoreline of Boston Common, projects farther out into the Back Bay than indicated on Bonner's 1722 map. *(Courtesy of The Bostonian Society/Old State House.)*

Bay was to prevent enemies from approaching the Neck and the west side of the peninsula through the Stony Brook and Muddy River, tidal drainage channels or small creeks that would float small boats at high tide.

The pre-nineteenth-century Charles River, Muddy River, and Stony Brook discharged into a broad and shallow estuary that was situated between the Boston peninsula and the Cambridge shore, with wide marshes on both sides. This estuary, forming the western shore of the Boston Peninsula, broadened out into a wide, marshy bay before passing through a relatively narrow channel between Boston and Charlestown into Boston Harbor.

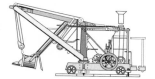

CHAPTER 2

Why Fill the Back Bay?

Early Efforts to Fill Parts of the Back Bay

In 1800, at the dawn of Boston's century of greatest change, the town held only about twenty-five thousand people, who were nearly all of English origin. The town was confined to a tiny peninsula of about 750 acres that was surrounded by the Atlantic Ocean and the Charles River Estuary. This was alluded to by Ralph Waldo Emerson in his poem "Boston":

> And twice each day the flowing sea
> Took Boston in its arms.[1]

Boston was basically an island that was connected to Roxbury by the low-lying, narrow Neck, which had room for only one road, which is now Washington Street. A very large tidal marsh lay behind the town, with the Charles River running through it. This "Back Bay" separated Boston from Cambridge, Brookline, Brighton, and Roxbury.

Most of Boston's residents in 1800 lived in today's downtown area, the North End, the West End, and Beacon Hill. Protestant churches dominated the town's religious life, and Congregational churches, directly derived from Puritan origins, were still influential but less dogmatic than before. Successful maritime trade and a growing wealthy class led to a self-image of Boston as a cultured and educated place. In 1822 the Town of Boston became a city, and an era of amazing growth began, as the population increased drastically and thousands of acres of territory were added to the small original land area.

In the first two decades of the nineteenth century, the town of Boston began to grow rapidly and to embrace its potential as the metropolis of

New England. Boston's population expanded steadily as its maritime trade boomed because of its large, protected harbor and the willingness of its merchants to take big risks in world trade for the chance of huge profits. Long deepwater wharves stretched out along the shore for more than a mile both north and south of Long Wharf and served hundreds of ships bound for Europe, the Caribbean, South America, the Pacific Islands, and the Far East. Long Wharf, true to its name, extended one-third mile into the deepest part of the harbor. To support this lucrative trade, warehouses and financial institutions quickly expanded, which created many new fortunes in maritime trade among Boston's well-established Protestant families. More wealth was created as Bostonians developed the textile mills of Waltham, Lowell, and other communities by harnessing the waterpower of local rivers. The growth spurred by maritime trade and Boston's emergence as a "machine metropolis" by the middle of the nineteenth century led to a severe shortage of space that required the creation of more land around the original peninsula.

The idea of filling parts of the Back Bay grew out of the limitations of Boston's cramped peninsular location. The filling of the former tidal marsh began with small efforts around its edges to create new land for commercial and residential purposes.

The manufacturing of rope needed for sailing ships and other uses was an important industry in early Boston. Using hemp fibers and flammable tar, ropes were woven in a straight line while the rope makers walked backward in long wooden sheds, called ropewalks. In 1796 six ropewalks burned on Boston's Fort Hill and destroyed ninety-six other buildings near the center of Boston. Because of the fire hazard, the Town of Boston soon granted rights to the ropewalk owners to rebuild on the marsh and mudflat extending three hundred feet west of Boston Common, where the threat to the town would be minimal. The grant required ropewalk owners to build a seawall at the outer edge of their plots in order to fill the area behind it.[2] The Association for Town Improvement began filling Charles Street in 1803. Gravel brought down from Mount Vernon near the west end of Beacon Hill was transported to the site in tipcarts. Much of the gravel sank into the soft, marshy ground, and so more filling material was required than had been expected. In 1807 Boston had to add more fill to a ten-foot-wide strip of Charles Street beside the Common because of flooding during high tides.[3] The land used then for new ropewalks would become part of the Public Garden a few decades later.

In 1804 or 1805 the developers of Beacon Hill's south slope, the Mount Vernon Proprietors, created Charles Street by removing the top of Mount Vernon, the westernmost peak of Beacon Hill. This filling allowed them to sell lots along Charles Street and to connect Charles Street with the new West Boston Bridge or Cambridge Bridge, at Cambridge Street.

A remarkable new technology was used, starting in 1804, to move material from Mount Vernon in a more efficient manner. The ingenious contractor was Silas Whitney, who set up a "gravity railroad" to expedite the work. This was apparently the first railroad of any kind to be employed in this country and it allowed gravel excavated on the upper slopes of Mount Vernon to be carried diagonally down to the edge of the marsh to fill the area along Charles Street and River Street, one block to the west.[4] The gravity railroad operated with a large pulley at the top and a rope around it, fastened to two sets of carts on board tracks. One set of cars went down while the other went up; the weight of the full cars going down pulled the empty cars back up the hill. Branch rails at the bottom delivered cars to locations where they were to be unloaded (see fig. 2.1).[5]

Most of the new land filled by the gravity railroad was at the base of Charles Street and used for residential construction and for extending Boston Common. An exception, however, was the Charles Street Meeting House, built as a Baptist church in 1804 on the riverside of Charles Street where full-immersion baptisms could be performed on the property.[6]

The filling of the Beacon Hill flats at the east end of the Back Bay continued over about sixty years' time to expand the land west of Charles Street and north of Beacon Street. In the 1820s a small section was filled just north of the Mill Dam and in the 1840s a few wharves were built into the river on the west side of Charles Street.[7] As late as 1850 the Charles Street Meeting House stood at the water's edge. This area is now known as the "Flat of Beacon Hill" because it is a continuation of that neighborhood on the flat, filled land west of Charles Street. Bainbridge Bunting notes that demand for land in this area did not increase until the 1850s, when several moderately large residences were constructed.[8]

In the 1820s a small neighborhood, developed by private owners, lay between Boston Common and the narrow part of the Neck connecting Boston to Roxbury. This "Church Street District," now called Bay Village, began on a marsh that became low-lying land when construction of the Mill Dam across the mouth of the Back Bay, completed in 1821, kept the water level there lower than the mean high tide. Owners of that land requested that the City of Boston build a dike across the northeast

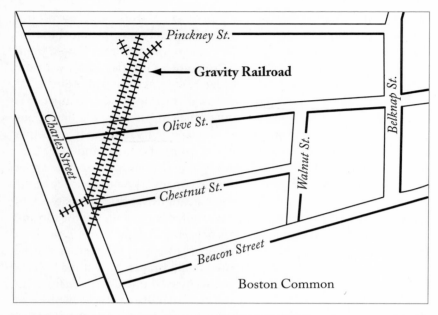

FIGURE 2.1. Map of the gravity railroad on Beacon Hill. In 1804 and 1805, a gravity rail-road was used to move sand and gravel efficiently from Mount Vernon, the westernmost peak of Beacon Hill, to filling sites along Charles Street. A rope around a pulley at the top of the steep slope was attached to two carts on the wooden tracks. Men with shovels filled a cart on the top, and while the first cart descended the pulley would pull up an empty cart on the adjacent track. *(Modified from Osgood Carleton, "A Plan of Boston from Actual Survey in Boston Directory" [Boston: Edward Cotton, 1805].)*

corner of the Back Bay to increase the value of their land, but the dike was never finished. The Bay Village land was graded at a level of only five to six feet above mean low tide, well below the level of mean high tide. This was possible because the Receiving Basin was kept nearly empty for the tidal power project, and sewers in Bay Village could flow into the Back Bay most of the time.[9] We will see that this low-lying area would flood by the 1860s, owing to the filling of the Back Bay, and drastic measures would be required to solve the problem.

In 1824 the Boston and Roxbury Mill Corporation was given permission to fill some mudflats along its dam on the Charles River side, extending up to two hundred feet north of today's Beacon Street.[10] This process continued slowly, beginning with granite and brick buildings being built on Beacon Street opposite the Public Garden, and in the early 1850s this new land extended only about to the future location of Clarendon Street.

In 1839 the Massachusetts Legislature made Horace Gray and Associates a corporation, the "Proprietors of the Botanic Garden in Boston," and charged it with creating the Public Garden on the filled land west of Charles Street where the ropewalks had been.[11] This is the same Horace Gray who built an iron foundry on Gravelly Point in 1821 and 1822. Eventually, this filling would reach nearly to the line of present-day Arlington Street. Even so, until the mid-1850s there were attempts by the City of Boston to develop the Public Garden land for residential purposes, but these moves were always defeated.[12] Nearby, the block of Boylston Street opposite the new Public Garden was extended to the water line in 1843. Bunting shows that the property values were very low on the water end of this block until the mid-1850s. Within a few years after that, however, "confidence had been established and dwellings of uniformly good quality were constructed upon these lots."[13]

In the mid-1850s, when planning for the Back Bay landfill project was well under way, there were still several hundred acres of mudflats and channels in the former tidal marsh between the Public Garden and Gravelly Point. Increasing pressures for filling the Back Bay evolved until an enormous engineering project was seriously considered. The three primary motivations for filling the Back Bay were pollution, overcrowding in Boston, and social pressures to keep wealthy Protestant families in the city in the face of an increasing immigrant population.

Dams in the Back Bay Cause Serious Pollution

Boston as a potential manufacturing center faced problems from the beginning because it had no fast-flowing rivers that could be dammed to harness waterpower for grinding grain or doing other work. Traditional waterpowered mills would not function along the final seven miles of the Charles River because it was a tidal estuary. The nearest such mills were at Watertown on the Charles River, Dorchester Lower Mills on the Neponset River, and Medford on the Mystic River. Therefore, alternative forms of waterpower had to be developed if Boston was to become a manufacturing center. Tidal power was harnessed in the early Colonial period by damming off the cove lying between the North End and West End near the center of Boston. Mills there were successful for several decades, but the Mill Pond became very polluted and was filled with silt by 1800. This pollution problem was repeated when dams closed off the Back Bay in 1821.

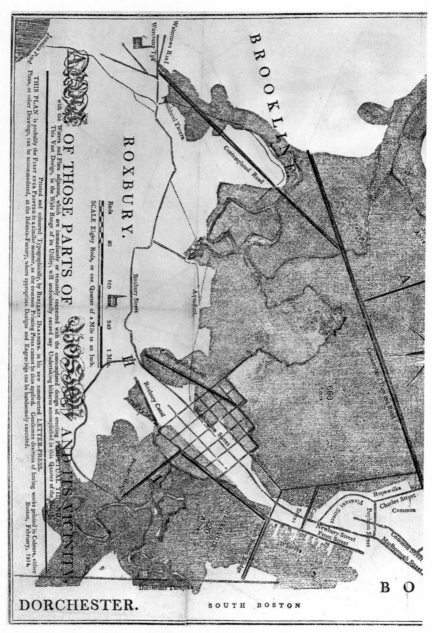

FIGURE 2.2. The Dearborn Map of 1814 with an expansive plan for tidal mills. This plan for tidal power involving the Back Bay, including flooding over Gravelly Point with a dam along the line of Beacon Street, would have turned the entire area into a full basin. As many as one hundred mills were to operate on the neck, and the South Bay would be dammed near the South Boston Bridge. *(Courtesy of The Bostonian Society/Old State House.)*

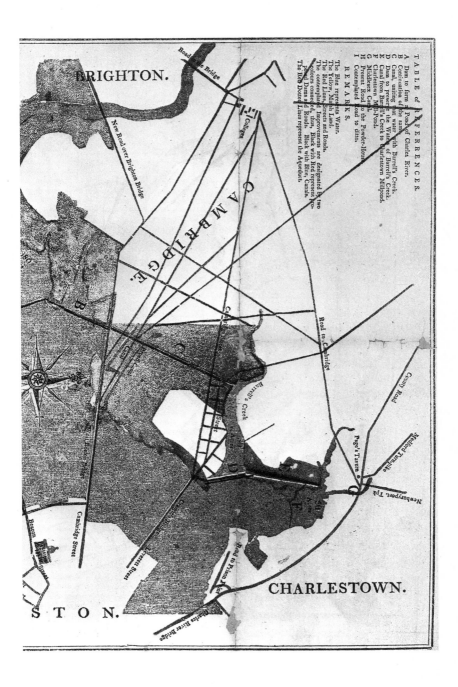

BRIGHTON.

CAMBRIDGE.

CHARLESTOWN.

STON.

Early in the nineteenth century, as the Industrial Revolution took hold, waterpowered mills symbolized progress. Boston's geographic setting led to grandiose plans to capitalize on its ten-foot tidal surges twice each day. In 1813 a Boston town committee gave tentative approval to Isaac P. Davis and Uriah Cotting's plan for a tidal power scheme that included the Back Bay and the South Bay on the other side of the Neck.[14] In this first plan, Cotting claimed that a row of about a hundred mills would be built along the Neck, powered by water rushing from the high water in the former Back Bay marsh into the lower basin on the southeast side.[15] Early in 1814 Benjamin Dearborn proposed an even more complex scheme with additional dams across the Charles River and coves in Cambridge and Charlestown for more mills, connected by canals.[16] Both of these plans called for "perpetual mills," which could run twenty-four hours a day by keeping one basin full and a second basin mostly empty (see fig. 2.2). The huge tidal power scheme was intended to make the town a major manufacturing center.

Although the tidal power plans involving the Back Bay were supported by several business and civic leaders, opponents raised environmental concerns. A letter writer to the *Boston Daily Advertiser* in 1814 foresaw future problems when he asked: "What think you of converting the beautiful sheet of water which skirts the Common into an empty mud-basin, reeking with filth, abhorrent to the smell, and disgusting to the eye?"[17] This anonymous writer proved to be absolutely right: as soon as the Mill Dam was completed along the line of today's Beacon Street, pollution fouled the newly enclosed Back Bay. Twice-daily high tides no longer washed out the sewage and trash deposited from the rapidly growing city.

In spite of some opposition, the charter to build the tidal mills on a more modest plan was granted by Boston on June 14, 1814. The Boston and Roxbury Mill Corporation, led by Uriah Cotting, would build Mill Dam one and one half miles long along the extended line of present-day Beacon Street. The shorter Cross Dam, from the north end of Gravelly Point to the Mill Dam, near the location of today's Massachusetts Avenue, would separate the two basins. Power for eighty-one mills on Gravelly Point would be generated by water flowing rapidly through their waterwheels from the Full Basin to the west on the Brookline side into the Receiving Basin east of Gravelly Point (see fig. 2.3).

The ambitious tidal power plan in the Back Bay faced delays caused by the difficulty of attracting private investors and by the complex construction challenges for building massive dams, sluices to fill the Full Basin at high tides and to empty the Receiving Basin as well as efficient millraces

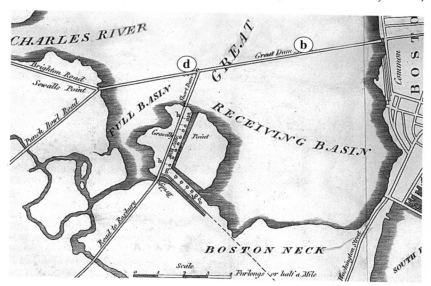

FIGURE 2.3. The 1821 plan of the Back Bay tidal project as built. Hales surveyed the Back Bay dams and sluices soon after they were built. The Mill Dam and the short Cross Dam create a full basin west of Gravelly Point and a receiving basin between there and Boston Common. The filling sluices just west of the Cross Dam and the emptying sluices are shown as V-shaped symbols. Several mills are shown on Gravelly Point, more than what actually operated at one time.

The Hales 1821 plan of the Mill Dam project shows the Mill Dam ("Great Dam") extending west along the line of Beacon Street from the lower side of Boston Common. Water entered the Full Basin through sluices (d) just west of the Cross Dam (labeled "Short Dam") that would run north from the end of Gravelly Point. Muddy River and Stony Brook are shown flowing into the Full Basin from the lower left. Mills were proposed to stand in two rows, angled along a canal, powered by water rushing from the high Full Basin through their mill wheels. After powering the mills, water would flow into the Receiving Basin. The Receiving Basin would be emptied near times of low tide into the Charles River through emptying sluices (b) located about half way along the Great Dam between Charles Street and the Cross Dam. (*Courtesy of The Bostonian Society/Old State House.*)

and mill wheels for getting the most power out of the available flow. The recession following the War of 1812 reduced the willingness of Bostonians to invest in this scheme, and the work came to a halt. In an 1818 pamphlet Uriah Cotting stated that the delay had been caused by a depression following the War of 1812 and the need to gather more information and make appropriate calculations on technical matters.[18] Cotting also issued an impressive appeal for investors, claiming that Boston desperately needed the projected eighty-one mills, including sixteen cotton

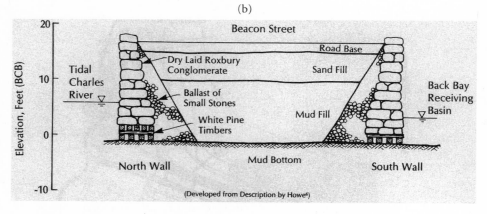

FIGURE 2.4. Photo of Cross Dam timbers and diagram of the Mill Dam cross section. The upper photo shows Cross Dam timbers found in 1937, when the Commonwealth Avenue underpass was built at Massachusetts Avenue (a). The timbers have been placed on the ground in the same way they were built to support the Cross Dam, as platforms of criss-crossed timbers were held together with wooden pegs. The lower diagram shows how the Mill Dam was constructed (b). Each side of the dam consisted of a high stone wall of Roxbury puddingstone (conglomerate) resting on a platform of timbers similar to those

mills, twelve rolling and slitting mills for processing iron, eight woolen
mills, eight flour mills, six gristmills, and six sawmills.[19] Cotting asked in
a public notice, "How shall the people of Boston fill their empty stores?"
and went on to answer his own question: "ERECT THESE MILLS, AND
LOWER THE PRICE OF BREAD." When new stock went on sale in 1818, the
demand was overwhelming because of Cotting's appeal to civic pride.[20]

The project continued to be built for another three years. The one-
and-a-half-mile-long dam was a huge undertaking, built with two parallel walls of Roxbury conglomerate blocks, six feet thick at the bottom
and three feet thick at the top.[21] The walls rested on massive timbers laid
directly on the mud and an elaborate cribbing structure of large timbers
laid crosswise. This type of structure was found when the Cross Dam
was uncovered during construction of the Commonwealth Avenue underpass at Massachusetts Avenue in 1937 (see fig. 2.4).[22] The Cross Dam
was constructed of granite.

Sluices in the dam at two points allowed water to be let in or out of
the Charles River Estuary, depending on the level of the tide (see fig. 2.5).
Each set of sluice gates would be opened wide when higher water on one
side was to be let through, and closed tight when the water level in a basin
was at the appropriate height. Six watertight "filling sluices" brought tidal
Charles River Estuary water into the Full Basin when the water level was
higher in the Charles River. As high tide neared, the inflowing brackish
Charles River Estuary water, combined with the discharges from the
Muddy River and Stony Brook to keep the water level in the Full Basin as
high as possible and thereby maximize the flow of water through mills
on Gravelly Point. The "emptying sluices" in the Mill Dam, five flood
gates that closed so water could not enter at high tide, drained water
from the Receiving Basin into the Charles River Estuary around the
times of low tides, twice daily.

John Hales described the filling sluices and the emptying sluices, and
"flood doors." He said that the doors of both kinds of sluices were grooved

---

under the Cross Dam. Stone ballast was placed inside each wall with mud fill in the central section, and was covered by a layer of sand and topped with the road base for Beacon Street. Much of the Mill Dam still lies beneath Beacon Street today. *(Photograph courtesy of The Bostonian Society/Old State House. The Mill Dam cross section is from Harl P. Aldrich, Jr.,
and James Lambrechts, "Back Bay Boston, Part II: Groundwater Levels," Civil Engineering Practice:
Journal of the Boston Society of Civil Engineers Section/ASCE 2 [1986]: fig. 5. Reproduced by permission from the Journal of the Boston Society of Civil Engineers Section/ASCE, Civil Engineering Practice, Journal of BSCES.)*

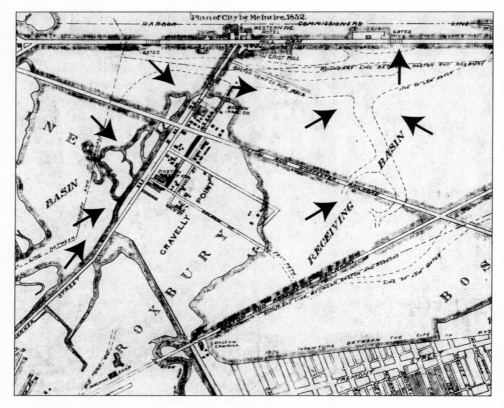

FIGURE 2.5. Map showing the flow of water in the Back Bay tidal project. The Fuller and Whitney reconstruction map of the Back Bay for 1851 illustrates the flow of water through the mills on Gravelly Point. Near each high tide, water was let in from the Charles River Estuary through the filling sluices shown at the top left side of the map. By 1835, the filling sluices were moved two blocks westward from their position in 1821. Water from the Muddy River and Stony Brook flowed into the southern part of the Full Basin.

High water in the Full Basin entered a wide channel above the mills through both ends and several smaller channels. Millraces carried water down into mill wheels beneath the three large mills shown on Gravelly Point, and below the mill wheels water exited through a narrow canal emptying into the Receiving Basin north of the Boston and Worcester Railroad line. The Receiving Basin was emptied into the Charles River Estuary at low tide through emptying sluices that were just off the upper right corner map. *(Courtesy of the Bostonian Society/Old State House. Enhanced by Kirsten Lindquist.)*

in massive piers of hewn stone (probably granite), with iron pivots attaching the doors to the stone at the top and bottom. The doors would not close flat, but pointed toward the higher water side when they were closed, with a watertight seal where the doors came together. To strengthen the gates of the sluices to withstand high water pressures when closed, each door rested on a horizontal platform of stone with a raised, v-shape stone sill supporting the closed doors.[23] We have based fig. 2.6 on Hales's description of the sluices.

The mills on Gravelly Point were not typical tidal-powered mills because they could run constantly, since the water in the Full Basin was kept considerably higher than the water in the Receiving Basin. Tidal power was involved here only because during rising and high tides water flowed through the filling sluices to keep the level of the Full Basin as high as possible. In 1971 the Back Bay mill project was called "the most advanced in all America" because it operated on a two-basin or "perpetual" system that allowed mills to run twenty-four hours a day. The gates in the filling and emptying sluices were described as being opened and closed automatically by the difference in water pressure on opposite sides of the floodgates.[24]

During low tides, the Receiving Basin could be nearly completely drained to increase the waterpower generated. Pollution would be increased, however, because the dam would block the cleansing tides and the nearly empty Receiving Basin would accumulate concentrated sewage and garbage in shallow water on the exposed mudflats.

Building the dams and sluices was a very large and complex project requiring huge amounts of cut stone, pilings made from large tree trunks, and thick wood planking. The work on the dam was delayed considerably in 1819 and 1820 because of problems with getting building materials and carrying out the work.[25] Uriah Cotting died early in 1821 and Colonel Loammi Baldwin II, the engineer who had built the Middlesex Canal over a decade earlier, became superintendent of the construction.[26] The Mill Dam was completed on July 2, 1821, and a toll was charged for people traveling on the new Western Avenue (now Beacon Street), which improved access to Brookline, Brighton, parts of Roxbury, and Harvard College in Cambridge.

Experiments for the Mill Corporation at the Franklin Institute of Philadelphia compared the effectiveness of various types of mill wheels. The "breast wheel" design was judged to be most appropriate, with water flowing over the top of the dam being channeled at least halfway up the wheel into "buckets" or paddles on the outside of the wheel (see fig. 2.7).

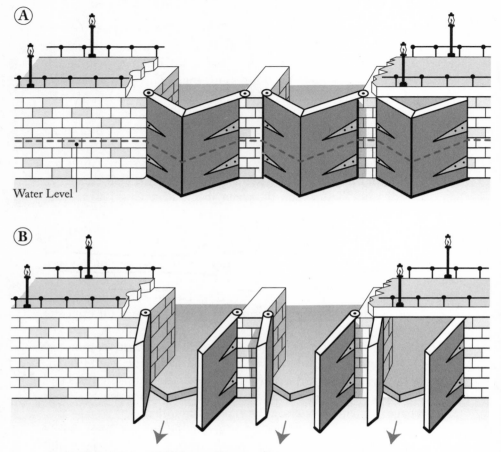

FIGURE 2.6. Schematic diagram of the Mill Dam sluices and sluice gates. This diagram is based on basic plans for the Mill Dam and general descriptions of the sluice operations there. Both sets of sluices worked in the same way, but the water flowed in opposite directions. This drawing shows the same three sluices when closed (A) and later, when they are opened (B). When closed, the sluices remained tightly shut because of the water pressure against their doors. Then, when the water level rose relative to the back of the closed doors, they would be pushed open automatically. When the sluices were open, water flowed through them from the higher water side to the lower water side. Then the relative water levels would equalize and shift, causing the doors to close automatically.

The doors seem to have been slotted in the granite walls and backed by a granite sill cut into the platforms when they were opened or shut, as described by Hales in 1821. In this way, the doors when closed could more easily resist the strong pressure exerted on them when there was higher water on the side behind them. *(Derived from newspaper reports, historical reports, plans of the dams and sluice construction, and from Hale's description in the pamphlet accompanying his 1821 plan of the Back Bay. Kirsten Lindquist.)*

FIGURE 2.7. Illustration of an operating breast-wheel and the basic gears for a grist mill. This drawing shows water flowing from the lower left into a wide breast wheel that turns counterclockwise. A curved breast of heavy planks fitted close to the back of the wheel keeps water in the buckets. The cutaway drawing shows sides on the buckets and spokes supporting the wheel. The main axle of the breast wheel turns a vertical gear that connects with a horizontal gear of equal size. All of the machinery in a grist mill was run by power from the axle that led up into the mill building. The water escaped at the bottom in the front of the breast wheel. *(Kirsten Lindquist from information provided by Wilfred E. Holton.)*

In this way, the portion of the wheel near the dam was pushed down by the force of falling water at a rate of speed determined by how far the water fell and the volume of water flow. Nine-foot-diameter breast wheels proved to be best for the fall of water available and were judged to generate enough power. Engineers prepared a diagram showing the output of power with various levels of water in the Full Basin, based on a fall of water ranging between three and seven feet (see fig. 2.8).[27] It was clear from the beginning that the water in the Full Basin would have to be maintained at a very high level to make the mills successful.

The relatively small size of the Full Basin reduced the potential water-power because the water level could be drawn down more quickly when the mills ran at full power. Keeping the Full Basin high was easier when large amounts of runoff entered it from the Stony Brook and Muddy

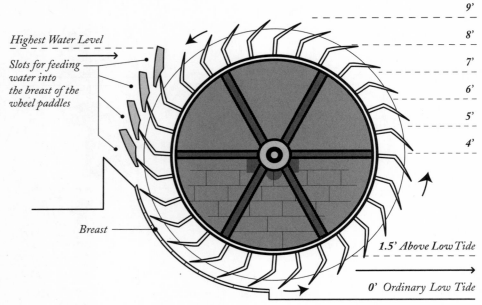

Highest Water Level

Slots for feeding water into the breast of the wheel paddles

Breast

9'
8'
7'
6'
5'
4'

1.5' Above Low Tide

0' Ordinary Low Tide

FIGURE 2.8. Diagram of the City Mill Wheel for the Back Bay, 1821. This diagram shows a cross section of the water wheel used at the City Mill on the Boston Mill Dam in 1821. The nine-foot-diameter breast wheel provided the power for grinding grains and corn in this grist mill. Levels of water in the Full Basin are shown ranging from 4.0 to 8.0 feet above the bottom of the mill wheel. It is clear that higher levels of water in the Full Basin were very important for generating effective power in the mills. Water levels in the Receiving Basin are shown at about 1.5 feet above the bottom of the mill wheel because the basin was not completely emptied, creating considerable backward pressure on the mill wheel in the backwater. *(Diagram of the City Mill Wheel, 1821. Redrawn by Kirsten Lindquist from the original in the Boston Water Power Co. Collection, Baker Library, Harvard Business School: Case 9, "City Mill Miscellaneous Papers".)*

River watersheds. The Receiving Basin could be drained during only two very short periods each day when tides were very low in the Charles River Estuary. There was about 1.5 feet of "backwater" remaining in the Receiving Basin, below the mill wheels, which impeded their movement and reduced the amount of power produced.[28]

Starting in 1821, a committee of the Mill Corporation rented "mill powers" for mill sites on Gravelly Point. One mill power would grind eight bushels of rye per hour into "good merchantable meal." Mill sites were sold to the highest bidders with a limit of ten mill powers for each site owner. Anyone buying or renting eight or more mill powers for manufacturing one product could have a monopoly on that type of man-ufacturing for ten years. The Mill Corporation guaranteed their dams and gates would be kept in good repair, with no decrease in power.[29] A few mills were established quickly, including a large ironworks owned by Horace Gray and a gristmill for grinding flour. In 1838 the ironworks would build a locomotive, the "Yankee," for the Boston and Worcester Railroad.[30]

Immediately following the completion of the Mill Dam and Cross Dam, there were bitter complaints about pollution in the Receiving Basin portion of the former tidal marsh. Several of Boston's sewers con-tinued to drain into the former marsh, a short distance from the shore-line near the Shawmut Peninsula and the Neck (see fig. 2.10). In May 1821 the Boston Board of Health received numerous complaints that the new dams had excluded tidal waters from the flats west of the Common (the Receiving Basin), "causing noxious substances, and sources of filth, to rest and remain on said flats, to the great injury of the citizens."[31]

The Boston Board of Health called a meeting to require the Mill Cor-poration managers to "show why they should not remove their dam or be required to again cover the flats with salt water."[32] Making matters worse, the Mill Corporation could operate its mills efficiently only if the Receiving Basin was kept nearly empty, so as to maximize the fall of water through the mill wheels on Gravelly Point. The pollution contin-ued to cause problems and over a year later, in August 1822, the Mill Cor-poration was ordered to appear before the Boston Board of Health about removing the nuisances "by making suitable drains to convey this Filth on said Flatts to the Channel."[33] The Mill Corporation apparently re-sponded by deepening the existing channels and facilitating the drainage of the exposed areas, but severe pollution continued to plague the Re-ceiving Basin of the Back Bay into the 1850s and until the filling was complete.

The Mill Corporation was unable to attract nearly as many mills to Gravelly Point as Uriah Cotting had prophesied. In a few years it became obvious that the tidal power produced did not measure up to claims that had been made. In March 1824 a Mr. Reed, the agent at the gristmill on Gravelly Point, complained that the warranties in the lease guaranteeing a minimum level of power had not been fulfilled.[34] Five years after com-pletion of the first mills, in 1827, there were only three mills operating on Gravelly Point and two other businesses were renting land there. Rents paid for mill powers totaled only $4,665 in that year, far short of the income that the Mill Corporation needed to cover expenses and pay dividends to its stockholders. In the same year, the superintendent of the Mill Corporation recommended repairing the wooden sluices during the next summer because he felt they were not secure for any period of time.[35] Ice floes probably caused the damage. Ten years after the mills began to operate, in 1832, the Mill Corporation "transferred all its mill franchise and water power to the Boston Water Power Company." After that time, the Mill Corporation only held the dams themselves.[36] The problems with providing sufficient, continuous power to the mills apparently resulted in failing to attract more than four mills at any one time, far short of the promoters' prediction that eighty-one mills would prosper in this tidal power project. On June 9, 1854, the Boston Water Power Company "virtually abandoned its public purpose of tide mills for a private purpose of land speculation."[37]

While international shipping and associated businesses continued to drive Boston's economy, its growth and prosperity after its incorporation as a city in 1822 depended on the emergence of efficient inland transportation by railroad and on the filling of small downtown coves to create land for more essential business functions.

Railroads Worsen Pollution and Reduce Water Power

Boston was one of the first American cities to bring in the railroad technology that had developed in England in the preceding decades. In the early 1830s two railroads were chartered in Massachusetts, which began to plan lines into Boston from the west and south that would lead to and facilitate the filling of the Back Bay more than twenty-five years later.

The Boston and Worcester Railroad faced a difficult choice on how to enter Boston from the west, with two possible routes. The first was to cross to the north side of the Charles River in Cambridge near today's Boston University Bridge, skirt large marshes on the Cambridge side, run into present-day Central Square, cross the river again to enter Boston near the present Longfellow Bridge, and end near today's North Station. The other choice was to stay on the south bank of the Charles River and cross the Full Basin, Gravelly Point, and the Receiving Basin on a mile and a half of embankments, trestles, and arched stone bridges before continuing eastward into a station with harbor access near today's South

Station. The first choice was a longer route and would require two costly bridges across the Charles River. The decision was made to run the Boston and Worcester tracks directly across the former Back Bay tidal marsh before curving eastward into a station near today's South Station.[38]

Ending the railroad this far to the east would allow it to connect to maritime trade on the docks of Boston. Finding a suitable location for its Boston station led the Boston and Worcester to work with the South Cove Corporation, which had bought and was filling the seventy-five-acre mudflat lying east of Washington Street and south of Kneeland Street. The South Cove Corporation wanted to attract a railroad station, so they offered a very good deal and sold slightly more than two acres to the railroad. The parcel had a 150-foot frontage on the South Bay, where the railroad could build piers next to its tracks. The benefits for the railroad did not materialize as expected because the South Cove was too shallow for newer, deepwater ships.[39]

Work on the Boston and Worcester Railroad's line proceeded from the west into Boston. The Boston and Providence Railroad built its tracks across the Receiving Basin, from near today's Massachusetts Avenue Station on the Orange Line subway, to its station in Park Square, near the present-day Boston Park Plaza Hotel. The two railroads crossed on the same grade near the middle of the Receiving Basin, close to today's Back Bay Station (see fig. 2.9).

The value of the Boston Water Power Company (an offshoot of the Boston and Roxbury Mill Corporation) stock plummeted when news emerged of plans to extend the Boston and Worcester and the Boston and Providence tracks across the Back Bay. The Boston and Worcester filed for eminent domain rights to build a right-of-way five rods (eighty-two and a half feet) wide. Mill owners feared that their waterpower potential would be reduced and objected to the Boston and Worcester's plans, refusing to negotiate with the railroad for the right to cross the Full Basin and Receiving Basin. The Boston Water Power Company sought an injunction in the Massachusetts Supreme Judicial Court to block the railroad on the ground that their charter gave them the exclusive right to use the Back Bay marshland.[40] The court denied this lawsuit because it challenged the basis of eminent domain, but the issue of compensation for damages to the Boston Water Power Company dragged on until the lawsuit was resolved in favor of the railroads in 1839.[41]

The Boston and Worcester faced the challenge of building a combination of embankments and low bridges across a mile and a half of soft

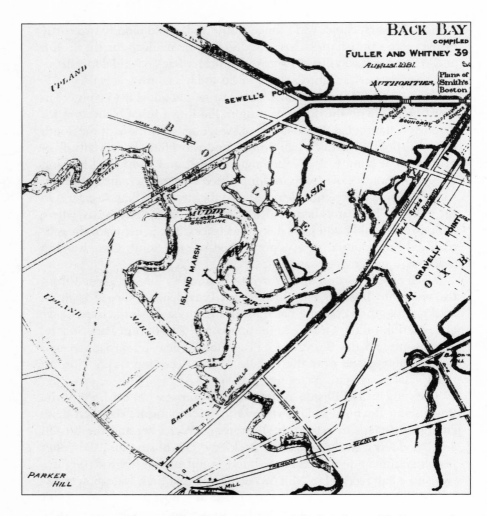

FIGURE 2.9. Map of the two railroad embankments and the dams in 1836. The Boston and Worcester Railroad crossed the Full Basin, Gravelly Point, and the Receiving Basin. The Boston and Providence Railroad crossed only the Receiving Basin at the first rail line about where Back Bay Station is now located. These railroads altered the flow of water in both basins and contributed to worsening pollution. *(Fuller and Whitney Map for 1836, recreated in 1881. Courtesy of The Bostonian Society/Old State House.)*

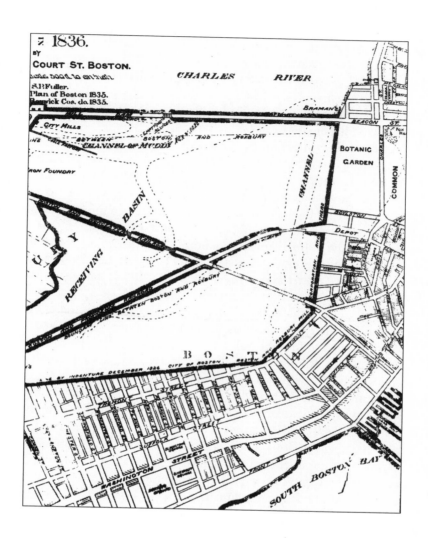

N. **1836.**
BY
COURT ST. BOSTON.
S.P.Fuller.
Plan of Boston 1835.
Bonwick Cos. do. 1835.

CHARLES RIVER

CITY MILLS

BETWEEN BOSTON AND ROXBURY
CHANNEL OR MUDDY

IRON FOUNDRY

BASIN

RECEIVING

BRAMAN'S

BEACON ST.

BOTANIC GARDEN

COMMON

CHANNEL

DEPOT

BETWEEN BOSTON AND ROXBURY

BOUNDARY BETWEEN BOSTON

B O S T O N

CITY OF BOSTON

LINE BY INDENTURE DECEMBER 1836

WASHINGTON STREET

SOUTH BOSTON BAY

mud, organic matter, and Boston blue clay. To preserve the discharge channels in the Receiving Basin so water and polluting materials could reach the sluices in the Mill Dam, the railroad built 1,700 feet of wooden trestles. The remaining 6,220 feet of track required an embankment flanked by granite walls and filled with stone rubble brought in from Wellesley on flatcars.[42]

Water was allowed to flow from one side of each basin to the other side through bridges with several graceful stone arches; the bridges were supported by piles driven below the low tide level. The Boston and Worcester took care to avoid having their embankments reduce the water storage capacity of the Full Basin. They enlarged the volume of that basin by removing over nine thousand cubic yards of earth from the marshes surrounding the railroad embankments.[43] The entire railroad cost more than $1,600,000, about $38,000 per mile. Some of the $700,000 cost overrun resulted from the expense of the viaducts over the Boston Water Power Company's basins in Roxbury and Boston.[44]

The pollution of the Back Bay increased markedly after the railroads blocked off smaller sections of the former tidal marsh while sewage and refuse continued to foul the Full Basin and the Receiving Basin (see fig. 2.10). Pollutants also flowed into the Full Basin from factories and communities along Stony Brook and Muddy River. The most severe pollution accumulated in the closed-off segments of the Receiving Basin, between the two railroads and east of the Boston and Providence Railroad, where the lack of flowing water resulted in heavy concentrations of sewage and other contaminants. As a result of Boston's remarkable growth (its population was about 130,000 in 1850), the Back Bay's pollution continued to become more extreme and intolerable.

In 1849 the City of Boston launched a special investigation into the condition of the Back Bay.[45] The report described the awful condition of the former tidal marsh in evocative Victorian language: "In fact, the Back Bay at this hour, is nothing less than a great cesspool, into which is daily deposited all the filth of a large and constantly increasing population."[46] The report went on to blame the Mill Dam for the pollution and to describe the "daily accumulations of decaying and offensive animal and vegetable substances" in this open cesspool cooked by the sun and weather. The report concluded, ". . . every west wind sends its pestilential exhalations across the entire City."[47]

As the pollution worsened, the City of Boston commissioned another report on the Back Bay a year later, in 1850.[48] This report described the

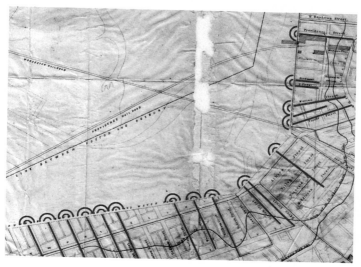

FIGURE 2.10. Map showing sewer outfalls on the Back Bay shoreline in 1850. Many older sewers continued to empty into the Back Bay even after the Mill Dam prevented high tides from washing it out somewhat twice each day. Because the Receiving Basin was kept as close to empty as possible, sewage tended to accumulate near the shoreline and to extremely pollute what shallow water there was. This 1850 map of the east and south shorelines of the Back Bay shows eighteen sewers emptying directly into the former tidal marsh, then cut off by the Mill Dam and two railroads. *(1850 Plan for New Sewers. Courtesy of the State Library of Massachusetts.)*

accumulations of polluted matter around the mouths of sewers that sometimes backed up into the basements of homes nearby. In the shallow water of the Receiving Basin, the report noted, foul substances blocked the weak currents that remained. A sickening description sums up the problem: "A greenish scum, many yards wide, stretches along the shores of the basin as far as the Western Avenue" (the toll road on the Mill Dam, now Beacon Street). Farther out in the Receiving Basin, the "surface of the water beyond is seen bubbling, like a cauldron, with the noxious gases that are exploding from the corrupting mass below."[49]

The 1849 and 1850 reports focused on assumed health hazards, such as the "pestilential exhalations" mentioned in the 1849 quote. The committee reports warned that the pollution would become so extreme that it would cause fatal diseases in the area. Medicine and public health did not understand disease process in the mid-nineteenth century, so it was assumed that the awful smells from the polluted Back Bay caused the

FIGURE 2.11. Trains crossing the Back Bay in 1844. This view, from near today's Massachusetts Avenue Station on the MBTA Orange Line, shows much of the Receiving Basin with polluted water and marsh grasses around the railroads. A passenger train of the Boston and Providence Railroad is in the foreground, and another is on the Boston and Worcester Railroad at the far left. The two tracks cross near the center of the Receiving Basin of the Back Bay, close to the present-day Back Bay Station. *(Courtesy of the Bostonian Society/Old State House.)*

epidemics and other serious illnesses that plagued Boston. The "miasma" theory of diseases held that they were spread in the air, at close range from infected people or more widely from sources of pollution.[50] The stench was most obnoxious in the summer months, when the committee said it was "highly prejudicial to the comfort and health of the neighboring inhabitants and the citizens generally."[51] In his 1850 report for the City of Boston, Dr. Jesse Chickering included a table showing that deaths from diseases such as cholera in infants and dysentery were much more likely in the warmer months of July, August, and September. He explained that more moisture is held in warm air and moist air contained more dangerous odors from "corrupt and corrupting matter."[52] The pollution of the Back Bay was seen as a serious public health problem.

By the time the State Commission was established in 1852 to deal with the future of the Back Bay, it was generally agreed that the severe pollution required the filling of the Back Bay, if the massive project could be made possible on technological and financial grounds. Presumed health hazards caused by the pollution thus created a crisis that was one of the primary motivations for the filling of the Back Bay.

Severe Overcrowding

The tiny Shawmut Peninsula had met Boston's needs in Colonial days. Its hills provided not only an excellent point for a lookout and a warning beacon on the highest point on Trimountain (now Beacon Hill), but also sites for strategic cannon emplacements on Copp's Hill and Fort Hill, near the ship channels. The Neck was secured easily by a wall and gate to deter attacks by land. Plentiful springs and wells on the peninsula supplied clean drinking water for almost two hundred years. Near the middle of the nineteenth century, however, the small land area of Boston was a serious liability because there was very little room for more residences and businesses as the city grew rapidly.

Before 1850 three coves were filled along Boston's waterfront. Also two edges of the Back Bay were filled, adding about four hundred acres in all to Boston's land area.[53] But nearly all of the new land was developed for commercial uses, and so little was done to relieve the growing population pressure. By 1850 the exploding population was confined to a few residential areas: the North End; Beacon Hill; Fort Hill (near today's South Station); the West End (encompassing today's Massachusetts General Hospital and Charles River Park); the former South Cove shoreline (today's Chinatown); Bay Village (on the Back Bay shoreline near today's Theater District); and a partly developed wedge of land just east of Tremont Street that had been filled recently.

The population of Boston had grown very rapidly in the decades before 1850, with most of its people crowded into the slightly enlarged original peninsula, now totaling about a thousand acres. The population of Boston nearly quadrupled between 1800 and 1840, reaching 98,383 (see Table 2.1).[54] In the 1840s, the last decade before planning commenced for the Back Bay landfill project, the population of Boston increased by 39.1 percent, and 83.1 percent of the population lived on the original peninsula.[55] The 113,721 residents in the original part of Boston in 1850 were being compressed into an even smaller area as businesses expanded and railroads and shipping demanded more land near the terminals and docks. The density of about 150 people per acre in 1850 was actually much higher in residential neighborhoods because so much land on the pen-

TABLE 2.1. Boston Populations and Increases, 1800–1860

Year	Total Boston Population	Increase since previous census	1630 Boston land area population	Increase since previous census
1800 (U.S.)	24,937	—	24,656	—
1810 (U.S.)	33,787	35.5%	32,896	33.4%
1820 (U.S.)	43,298	28.1%	—	—
1830 (U.S.)	61,392	41.8%	—	—
1840 (U.S.)	98,383	60.3%	85,487	—
1845 (City)	114,366	16.2%	99,036	15.8%
1850 (U.S.)	136,881	19.7%	113,721	14.8%
1855 (State)	160,490	17.2%	126,296	11.1%
1860 (U.S.)	177,340	10.5%	133,563	5.8%

insula was given over to business and commercial uses. And the crowding was worse than we would think today because residential buildings did not exceed four stories in the 1850s.

In 1850 the Boston City government was concerned enough to commission Dr. Jesse Chickering to prepare a special report, based on the census, on population growth and immigration trends. Chickering described how commercial expansion resulted in a loss of family housing and showed that residents were moving out of some sections of the city. He stated that some entire streets had "been converted to stores, and the former occupants have removed to other locations, in or out of the City."[56] Chickering was referring particularly to the "Old South End" area near the Boston Common, which was overtaken for commercial and retail purposes as business expanded rapidly southward from the original center of the city around the docks.

Five years later, the City of Boston published another special report on population growth and change. Boston's crowding continued to increase, as the total population grew by 17.2 percent, to 160,490, between 1850 and 1855. This slower rate of growth was similar to the 19.7 percent increase between 1845 and 1850, in part because space was at such a premium.[57] A commission report published in 1857 noted that there was little land available for homes either in or near Boston.[58] There simply wasn't enough space for more people—unless land was added.

After 1860 the population growth slowed in the original area of Boston while the total population of the city increased rapidly because of the annexation of nearby towns and cities and because of landfill. Boston's population grew by 40.9 percent in the 1860s and by 52.8 percent in the 1870s, reaching 382,839 in 1880.

The rapid influx of Irish immigrants made Boston a very congested city by 1850. The Harvard historian Oscar Handlin pointed out that between 1845 and 1855 more than 230,000 people entered Boston as immigrants, and enough of them remained to raise the population by more than a third and to transform Boston from a densely settled city into an over-crowded city.[59] Boston's poor Irish areas became horribly congested with new immigrants who had escaped the potato famine in Ireland. Handlin described the unsanitary living conditions in areas such as the North End and Fort Hill, where slumlord landowners used yards, gardens, and courts to throw together poorly constructed hovels to rent to poor Irish immigrants. Thus were created the most vicious of Boston's slums.[60]

Housing for wealthy families was also in short supply because of the city's economic growth and crowding. Large homes in the old South End, now the downtown retail district, were replaced by commercial build-ings by about 1850. The south slope of Beacon Hill, a high-status neigh-borhood since about 1800, had filled completely with town houses for wealthy families. In the 1850s the new South End was being developed with attractive brick town houses on the old Neck leading to Roxbury. These elegant homes were designed for wealthy families, making up in part for the housing lost in other parts of Boston.

Moving the major city of the region would have been an option, but Boston, with its historical sites and thriving business center, was very well established after more than two hundred years. Abandoning the old city center would have brought severe financial losses to many people. As a consequence, Boston's leaders were understandably reluctant to abandon their heritage and business investments on the peninsula and move the city center to a nearby mainland site such as Cambridge or Roxbury. This contributed to the desire to add more land to the original peninsula.

By the 1850s overcrowded housing conditions and severe pollution, with its perceived health risks, created compelling reasons for filling the former Back Bay tidal marsh. These motivations have long been recog-nized, but they do not account entirely for the way the new Back Bay neighborhood was planned and created. To understand why extreme efforts were made to fill the Back Bay as an exclusive enclave for wealthy Bostonians, we look at what can be called "social motivations" underlying the massive project. These social motivations focus on Otis D. Duncan's "social psychology" factor in the "Ecosystem Model" for understanding regional change. The values and desires of powerful groups in Boston shaped the project in fundamental ways. The other factors in Duncan's ecosystem model are population, organization, environment, and technology—all important elements in the filling of Boston's Back Bay.[61]

Social Concerns Leading to Filling the Back Bay

Planning for the new Back Bay strongly emphasized keeping as many wealthy families in Boston as possible. In the 1850s nearly all Boston's high-income families were Protestant and their primary breadwinners were businessmen and professionals who worked in downtown Boston.

Understanding social motivations in planning for the Back Bay project requires looking at the demographic and social changes revealed in the 1850 and 1855 census data and examining the reactions of community leaders to those changes. Dr. Jesse Chickering's special report in 1850, discussed above, was commissioned by the city to investigate "some facts and considerations relating to *the foreign population* among us, and especially in the City of Boston."[62] Although the possibility of filling the Back Bay is not mentioned in Chickering's report, he indicated clearly the need to keep native-born residents in the city so the "foreign class" would not completely dominate Boston.

Between 1845 and 1850 Boston's population grew from 114,366 to 136,881, and the "foreign portion" (including children of foreign-born parents) increased from 32.6 percent to 45.7 percent, nearing half of Boston's population. Most remarkably, the "foreign" population had grown by 70.2 percent in five years' time, while the "American" portion had decreased by 2.3 percent. Chickering stated that "most of this foreign population are Irish . . . mostly poor, downtrodden and uneducated." He did note that, while these immigrants required charity, they tolerated their "trials" well and made their "scanty means" go as far as possible.[63] Chickering was concerned that a large majority of the children in public primary schools were "foreign" children. These young people would soon become adults, gain citizenship, and form a large voting bloc.[64]

In 1850 large portions of the populations in several Boston neighborhoods consisted of "foreigners"—foreign-born people and their children. Fully 83.4 percent of this group originated in Ireland, and their Catholic religion was hated and feared by many Protestants because of prejudices brought from England. The neighborhoods with the highest percentages of Irish residents in 1850 were the Commercial District and the old South End (62.6 percent), the North End (42.7 percent), South Cove (42.5 percent), South Boston (42.1 percent), East Boston and the Islands (40.9 percent), and Haymarket and the West End (40.4 percent).[65]

Chickering then considered the causes of the recent decline in the "American," or native-born, population. He estimated that two thousand men had gone to California from Boston in the past year, lured by "that golden expedition," the gold rush. That emigration was of little concern to Chickering, however, compared with the much larger number who had moved to the suburbs of Boston. He noted the impact of commuting by train, showing that many "merchants and others doing business in the City" had recently moved to neighboring towns and could commute to their downtown jobs "as quickly and cheaply as if they had continued in their former residences." Chickering estimated that twenty thousand people were commuting to Boston by train daily in 1850.[66]

The railroad commuters were well-to-do Protestants who had moved out of Boston—pushed out by crowded conditions in the city and the influx of poor Irish immigrants, and attracted to the suburbs by available land, large houses, and efficient transportation. This emerging suburban movement of high-income Protestant families threatened to increase rapidly the relative population of Irish Catholic immigrants. It is clear that Chickering feared this trend would continue and he felt that Boston's character would change for the worse.

The considerations of ethnicity, religion, and class were very important to the established "American" group, which was indeed losing the tight grip it had held on Boston's politics and culture for more than two hundred years. Until the early decades of the nineteenth century, English-descendant families who could trace their residence in Boston and New England from the seventeenth century had dominated Boston at all levels of the social structure. Chickering did hold out some hope for retaining the elite Protestants of English origin, whom he clearly valued and wanted to keep in Boston.[67] As he wrote, the South End development was beginning to hold some wealthy Protestant families in the city. Social motivations for the Back Bay project centered on providing housing for this group in Boston, and on giving them ample social and cultural reasons to remain in the city.

George Adams's report on the 1850 Boston census stressed the need to give wealthy people who might move to the suburbs more reasons to stay in Boston. He noted that the city already provided ample water piped from Lake Cochituate in Framingham and operated good public schools. Adams went on to say that, even without landfill for residential areas, Boston had the potential to double its population by developing East Boston and South Boston, but he overlooked the fact that those neighborhoods were too far from downtown Boston to be convenient for "the business class."[68] A filled Back Bay would be an ideal location, essentially an extension of the prestigious Beacon Hill neighborhood and near the workplaces of many wealthy Protestants.

The population of immigrants and their children increased at a slowed rate of 34.7 percent between 1850 and 1855. In the same period the "American" population barely held its own, increasing by only 0.8 percent. The net result of these changes was that the "foreign" population grew to represent 53.0 percent of Boston's residents in 1855.[69] Curtis concluded, with a tinge of dread, that it was unlikely that, in the foreseeable future, "native" Americans would again constitute a majority of Boston's population.[70] Boston would be a largely Catholic city and the Protestants' views of the Catholic religion were very negative in the mid-nineteenth century, based on fears carried from Protestant Europe. This was the time when "no Irish need apply" was a common discriminatory phrase in job listings in Massachusetts.

In 1855, 80.2 percent of the immigrant group had Irish origins, and the political implications of the growing "foreign" population were not lost on Curtis.[71] He emphasized that "native" American voters had increased only 30.38 percent since 1850, but the number of "foreign" voters had almost tripled—a 194.64 percent increase. Curtis also pointed out that "a very large number of those who do business in Boston reside out of town with their families and households (estimated at 40,000)."[72] This represents a doubling in railroad commuting from the 20,000 daily commuters estimated by Chickering only five years earlier.

Curtis expressed concern about the 200 percent higher birthrate in the "foreign" population in Boston than in the "native" population since 1850.[73] The projected impacts on the public schools and on the future political balance of power were of deep concern to the established "American" population in Boston. Curtis wrote that "the native inhabitants" should "guard with patriotic care the glorious institutions bequeathed by a noble ancestry"; he concluded that proper efforts should be made to maintain a large majority of native-born citizens in Boston.[74] The "glorious institutions bequeathed by a noble ancestry" were the legacy of

English Puritans dating from Boston's seventeenth-century origins. This reflects the growing anti-immigrant sentiments of the time.

Keeping much of the influential wealthy Protestant group in Boston promised at least to postpone the time when Irish Catholic immigrants would dominate the political power of the city. Creating the Back Bay as an attractive, exclusive neighborhood close to downtown offices, Beacon Hill, and the new Public Garden gave promise of maintaining the "Old Yankee" character of Boston. Though Curtis does not mention the planning for the Back Bay project, which was then under way, it was clearly designed to keep wealthy Protestants in Boston.

Curtis also commented favorably on efforts by Governor Henry J. Gardner of Massachusetts to reduce the influx of undesirable immigrants.[75] Gardner was swept into office in 1854 by the astounding success of the American Party in Massachusetts.[76] This political party, organized through secret lodges of Protestant men in towns and cities, attacked the ineffectiveness of existing parties and the corruption of politicians, and it claimed to champion the interests of common citizens—meaning native-born Americans, excluding American Indians. The members of the American Party were called "Know-Nothings" by their opponents and the press because they would not reveal anything about the workings of their organization. The American Party's power in Massachusetts coincided exactly with the planning of the Back Bay landfill project: the final plan of the State Commission was approved in 1856. The anti-immigration ideology of this political party seems to have influenced the strong efforts of the commission on the Back Bay and the state legislature to attract wealthy Protestant families to the new Back Bay neighborhood.[77]

Governor Gardner was reelected in 1855 and 1856 by smaller margins, but the American Party was weakened when Gardner took control from the secret lodges because the members distrusted authority. In his 1856 inaugural address, Gardner announced that he would not run for reelection and continued to stress the dangers of immigration and the role of the "horde of foreign born" in the growth of the Democratic Party.[78] Although the "Know-Nothings" lost power quickly, the desire of the State government and other leaders to attract wealthy Protestants to the Back Bay continued unabated.

The planning for the new Back Bay would soon demonstrate an emphasis on this desire. The layout of streets, avenues, and parks would create an elite neighborhood. Zoning restrictions and measures taken to keep the prices of house lots high would maintain the high status of the neighborhood for many decades to come. Attracting some of the most prestigious Protestant churches and important cultural institutions to the Back Bay would keep many wealthy Protestant families in Boston.

Pollution, overcrowding, and a desire to keep wealthy Protestants in Boston were three compelling reasons for filling the Back Bay. While these motivations generated interest in creating the new neighborhood, carrying out such a massive project would be possible only if political and financial considerations could be worked through by several governments and business interests. Leaders faced the challenge of making real the dream of a new, elegant neighborhood to replace a badly polluted former tidal marsh. Planning for filling the Back Bay would start in 1852 and the complex project would begin in 1858.

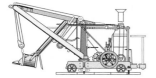

CHAPTER 3

Planning and Financing the Back Bay Landfill

Filling parts of the Back Bay began to be considered soon after the tidal power project was completed in 1822. Several early plans and false starts were motivated by the increasing pollution and crowding as Boston's population grew. The various unrealized ideas for filling in the Back Bay reflected key considerations that would remain strong when the Back Bay Receiving Basin was finally filled, starting in 1858. Objections that were raised to some plans revealed concerns that would later shape planning for a new, elegant neighborhood. Making the Back Bay project happen required getting through bitter conflicts among several government groups and private parties: the Commonwealth of Massachusetts, the cities of Boston and Roxbury, the Boston Water Power Company, and individual landowners and planners. In the end, the State Commission would be the most powerful player in pushing the project through to successful completion.

Early, Unsuccessful Plans

In 1824 a plan was proposed to fill and subdivide the area west of Charles Street, just west of the Boston Common beyond Charles Street (see fig. 3.1). As described by its promoters, the plan called for an elegant development with 321 house lots, spacious streets, and squares.[1] Five streets, each one block long, would run parallel to Beacon Street (the Mill Dam) and stop near the edge of the Eastern Channel in the Receiving Basin. The City of Boston committee appointed to investigate this plan feared that the new area would not attract wealthy buyers and instead would

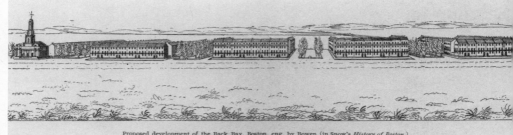

Proposed development of the Back Bay, Boston, eng. by Bowen, (in Snow's *History of Boston*.)

FIGURE 3.1. Drawing of the proposed streets and buildings west of Charles Street, 1824. A residential development proposed in 1824 would have filled most of the present-day Public Garden area. Developers promised elegant homes on large lots but the City feared that slum housing would result. The project was not allowed. *(Boston Athenæum.)*

become a poor neighborhood near the new mansions on Beacon Hill's south slope.[2]

The 1824 plan was rejected on the recommendation of the committee. The City's concern about the proposed new blocks west of Boston Common was the same kind of social consideration that would dominate the project about thirty years later. Powerful interests in Boston wanted to attract only wealthy families to the new housing. Although the rapid immigration of Irish Catholics had not begun in 1824, the value of creating an exclusive neighborhood for rich Protestant families was already a compelling argument.

Nineteen years later, Robert Fleming Gourlay, a Scotsman from Edinburgh, appeared somewhat mysteriously in Boston. Gourlay had spent some time in New York City, producing several small plans for improving that city. He claimed to be able to accomplish huge amounts of work because he was an insomniac who had slept only two hours over the past five years. In his native Scotland he had planned redevelopment projects and begun to create what he called the "science of City-building."[3] Soon after his arrival, Gourlay proposed bringing a flock of sheep into Boston Common[4] and building a six-story pagoda tower there, with a telescope on the top level.[5]

Failing to have these eccentric plans enacted, Gourlay set out to design a nearly complete rebuilding of the city of Boston, with a focus on the Back Bay. Gourlay proposed a very ambitious plan designed to provide excellent housing, parks, and transportation systems. Most of the Back

Bay area would be taken up by a body of water into which the Charles River flowed, thus doing away with the Mill Dam, the Cross Dam, and the tidal mills. "Elysian Fields," an oval island south of Mill Dam Avenue, would hold elegant housing. South of that, on a round "Circus Island," there would be housing and a "Transfer Depot" where the Western (Boston and Worcester) Railroad already crossed the Boston and Providence Railroad (see fig. 3.2).[6]

Three elegant "Boston Boulevards" would be two hundred feet wide and curve around the body of water in the former Receiving Basin, from Dover Street in today's South End in a broad sweep to the west into Roxbury and then through Cambridge to the north and northeast, ending in Charlestown. The large body of water would be dredged continually to keep it three or four feet deep. Mud from the dredging would go into forming the islands and boulevards that would provide space for many fine mansions for wealthy families. The innovative underground railroad lines would serve Boston's suburbs well, with a central station near the New State House on Beacon Hill.[7] Gourlay considered the fact that much of his planned development would be in Norfolk County (Roxbury and Brookline) and Middlesex County (Cambridge), and he recognized that the Mill Dam Corporation had rights in the Back Bay. He also knew that only the Massachusetts State Legislature could approve his grand plan and carry it through to reality.[8]

Robert Gourlay gave some thought to the technology needed for transforming the Back Bay and came up with a strange plan. Where the front edges of the curving boulevards would be located, he would drive coarse lumber planks into the mud to make two walls, twenty feet apart. The new shoreline would be established by filling between these wooden walls with stones and gravel. Then, behind the edges of the future boulevards, Gourlay would drive lines of stakes warped with brushwood (much like the buried Indian fish weir that was unknown to Gourlay). To bring water and mud into the area after the Mill Dam was removed, he would cut channels from the Charles River Estuary into these flats. Gourlay thought that large quantities of mud and floating substances would accumulate around the lightweight barriers, so very little "travelled earth" would be needed. He prophetically mentioned that, if it was needed, supplementary filling material could be brought in "by temporary railroads."[9]

Gourlay's plan seems to have been dismissed as too grandiose and expensive, and he was probably seen as something of a crank. This im-

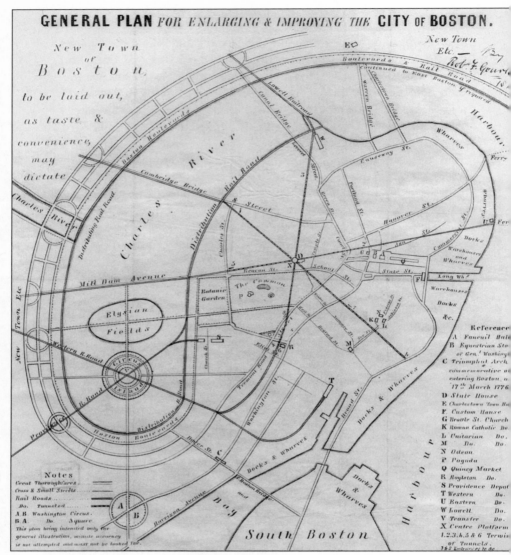

FIGURE 3.2. The 1844 Gourlay plan for the Back Bay and surrounding areas. Scotsman Robert Gourlay proposed a grandiose scheme of watery expanses, elegant boulevards, artificial islands, railroad lines tunneling though the city, and massive redevelopment. Most of the Back Bay would have been flooded and Boston would still be a small peninsula.

The Gourlay plan shows the Back Bay as filled mostly with water and the mill operations having been removed. The Charles River enters the new basin from the far left as a narrow channel north of Mill Dam Avenue. The Mill Dam would apparently be maintained, but Gourlay shows no sluices or openings through it. The new basin would extend from the Brookline and Roxbury shores on the west all the way to the Public Garden and pression was likely reinforced by his immodest statement that, because he had studied city building for many years and had been in Boston for twelve months, he had produced plans "which I flatter myself are perfect."[10] His emphasis on elegant avenues would be partly incorporated into the final plan: Commonwealth Avenue, like his boulevards, would be two hundred feet wide.

In 1849, a few years after Robert Gourlay left Boston, another visionary plan for transforming the Back Bay was proposed by David Sears. This proposal would have much more staying power and gain considerable support. Sears was a wealthy businessman and developer who lived on Beacon Hill in a large granite mansion he built in 1819 at 42–43 Beacon Street, which is now the Somerset Club. Sears traced his family history in Boston to 1630 and married into the Winthrop family, thus linking him to the first governor of the Massachusetts Bay Colony, John Winthrop. He invested in land all around Boston and developed the exclusive Longwood neighborhood in Brookline.

David Sears promoted a plan for the Back Bay that featured an oval "Silver Lake" near the center, just north of where the two railroads crossed. Sears's original plan shows a seventy-five-acre lake extending westward from near today's Berkeley Street, a block west of the Public Garden. The lake was to be filled by a slightly curving sluice leading in from the Full Basin (marked "Receiving Basin" on Sears's plan) and was to drain into the Charles River by a short sluice or canal leading out of the northwest side of the lake. "Sears Avenue" immodestly runs along the lake's south shore and extends westward through the area to be filled to Gravelly Point. An unnamed tree-lined avenue, similar to Gourlay's boulevards, encircles the lake, and a similar avenue runs to both the east and west ends of the lake, following the line of Boylston Street from the corner of the Public Garden (see fig. 3.3).[11]

Bay Village. A new street would cut across Boston Common and the Public Garden, parallel to Beacon Street, and then continue across the basin, crossing another new street on an oval island, labeled "The Elysian Fields." South of that island is the round "Circus Island," to be filled where the two railroad lines already crossed in the middle of the former tidal marsh. This island would contain housing and a major transportation hub. Gourlay shows the Western (Boston and Worcester) Railroad as splitting near Tremont Street to serve both its existing station and two stations to the north. The new railroad branch would go underground across a corner of the Boston Common to reach a station beside the Massachusetts State House and then continue under Beacon Hill to a terminus near today's Green Line station at Science Park. (*Boston Athenæum.*)

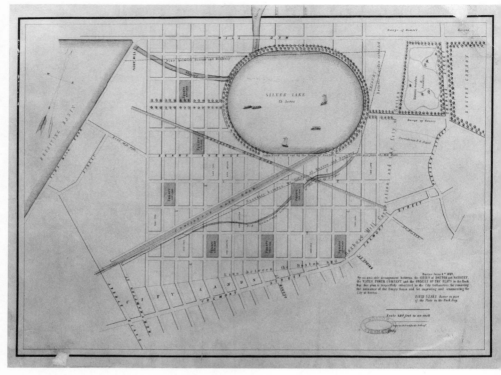

FIGURE 3.3. The David Sears plan of 1849. The seventy-five-acre "Silver Lake" near the center of the new Back Bay neighborhood was the first and largest version of the lake promoted by David Sears for more than ten years. The south shore of the lake would lie just north of the point where the two railroads had crossed since 1835. The plan shows the Boston and Worcester Railroad tracks ending near Tremont Street, but it probably was to continue to its existing station. The Boston and Providence Railroad, however, seems to end in the southeast edge of the lake, although the "Providence R.R. Depot" is indicated where it stood then, south of the Public Garden. Silver Lake was to be fed with brackish water from the Charles River and the Full Basin. Sears Avenue is planned to run along the south shore of Silver Lake, and a tree-lined boulevard (not named) wraps the rest of the way around the lake. The east end of the lake would be near the present-day Berkeley Street, and the west end would be near the edge of the approximately one hundred acres that would later be determined to be the State's. This Sears plan also includes seven block-sized park squares, scattered south and west of Silver Lake. *(Boston Athenæum.)*

Sears expressed concern with making the new neighborhood as attractive as possible, bringing wealthy families to the area, and improving conditions of public health. He argued that his plan would combine elegance with the health benefits of fresh air passing over water.[12]

Others, however, feared that Silver Lake would soon revert to being polluted with stagnant water and contamination. An anonymous critic of David Sears, writing in 1859, questioned the desirability of creating a lake in the middle of the Back Bay neighborhood. The writer claimed that most practical men believed that any sort of lake in the Back Bay would fill with filth and sediment, even if less extensively than the badly polluted, empty Receiving Basin.[13] Although his plan was not embraced when he proposed it in 1849, David Sears and his associates persisted in pushing versions of it for more than fifteen years.

The Commonwealth of Massachusetts Enters the Scene

Integrated urban planning for the Back Bay development began on May 19, 1848, when the General Court (the State Legislature) established the Commissioners on Boston Harbor and the Back Bay (the State Commission) to consider and report on the rights and duties of the Commonwealth in the harbor and Back Bay and to make recommendations on filling the Back Bay.[14] The commission held a large number of meetings, hearing from all interested parties.[15] This was a key political move, signaling that the State had given the filling of the Back Bay a high priority and determined to take the controlling role in carrying out the project. In 1852 a report of the State Commission was completed. The commission clearly articulated the social motivations discussed in chapter 2. The report begins with the goal of making the area valuable to all interested parties.[16] The objective was to develop a neighborhood for "a healthy and thrifty population and business." This is code for restricting the area to residences and businesses of wealthy Protestants. The report goes on to stress the goal to "prevent this territory from becoming the abode of filth and disease." This caution expresses the fear of the new neighborhood's becoming occupied by poor immigrants, especially Irish Catholics.[17]

In 1852 the state legislature charged the State Commission to investigate any conflicting interests among cities, corporations, and private parties. At the same time, the State Legislature spelled out overall objectives for the planning and filling of the Back Bay, staking out the State's role in controlling the entire project even though much of the acreage would not be filled by the State. The objectives were as follows:

1. The State should authorize the parties in interest to change the use of the receiving basin from mill purposes to land purposes, and to fill up the same . . .

2. The filling should be done with clean gravel, and as high as the Mill Dam, or Western Avenue [Beacon Street].

3. Perfect drainage should be secured; and the common sewers should discharge, either into South Bay or into Charles River, under water at low tide, below the main dam.

4. The public streets, squares, and ponds, should be wide and ample, so as to admit of a free circulation of the air.

5. The Western avenue, and all dams, should eventually be made major highways, without a toll.

6. The present scouring force of the water issuing from the two basins should not be diminished to the least degree, but should be increased as much as possible.

7. The strip of flats, two hundred feet wide, north of the main dam, should be filled up solid as high as the dam, or somewhat higher, with a strong, smooth sea-wall next the river, leaving ample sluiceways for the flow of the tide into and out of the full basin, and any ponds that may be left in the empty basin.

8. The receiving basin, embracing between four and five hundred acres, should be filled up, and laid out into building lots, streets, squares, and ponds as to secure upon the premises a healthy and thrifty population and business, and by inherent and permanent causes, forever to prevent this territory from becoming the abode of filth and disease; and the same thing should be done with the full basin, whenever that may be discontinued and filled up.

9. Any improvements in the Back Bay, involving the change in use from water to land, whenever and however made, should be done under the direction of the State, and in such ways as to secure the above-named objects in the most certain and thorough manner.[18]

The Cities of Boston and Roxbury Raise Objections

In 1849, as the State Commission began its work, a committee appointed by the City of Boston studied the Back Bay and reported that the severe public health hazard there required filling and proper drainage. This committee recommended that the Back Bay's former tidal marsh be filled on a plan that would "promise" to become a benefit and ornament to the City."[19] The City took steps to secure the right to fill and develop the area within is boundaries. Since 1827 Boston had held title to the mudflats west of Charles Street that later became the Public Garden, and out to the channel in the marsh somewhat beyond that. The Roxbury city line followed the main channel, near today's Clarendon Street, (see fig. 3.5). Starting in 1849 Boston pushed to fill house lots on this territory and to expand its borders at the expense of Roxbury.

The State Commission, after a long conflict with the City of Boston, concluded that Boston did not own any part of the Back Bay, much of the land was in the city of Roxbury, and new land filled by the State would be of great value to Boston as taxable property. The commission rejected the City's demand for "large grants of land" in the Receiving Basin and pushed ahead on a plan for development under State control.[20] The State report in 1852 totally negated Boston's move, giving the City no authority or share in future profits from selling land.

As the State Commission established the State's right to fill the Receiving Basin starting at the present-day Arlington Street, the City raised the possibility of developing the Public Garden land. That action would have brought considerable profit to the City and it would have been harder for the State to create an elegant neighborhood. Without the Public Garden, the first blocks of State land would have been less valuable.

The State Commissioners took a stand against the development of the Public Garden and tried to compromise with the City of Boston. In 1854 the commission produced a plan that would give the City some land to develop for its benefit and would preserve the approximate size of the Public Garden. The Public Garden would be reduced in width on both its north and south sides, extending only between the proposed Marlborough and Newbury Streets. The City of Boston could develop and sell the mostly filled land flanking this park area, out to approximately present-day Arlington Street, between Marlborough and Beacon Streets to the north and Newbury and Boylston Streets to the south. The parkland would be extended westward another block to the present Berkeley Street, providing a green corridor leading to the future Commonwealth Avenue. The State would fill this space and the residential blocks north and south of it (see fig. 3.4). This plan to extend and narrow the Public Garden was rejected by the City of Boston. The City then demanded a huge portion

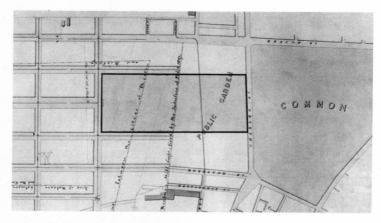

FIGURE 3.4. The Commissioners' 1854 plan proposed to the City of Boston. This map shows the narrowing and extension of the Public Garden that the State Commission proposed to the City of Boston as a compromise. The City would receive two blocks of land to develop and the park would be extended out to Berkeley Street. The City refused this offer, instead demanding much more land in the planned Back Bay. The width of the future Commonwealth Avenue (called Avenue V) is much narrower than it was finally planned and built. (*Courtesy of the State Library of Massachusetts.*)

of land totaling nearly three and a half million square feet, extending over 2,500 feet westward along the Mill Dam. The State Commission rejected the City's counter offer and withdrew all of its previous offers.[21]

The City then proposed to fill and develop the Public Garden territory first. Boston objected to the State's claim of exclusive rights to fill and sell the Back Bay lands starting at Arlington Street, the proposed street a few yards west of the existing Public Garden border. Boston set forth a plan to extend the anticipated Commonwealth Avenue through the Public Garden, along with parallel streets, and to subdivide the area into house lots. The commission concluded that the City's proposal to subdivide the Public Garden for housing would seriously damage the interests of the Commonwealth in the Back Bay.[22] A special two-man commission was set up to judge the City's claims, and a compromise strongly favoring the State was reached in which Boston received only a narrow strip of land along Arlington Street in return for not developing the Public Garden.

Two social motivations are revealed in this conflict between Boston and the State. The commissioners ruled that developing the Public Garden plot would reduce the elegant image of the new district by eliminating the formal park, making the Back Bay less attractive to the wealthiest families and reducing the value of the State's land. Additionally, the commissioners claimed to be more concerned than the City with attracting the highest-status families.[23]

David Sears reappeared in 1852, represented by R. H. Dana at early hearings of the Board of Commissioners on Boston Harbor and the Back Bay. Sears contended that the Boston and Roxbury Mill Corporation and the Boston Water Power Company had not lived up to their original commitment of providing adequate waterpower for mills and should be given no rights in the filling of the Back Bay.[24] If these companies' rights were negated, the value of his marshland plots east of Gravelly Point would be increased.

In 1853 David Sears tried to make a deal with the State for including a lake in the Back Bay. Sears repeated his claim of 1849 that a lake was needed to create an attractive neighborhood with healthful breezes blowing over open water. The commission rejected his offer because it had too many conditions that benefited only him.[25] The report of the commissioners stated that Sears's conditions would require them to lay out and construct a lake covering at least twenty-four acres, surrounded with marginal streets at least eighty feet wide. The lake would be completely on land belonging to the State, thus reducing the amount of land the State could sell.[26]

David Sears did not give up when the commission failed to adopt his plan. He wrote to Governor Clifford recommending action on a plan providing for a lake in the Back Bay. He painted a bleak picture of the future without such a plan: "narrow and filthy streets—with bad sewerage and imperfect ventilation and filled with receptacles of misery, vice, and crime." This raised the specter of the new neighborhood becoming a poor district occupied by Irish immigrants.[27]

Another political conflict arose between the State and the City of Roxbury. In 1836 most of the territory in the Back Bay had been determined to be in the town of Roxbury (see fig. 3.5). This boundary between Boston and Roxbury followed the early Colonial boundary lines established when Boston was confined to the tiny Shawmut peninsula. Boston's territory ended at the channel in the tidal marsh near the line of today's Berkeley Street. Roxbury became a city in 1848 and lost about two-thirds of its territory in 1852, when the town of West Roxbury was formed by residents who wanted a more rural community in the area that includes today's Jamaica Plain, Roslindale, and West Roxbury. Roxbury residents would not vote to be annexed to Boston until 1868.

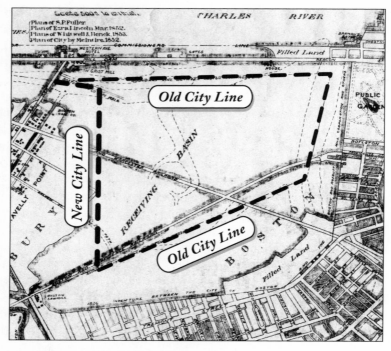

FIGURE 3.5. 1852 map of the Back Bay showing the old and new city lines. Before the State plans were completed, the city of Roxbury included most of the Back Bay within its boundaries. The map clearly demonstrates the serious threat to Roxbury's tax base posed by the commissioners' desire to put all of the Back Bay land in the city of Boston. The line between Roxbury and Boston ran just east of the Boston and Providence Railroad, from the southwest to the northeast. Then the line turned to the north and angled toward Beacon Street, between the present Clarendon and Berkeley Streets. The line then turned west, approximately along the line of Marlborough Street, which put the Mill Dam in Boston. The new Roxbury city line was moved almost to the east shore of Gravelly Point, which put all of the state's land in Boston.

The State Commission recommended in 1856 that the boundary line between Boston and Roxbury be changed so that most of the new Back Bay neighborhood would lie in the city of Boston. Mayor Sleeper of Roxbury wrote that the governor called the existing boundary "arbitrary, irregular and inconvenient." He pointed out that in the new Back Bay the Boston sewers would have to pass through Roxbury for suitable drainage. Also, the area in Roxbury would have less value to the State because it would not get the Boston water brought from Lake Cochituate in Framingham. The governor advised that the boundary line should be moved to bring nearly all of the new Back Bay into the city of Boston.[28]

These practical considerations were apparently only part of the State's motivation in wanting the city lines changed drastically. Deep concern about the rapid invasion of Boston by Irish immigrants had been generated by the 1850 census. At the same time, the city of Roxbury was attracting foreign-born Irish at an even faster rate than Boston. Although Roxbury had only 18,316 people in 1850, it had seen an increase of 249 percent since 1830. The "foreign population" (including children of immigrants) in Roxbury, growing faster than that in Boston, was up to 42.6 percent in 1850—just short of the figure of 45.7 percent for Boston.[29] Roxbury, with factories in the Stony Brook Valley and much vacant land, was not attracting many Protestant commuters. Moving the boundary to put all or most of the Back Bay in Boston would result in reducing the impact of poor Irish Catholic immigration on the city by creating a very large elite neighborhood.

Roxbury, predictably, bitterly opposed the State Commissioners' plan to take away a large tract of land with an estimated value of millions of dollars.[30] Mayor John S. Sleeper of Roxbury attacked the State's plan to set an arbitrary new boundary line that would deprive the City of Roxbury of jurisdiction over all the lands in the Back Bay, which totaled at least 450 acres.[31] In 1857 the State Commission delayed the sale of land in the disputed area until Roxbury's legal claim was settled in the Massachusetts Supreme Judicial Court.

The City of Roxbury was sued by the Commonwealth of Massachusetts over its claim to land areas below the line of "riparian rights" in the Back Bay. By Colonial law, riparian rights of shoreline landowners extended to the low tide line or 100 rods (1,650 feet) from shore, whichever was less.[32] The Supreme Judicial Court reviewed the report of a special referee, the Honorable Marcus Morton of Taunton, and confirmed his findings. The decision upheld the claim of the State to be the owner of all the lands, channels, and flats in the city of Roxbury that lay below the line of riparian proprietorship and south of the Mill Dam [Beacon Street].[33]

The State Legislature passed a law in 1859 to move the boundary between Boston and Roxbury, putting most of the Back Bay mudflats in Boston and in Suffolk County rather than in Roxbury and Norfolk County.[34] The boundary between the cities of Boston and Roxbury was shifted westward from near Berkeley Street to Fairfield Street, putting the whole State portion of the landfill project in the city of Boston.[35]

In 1855, the Commissioners on Boston Harbor and the Back Bay were replaced with the Commissioners on the Back Bay. The State Commission repeatedly rejected David Sears's proposals. In 1855 Sears again offered to donate some of his mudflats to the State in return for the State's placing a lake entirely on land belonging to, or claimed by, the Commonwealth of Massachusetts. Again, the State Commission determined that Sears's conditions were only to his benefit and would greatly reduce the amount of valuable land to be sold by the State.[36]

Early in 1856, while negotiations were going forward on plans for filling the Back Bay, the State Commission reported that the time was right to fill and sell the State's Back Bay land because of the great demand for housing in the city of Boston.[37] A few months later, a committee comprising two members from the Senate and two from the House recommended a joint special committee to look into selling the State's portion of the Back Bay before it was filled, and to take steps to control the plans and establish strict zoning regulations for the new neighborhood. The committee noted that the state auditor estimated this property to be worth over two million dollars. They warned against letting the land fall into the hands of speculators who would want quick profits, which could possibly lead to an undesirable population, poorly ventilated dwellings, and lack of suitable drainage to protect public health. Instead, under the proposal being considered, the State would sell to families who would build fine homes on wide avenues. By the end of 1856 the commissioners had completed their plan for the Back Bay and hammered out an agreement that would see the State filling its approximately one hundred acres and selling house lots to the public.[38]

The Tripartite Indenture of 1856

A key accomplishment of the State Commissioners was negotiating the Tripartite Indenture, a three-way settlement involving the Commonwealth of Massachusetts, the City of Boston, and the Boston Water Power Company. This legal document, signed on December 11, 1856, made the filling of the Back Bay possible; the final impediment would be removed when the State's lawsuit was settled against the City of Roxbury, which was then prevented from developing its mudflats east of Gravelly Point. Then, in 1859, the state legislature passed a law that moved the Roxbury city line westward, putting all the State's land in Boston.

The Tripartite Indenture divided the development of the Back Bay essentially between the State and the Boston Water Power Company and imposed an overall plan that also applied to private developers. The commissioners worked out a deal designed to favor the State. The Boston Water Power Company gave up the right to flood about half the mudflat below the line of riparian rights, which was controlled by private owners.[39] This agreement gave development rights over about a hundred acres to the State, and the Boston Water Power Company would fill and sell another hundred acres (see fig. 3.6). Much of the western part of the marsh was still controlled by the riparian proprietors who owned "uplands" along the shoreline on Gravelly Point and wetlands above mean low tide, although this section was in the area to be filled by the Boston Water Power Company. In 1856, riparian proprietors protested the Boston Water Power Company's use of its right to flood their land at that time to force the owners to give up half of their land to the company.[40]

The conflict with the City of Boston was settled by a compromise in the Tripartite Indenture. The City gave up all rights to develop the Public Garden for housing, with a new city hall being the only possible building to be placed there. In return, Boston was given a narrow strip of land extending the Public Garden westward and reaching south toward the Neck (see fig. 3.7). This change made the Public Garden rectangular. The State and Boston were required to "lay out and build a street [Arlington Street] eighty feet wide from the land to be released to the city, and a strip forty feet wide from the remaining land of the Commonwealth."[41]

The drainage of the Back Bay by a new system of large sewers on selected streets, connected to smaller sewers under the other streets, was required by the Tripartite Indenture. The agreement spelled out the responsibilities of Boston, the State, and the Boston Water Power Company to finance and build the new sewers. Boston was given the right to charge owners of house lots fair portions of the costs required to build and maintain the new sewers.[42]

The State Commission emphasized the advantages of the State's approximately one hundred acres of land. The commission pointed out that, while the territory in the Back Bay was divided equally between the State and the Boston Water Power Company, the State's portion was slightly larger. More important, the State's land was located in the most valuable part of the territory, adjoining the Public Garden and Beacon Street.[43] The State Commission concluded: "The conversion of a waste of water into a magnificent system of streets and squares, with dwelling

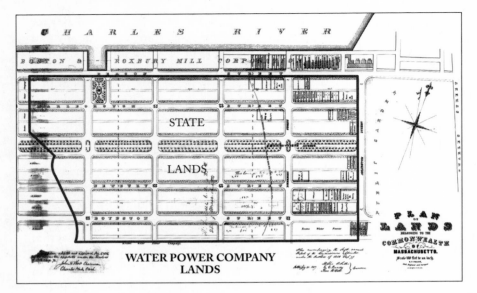

FIGURE 3.6. Map showing the boundaries of the State and the Boston Water Power Company portions of the project. The Commonwealth of Massachusetts successfully claimed control of about one hundred acres of mud flats in Back Bay. The state lands extended from the alley south of Boylston Street northward to Beacon Street on the Mill Dam. From east to west, the state portion went from Arlington Street to an irregular line between the future Exeter and Fairfield Streets. At first the western line of the state land had a curve in it, but it was later negotiated with the Sears brothers to zigzag in a way that would not cross any house lots. Most of the Boston Water Power Company lands were south of the state lands, thus connecting with the developing South End neighborhood. To the west, David Sears is shown as the owner of large tract of land, south of the area owned by the Boston Water Power Company. The two-hundred-foot-wide strip of land north of Beacon Street and the former Mill Dam was owned by the Boston and Roxbury Mill Corporation. *(Courtesy of the State Library of Massachusetts.)*

houses for a numerous population, is a transformation dictated by the soundest statesmanship and the wisest political economy."[44]

The commissioners were very clear about the social motivations in this arrangement. They pointed out that, given the chance, private individuals might develop the area in a shortsighted way designed to increase their profits. The commissioners believed that the State would be more concerned about ensuring permanent value and the public welfare.[45] The commissioners took steps to assure that the rest of the Back Bay would also be developed in an elegant manner. The Boston Water Power Company was also required to make specific improvements in its

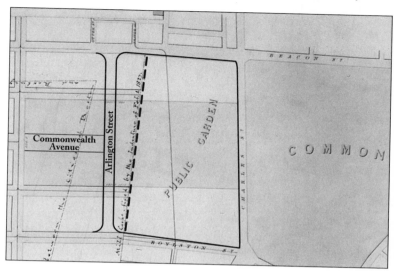

FIGURE 3.7. Map showing the minor extension of the Public Garden. The Tripartite Indenture of 1856 nearly removed the City of Boston from the project of filling the Back
Bay. As this map shows, the deal did give Boston a narrow, nearly triangular strip of land
that made the Public Garden almost rectangular by widening it considerably more on
the Beacon Street side than on the Boylston Street side. Boston got a slighter larger park,
but it was also required to fill the eastern half of the first new street in the Back Bay, Arlington Street. *(Adapted from the Commissioners' 1854 "Proposed Plan to the City of Boston." Courtesy of the State Library of Massachusetts.)*

area, and to follow the plan of streets determined by the State Commissioners.[46]

Details of the project were also laid out in this agreement with the
Boston Water Power Company. By the plan of 1856, streets and avenues
were to be filled to the level of the Mill Dam, and the building lots were
to be filled to a level five feet below that grade.[47] This procedure was
practical because the house lots and alleys within the blocks would
not have to be excavated soon after being filled to allow for the construction of buildings. When filling began in 1858, the contracts called
for streets eighteen feet above mean low tide, and the lots would be left
at 12 feet above mean low tide. The cross-streets would be completed in
a coordinated way by the State and the Boston Water Power Company so
each could be opened for its whole length at one time.[48] The Boston
Water Power Company was required to carry out a system of drainage
determined by the State, with arbitrators resolving disagreements with

the City of Roxbury over seventy-two acres of land between the new city line and Gravelly Point (see fig. 2.4).[49]

The commissioners favored an elegant but simple plan with wide streets in rectangular blocks. The successful plan of 1856 is generally credited to the architect Arthur Gilman, assisted by another architect and two landscape gardeners.[50] Mona Domosh tells us that Gilman's plan for the Back Bay was based on English precedents. She says that Gilman visited London, where several of the city's most famous architects showed him the sights. He saw the new grand boulevards in London's West End, particularly in Bayswater (north of Hyde Park) and Kensington (south and west of the park).[51]

Social motives are clear in the commissioners' description of how they developed the final plan. They listened attentively to the suggestions of several "gentlemen of taste and judgment" who planned to purchase lots in the new neighborhood when it was filled.[52] As a result of this process, Commonwealth Avenue was made more than 50 percent wider than originally planned, which was accomplished by narrowing other streets and reducing the depths of lots. Commonwealth Avenue was made 200 feet wide, and there were open spaces of 20 feet in front of the houses on each side. This made a total width of 240 feet between the houses for the central avenue. The increased width of Commonwealth Avenue created the "mall," the middle portion dedicated to trees, shrubbery, and other ornamental purposes.[53] The roadways on both sides were left the same width as originally planned.

The commission set aside about one-third of the Back Bay for public purposes, with the obvious motive of attracting appropriate residents. Priority was placed on establishing a good system of streets, avenues, and public squares to make the territory as attractive as possible and to convince people to select house lots in the Back Bay.[54] Domosh argues that the plan reflected the control of a small elite and was designed to benefit only that group so that Boston could become the cultural capital of the United States.[55] The design of the area, with Commonwealth Avenue as its focal point and rectangular blocks, served the Protestant elite's dual purposes of setting themselves off from the commercial city that had a tangle of curved streets, with the Common and Public Garden acting as an effective barrier, while they remained close enough to the downtown to exercise control. The elite did not flee the central portion of the city of Boston en masse, as the upper class in most cities was doing at the time.[56]

As the planning stage concluded and the filling process neared, an important decision was made that would increase the success of the new Back Bay neighborhood. It would have been easier to start the filling at the western end of the State's land, near Exeter Street, because the gravel trains would not have to go as far or to cross from the Boston and Worcester onto the Boston and Providence tracks before swinging onto the marshland. But that approach would have created the first new land in the middle of the polluted area, isolated completely from other residential neighborhoods. The land would not have been in demand because of its bad location. Instead, the plan was set to begin filling at Arlington Street on the State's land and to proceed westward block by block. In this way the first land would lie near the wealthy and well-established Beacon Hill neighborhood, the new Public Garden, Boston Common, and downtown businesses, making it much easier to attract high-income families to buy house lots there. Land could be sold at higher prices and elegant homes could be built as soon as the land was filled, with wide new streets providing easy access to the rest of the city. In a similar fashion, the Boston Water Power Company would fill its lands from the existing shorelines into the Back Bay, starting at the newly fashionable new South End along Tremont Street.

Strong evidence of social motivations in the planning process is seen in the selection of appropriate institutions for the Back Bay, and the reservation of key pieces of land for them (see fig. 3.8). A full block in a prime area was set aside and donated to the Massachusetts Institute of Technology and the Museum of Natural History.

Copley Square, the most important public space after the Commonwealth Avenue Mall, was planned to achieve this significance with the presence of the Museum of Fine Arts and two elite Protestant churches (Trinity Episcopal and New Old South Congregational). The massive Boston Public Library facing Copley Square would be built in the early 1890s. Other churches and institutions linked with wealthy Protestant society built new facilities in the Back Bay, firmly establishing their place in "Proper Boston." The commissioners bragged that nearly one-seventh of the land that could have been sold had been donated to the city of Boston and to prominent institutions.[57]

In 1859, a year after filling began and when the first buildings were under construction, a bold plan with a lake was put forward by George Snelling, a prominent Bostonian and a business partner of David Sears.

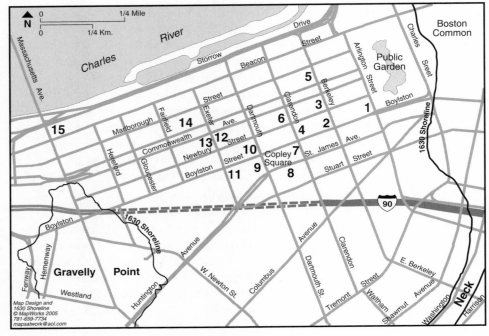

FIGURE 3.8. Map showing the key cultural institutions in 1895. Placing prominent institutions in the new neighborhood was an important way to attract wealthy families to the Back Bay and give the area a positive image. This 1900 map shows that higher-status Protestant churches were scattered broadly throughout the Back Bay. The churches in the Back Bay proper were Episcopal (Church of England), Congregational, Unitarian or Universalist, Baptist, and Spiritualist. The closest Catholic Church was tucked outside the southwest corner of the area, near Massachusetts Avenue, among stables and other service buildings. Educational institutions included the Massachusetts Institute of Technology, Harvard Medical School, and several Boston public schools. The Museum of Natural History and the Boston Museum of Fine Arts occupied prominent locations. The Boston Public Library was added to Copley Square in 1895 after earlier apartment buildings were removed from Dartmouth Street.

Institutions and Churches in the Back Bay in 1900:

1. *Arlington Street Church*
2. *Museum of Natural History*
3. *Church of the Covenant*
4. *Massachusetts Institute of Technology*
5. *The First Church in Boston*
6. *First Baptist Church*
7. *Trinity Church*
8. *Museum of Fine Arts*
9. *Boston Public Library*
10. *New Old South Church*
11. *Harvard Medical School*
12. *First Spiritualist Temple*
13. *Prince School*
14. *Algonquin Club*
15. *Mount Vernon Church*

(Mapworks © 2005.)

Under Snelling's design, there would be no Commonwealth Avenue. Instead, a narrow, long body of water would run the length of the Back Bay, filling the space between Marlborough and Newbury Streets from the Public Garden to the Cross Dam. West of the Cross Dam, the plan shows the body of water extending all the way to the Mill Dam at Beacon Street. Snelling acknowledged that a few houses under construction on Arlington Street would have to be removed to implement his plan.[58] The commissioners ignored Snelling's proposal and moved ahead rapidly on the filling. In 1861, the Commissioners on Public Lands replaced the Commissioners on the Back Bay.[59]

In 1861, five years after the State's plan was finalized and three years after the filling began, David Sears reappeared and succeeded in convincing the state legislature to require the State Commission to negotiate with the Boston Water Power Company and riparian owners to include a lake between the State's land and the Cross Dam. There were meetings on this, but no agreement was reached, even though the State offered to pay one-third of the cost.[60] Apparently, there was little interest in adding a lake that would reduce the amount of land that the Boston Water Power Company could sell.

Financial interests seem to have influenced David Sears in pushing the Silver Lake plan so long and hard. Years before, he had bought several plots of land on the eastern shore of Gravelly Point, which included riparian rights to large portions of the marsh extending well into the Receiving Basin. An 1862 map shows "D. Sears" owning an irregularly shaped area roughly equal to the hundred acres controlled by the State. David Sears is designated as the owner of about three-fourths of the lots in the Back Bay west of the future Exeter Street between Boylston Street and Commonwealth Avenue (see fig. 3.9).[61]

Creating a large lake near the middle of the Back Bay would have left David Sears owning much of the valuable land on the lake's western shore. After the State paid for the cost of most of the landfill project, Sears could sell his land to wealthy buyers at a very large profit.

The push for Silver Lake lived on and, late in 1865, George Snelling visited the commission offices to make another, even more drastic proposal to build a lake. Snelling wanted to improve the health of Boston by removing many of the structures now standing on land sold by the commissioners and to excavate a magnificent lake covering a few acres. This would have meant that many new brick and stone mansions would be destroyed. Snelling told the commissioners that he had done his best to

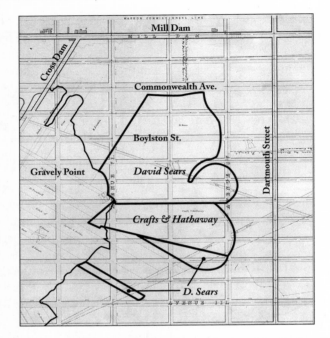

FIGURE 3.9. Map showing large plots of David Sears's land and the Craft and Hathaway lot in the Back Bay. A large part of the land between the State's section of the Back Bay and Gravelly Point belonged to Sears by riparian rights in the former tidal basin. This acreage promised to become very valuable after filling turned the Back Bay into a wealthy neighborhood. An oval lake in the Back Bay would have put much of the lake's western shore on Sears's land.

prevent the sales of land. His proposal that his plan should be presented by the commission to the next legislature was declined on the day of his visit and nothing more was heard of a lake in the Back Bay.[62]

The last change in state control of the Back Bay project came in 1877 when the Commissioners on Public Lands were abolished and their duties were transferred to the Massachusetts Board of Land Commissioners.[63]

Financing the Landfill Process and Land Sale Policies

People today often assume that taxes or government bonds financed the cost of the huge Back Bay landfill project. Early in 1856 the commissioners proposed a resolve to be debated and voted by the state legislature.

Among other issues, the resolve called for making some funds available before any land was sold by allowing the governor to draw up to ten thousand dollars from the state treasury to be used by the commissioners for the initial filling.[64] A short time later, the resolve was revised, with the only change being that the governor's power to draw the cash had been removed. Therefore, the State Legislature stipulated that, until land sales began, no money at all would be taken from the treasury for the project except to cover incidental expenses of the commission. The commissioners would have to find ways to fill the former tidal marsh economically with innovative approaches to financing so the project would not burden the taxpayers.

From the beginning, the commissioners faced a dilemma when the State Legislature refused to provide any start-up money for commencing the landfill process. The contractors' bids in 1857 had called for start-up payments so they could assemble their equipment and workers; without this, the cost per cubic yard for filling the area would have been much higher. The commissioners' solution in 1857 was to sell a large piece of unfilled land on Beacon Street about a year before the contractors began to fill the marsh. This land, in the first block of Beacon Street between Arlington and Berkeley Streets, would be filled by the two wealthy buyers; the proceeds of the sale could be used to pay the initial fees of the contractors to cover start-up costs. This first plot of land was sold at a very low price, $70,000 for 1.5 acres, most of a well-located block, only about $1.05 per square foot.[65] The commissioners were accused of favoritism and selling the land too cheaply, but their actions were found to be proper. The commissioners defended the sale by stating that the high status of the buyers, William W. Goddard and T. Bigelow Lawrence, would improve the chances of success for the landfill project and generate large amounts of money for the State.[66]

The commission's report for 1861 detailed the cautious approach and the slow beginning of land sales intended to maximize the long-term positive outcomes. At first the contractors, George Goss and Norman C. Munson, were paid in land rather than in cash because funds could not be drawn from the State treasury. For a few years after the first sale to Goddard and Lawrence, much more new land was paid to the contractors than was sold to the public by the State. In 1858, the first year of filling, 261,632 square feet went to Goss and Munson, valued at $305,000, or $1.17 per square foot; this was treated as a cash payment to the contractors equaling their charges for the work. The contractors then began selling their land as fast as they could to pay expenses and to make a profit. In 1858 the State sold only 54,832 square feet for $101,281, an average of $1.85 per square foot. The demand for land was even lower in 1859, and only two lots on Commonwealth Avenue were sold by the State; they totaled 6,972 square feet at $17,430, an average of $2.50 per square foot. The State's only sale early in 1860 was a strip three and a half feet wide to increase a lot purchased in 1858.[67]

This situation posed a very serious problem: the State was competing with the contractors to sell land. By March 1860 there had been so few land sales during the preceding fourteen months that the commissioners had hardly any resources for carrying on the work. The contractors had been paid with large quantities of land and had been able to compete in the market by selling land at prices starting at $1.71 per square foot. Meanwhile, the commissioners held out for prices of $2.50 on Commonwealth Avenue and $1.50 on the side streets. They could not sell State land at these prices because similar house lots were available at much lower prices from the contractors.[68]

This 1861 report shows that the State faced unfair competition for the sale of land from Goss and Munson, and this created a serious problem when demand was low, as it was in the late 1850s and early 1860s. Goss and Munson received prime lots near the Public Garden as payment for the filling work, which left some of the less desirable land for the State to sell. The State could not sell land at the prices it felt would guarantee only high-status buyers, and so it held newly filled land off the market. Therefore, the commissioners did not have the money they needed to push the filling ahead as fast as possible.

The commissioners appealed to the legislature in January 1860, suggesting issuing scrip (paper money issued for temporary, emergency use) to continue the filling before more sales could be made. This request was referred to the Committee on Finance.[69] After a delay, the commissioners' proposal was denied and they were forced to sell land to obtain funds.[70] In 1859 an offer to buy a large plot of land on Commonwealth Avenue at an average cost of $1.75 per square foot had been rejected. This offer was then accepted in 1860, and the buyer agreed to build immediately enough first-class residences to establish the character of the new neighborhood.[71] These moves first to demand higher prices, and then to place stipulations on the land sale that would guarantee a wealthy set of new homeowners, are direct evidence of the social motivations underlying the project.

The legislature authorized the issuing of scrip and required selling new land by public auction after May 4, 1860. All state land had to be sold at public auction until April 1879 (see fig. 3.10). The first auction was advertised in a catalogue dated October 24, 1860, and the bids were opened on December 1 of that year.[72] Each auction offered house lots in a few sections of filled land, and the minimum bids were set at specific prices per square foot for particular lots. Strict zoning restrictions were placed on the houses to be built and limited other uses of the land. In 1860, in all, private sales by the State accounted for 213,952 square feet sold for an average of $1.58 per square foot, and 126,701 square feet were sold at auction for an average of $1.91 per square foot.[73]

More auctions were held by the Commissioners on Public Lands at scattered intervals over the next several years. In all, twenty-four auction sales were held, and about three-fifths of all the State land was sold in this way.[74] For example, there was the "Catalogue of 19 Lots of Land on the Back Bay Belonging to the Commonwealth of Massachusetts, fronting upon Commonwealth Avenue and Marlborough Street to be sold at public auction, on Tuesday, October 21, 1862, at 11 o'clock, A.M., on the premises, by order of Franklin Haven, E. C. Purdy, Charles Hale (Commissioners on Public Lands)." The auctioneer was N. A. Thompson and Company. The auction catalogue has a fine map of the Back Bay that names only Arlington, Berkeley, Clarendon, and Dedham (later changed to Dartmouth) Streets crossing Commonwealth Avenue. The auction offered ten lots on the south side of Commonwealth Avenue: a corner lot with a minimum bid of $2.75 per square foot and nine other lots at minimum bids of $2.25. There were also one lot on the north side of Commonwealth Avenue with a minimum bid set at $2.25 per square foot and eight lots on Marlborough Street with minimum bids of $1.38.[75]

When enough money had flowed into the State treasury after a few years, the commissioners began to pay the contractor in cash or mortgages rather than in land, which gave the State more land to sell. The Boston Water Power Company followed the same pattern as the State, paying the contractors in land for the first few years and then shifting to cash or mortgages.

Land sales were strictly regulated by the State Commission to keep the sales prices high and to attract wealthy buyers as the filling of land proceeded. The commission sold segments of the filled land at irregular intervals in an effort to keep the prices up. In years when demand was low, no land was sold at all. This first occurred in 1861, although the filling

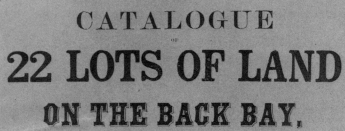

CATALOGUE
OF

22 LOTS OF LAND

ON THE BACK BAY,

BELONGING TO THE

Commonwealth of Massachusetts,

FRONTING ON BOYLSTON AND NEWBURY STREETS,

TO BE SOLD BY PUBLIC AUCTION,

On Saturday, Oct. 30, 1869,

AT 11 O'CLOCK, A.M., AT THE MERCHANTS' EXCHANGE READING-ROOM,

(Basement of the Old State House,)

BY ORDER OF   FRANKLIN HAVEN, ⎱ *Commissioners*
EDWD. C. PURDY,   *on*
ARTEMAS LEE,   ⎰ *Public Lands.*

N. A. THOMPSON & CO.,

AUCTIONEERS,

OFFICE, OLD STATE HOUSE, BOSTON.

BOSTON:
WRIGHT & POTTER, PRINTERS, 79 MILK STREET, COR. FEDERAL.
1869.

FIGURE 3.10. Auction catalogue cover. The State Commission sold various numbers of lots of land at auctions, spaced out over the years when demand for land was high. This catalogue, for the auction to be held on October 30, 1869, advertised twenty-two house lots on Boylston and Newbury Streets. Minimum bids were set for the lots, with higher minimums on Commonwealth Avenue and for corner lots. Text in the auction catalogues laid out the zoning limitations on the lots to be sold and described the payment process for purchasers to follow. *(Courtesy of the State Library of Massachusetts.)*

continued, with 733,482 square feet of new land completed by the contractor.[76] Land sales by the State resumed in 1862 and continued through the Civil War and beyond, but when a severe depression hit the country, the Back Bay land was held off the market from 1874 through 1878. Later, the land sales decreased steadily, dipping from 114,190 square feet in 1879 to 11,144 square feet in 1886, when the State sold its last house lots.[77]

Prices received by the State for Back Bay land varied widely, according to demand and the locations of the blocks being sold. Generally, the average annual sale price for house lots increased over time as the neighborhood became well established, reaching a high of $4.53 per square foot in 1884.[78] The most expensive building lot, at the northwest corner of Commonwealth Avenue and Dartmouth Street, sold for $6.55 per square foot and soon sported the magnificent brownstone Ames-Webster Mansion, built for Congressman Frederick Ames in 1872.[79] The highest average sale prices were obtained for house lots on the north side of Commonwealth Avenue because they shared the unique advantage in the winter of having bright sunlight streaming through front windows on all floors. The other east-west streets were too narrow for the low sun to reach all their front windows in the darkest months of a Boston winter.

The last report on the Back Bay project, submitted by the Massachusetts Board of Land Commissioners in 1886, summarized the land sales and the plots of land given to various institutions and the City of Boston. This report concluded that, of the 108.4 acres filled by the State, about 43 percent was "devoted to public avenues, streets, and passageways." The commission set aside about one-third of the remainder of the area for public purposes. The report goes on to give the amounts of land sold, and the average price per square foot, for the two time periods during which land was sold.

Between 1857 and 1872, 1,970,739 square feet of land were sold at an average of $2.00 per square foot, and between 1879 and 1886, 346,047 square feet were sold at an average of $3.28. No land was sold from 1873 to 1878.[80]

Obtaining donated land in the Back Bay was very important to educational and cultural organizations, and they made the argument that locating their facilities in the Back Bay would increase the land values around them. In 1861 the Committee of Associated Institutions of Science and Art published a report prepared by M. D. Ross. Ross showed that the house lots adjacent to the Public Garden and "Broad Avenue" (Commonwealth Avenue) had sold for more than twice as much (an average of $2.87 per square foot) as house lots on "ordinary streets" (an average of $1.33 per square foot). Ross's report concluded that reserving adequate land for such institutions would increase the total sales for the State by at least $150,000.[81]

As the filling went forward, the State and the Boston Water Power Company followed the commission's plan very closely; any changes had to be approved by the commission. One example of an important change in the plans came late in 1867, when the commission set forth conditions for construction of a privately owned horse-drawn streetcar line on Clarendon Street. The State would grade the street up to the standard level and tracks would be laid in the middle of the street and completed by July 1, 1868. The street railroad company would be required to run cars at least every half hour from 7 A.M. to 10 P.M. daily, except Sundays.[82]

The success of the Back Bay landfill project depended heavily on the elegant appearance of the new neighborhood and on strict enforcement of the zoning regulations. Innovative technologies had to be used to fill such a large area and to carry out the plans for the very attractive high status neighborhood.

CHAPTER 4

Locomotives and Steam Shovels

Yankee Ingenuity and Determination

As the drive to fill the Back Bay marsh gained momentum in the mid-nineteenth century, planners faced the reality that elegant homes now covered the former gravel pits on Beacon Hill. By 1850 the nearest sources of clean sand and gravel for filling the Back Bay lay at least five miles outside Boston in large glacial deposits. This distance made it prohibitive for horse-drawn carts to transport the vast quantities of fill required. The problem was how to excavate and transport large quantities of sand and gravel to the Back Bay quickly and economically. This project demanded new technologies for the rapid loading and unloading of sand and gravel. Local inventors were called on to contribute key technological improvements to solve the unique problems facing the Back Bay project.

Only small amounts of heavy sand and gravel could be carried in wagons for long distances on rough roads. Roads in New England, even toll roads, were muddy quagmires in the spring, rutted and dusty in the summer, and often blocked by snow and ice in the winter. The frequent breaking of freight wagon axles on these rutted roads resulted in extensive damage to the freight and long delays in its delivery. Even on a surfaced road, better than most roads of the period, one horse could pull only two tons of freight at very slow speeds.[1] Long distances and the necessity of loading and unloading four-wheeled gravel wagons with shovels made horse-drawn ground transport totally impractical for the Back Bay project.

Transportation of heavy loads across the countryside was greatly improved by canals, first in England and then in a limited way in New England during the early nineteenth century. One horse on a canal towpath could pull fifty tons of freight loaded in a shallow-draft barge.[2] The Back Bay contractors could not use this efficient method, however, because the Charles River could not be navigated beyond Watertown, and no canal was built westward toward the known gravel deposits along the Charles River Valley.

In England, James Watt's single-acting steam engine, patented in 1781, made possible Richard Trevithick's invention of the first successful steam locomotive in 1804. Only twenty-five years later George Stephenson's improved locomotive, "Rocket," pulled thirty-eight loaded carriages weighing ninety tons at speeds of twelve to sixteen miles per hour[3]; it was used in 1830 on the Liverpool and Manchester Railroad. Less than thirty years later, larger American locomotives would be powerful enough to pull heavy gravel trains.

The first locomotives to run on Massachusetts railroads were English locomotives manufactured by the firm of Robert Stephenson and Company of Newcastle-on-Tyne. In 1832 the Boston and Worcester Railroad purchased from the Stephenson company the "Meteor," a standard gauge, 2-2-0,[4] wood-burning, Planet-class locomotive weighing about six tons (see fig. 4.1). In 1835 the company purchased two standard gauge, 0-4-0, Sampson-class locomotives named "Mercury" and "Jupiter" (see fig. 4.2). A year later, in 1836, the railroad purchased two more Sampson-class locomotives, the "Comet" and the "Rocket," from the Stephenson company.[5]

In 1831 John B. Jervis, chief engineer of the Mohawk and Hudson Railway Company, designed a modified locomotive that had a swiveling four-wheeled truck in front and two driving wheels on a long wheelbase as an improvement on the rigid, short-wheelbase English locomotives. The stable, six-wheel engine of the Jervis locomotive (4-2-0) enjoyed a brief but intense popularity in the United States between 1835 and 1842.[6]

The Jervis locomotive was rapidly replaced by an enlarged version with four driving wheels (4-4-0), patented by Henry A. Campbell of Philadelphia in 1836. This more powerful and stable engine became the standard American-type locomotive for almost half a century.[7] Many of the earlier 4-2-0 Jervis locomotives were modified to 4-4-0, American-type locomotives. This 8-wheel engine was the most popular arrangement in nineteenth-century America. The limited power and poor tracking of the 0-4-0 Sampson-class engines (see fig. 4.2) soon reduced them to switching service, which was how they were used in the gravel pits.[8]

Although locomotives were improved quickly (see fig. 4.3), early rails were woefully inadequate and dangerous for heavily loaded gravel trains.

FIGURE 4.1. Photograph believed to be of the "Meteor" built in 1832 for the Boston and Worcester Railroad. The "Meteor," a 2–2-0, Planet-class locomotive, was built in 1832 by Robert Stephenson and Company for the Boston and Worcester Railroad. The locomotive was sold to the Bangor and Piscataquis Canal and Railroad Company in 1835 and scrapped in 1867. The photograph was taken at about the time of its retirement in 1867. The engine design was found to be unsuitable for the roughly laid American track, as its short wheelbase and lack of leading wheels caused the engine to rock and derail easily. *(John H. White, Jr.,* American Locomotive: An Engineering History, 1830–1880, *[Baltimore, MD.: Johns Hopkins University Press, 1998], figure 80; Smithsonian Photo 22, 707-M. Courtesy of Smithsonian Institution, National Museum of American History.)*

Heavier and more powerful steam locomotives required more durable and stronger rails. In the 1830s solid wrought-iron rails were used on Massachusetts railroads. This material was almost pure iron, with a negligible carbon content. Wrought iron had a relatively high tensile strength and was malleable enough to be rolled into required shapes. These wrought-iron rails, however, were deformed continually under the weight of the pounding gravel trains (see fig. 4.4). Even these improved rails broke quite easily under the heavily loaded gravel trains, particularly in cold weather, and caused many accidents. Steel rails did not come into general use until after 1865.[9]

Locomotives and gravel trains often were involved in horrific accidents. Safety features were not mandatory on trains for much of the nineteenth century. Because brakes did not contribute to the income of the railroad, driving wheel brakes seldom appeared on American loco-

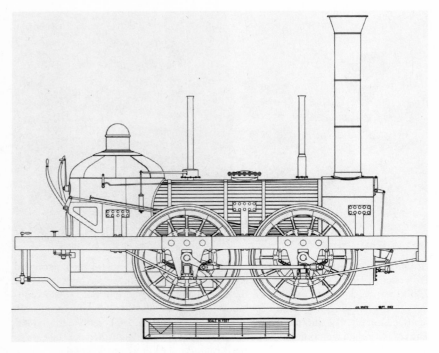

FIGURE 4.2. Plan of the "John Bull," a typical Sampson-class locomotive. The 0-4-0 locomotives "Mercury" and "Jupiter," purchased by the Boston and Worcester Railroad from
Robert Stephenson and Company in 1835, were Sampson-class engines similar in plan to
the "John Bull." Like the Planet-class locomotives, the short-wheelbase engines were
constantly breaking down or jumping the track. Shortly after their purchase they were
taken off the main line and converted to switching engines. *(John H. White, Jr., American
Locomotive: An Engineering History, 1830–1880. p. 255 (fig. 91). © 1998 by Johns Hopkins University
Press. Reprinted with permission of the Johns Hopkins University Press.)*

motives before 1875.[10] Single eccentric valve gears, used on most early
American locomotives, allowed a train to be slowed down and stopped
by throwing the drive wheels into reverse while the locomotive was still
in forward motion. This method was satisfactory until locomotives became larger and heavier.[11] Nor were there brakes on the small, four-
cubic-yard-capacity gravel cars. Some of the heavy locomotive tenders
carrying fuel and water had friction brakes on two or more of their
wheels that were operated by a single brakeman sharing space in the locomotive cab with the fireman and engineer, but those brakes were not
sufficient to stop a train quickly. If an obstruction on the track or a break

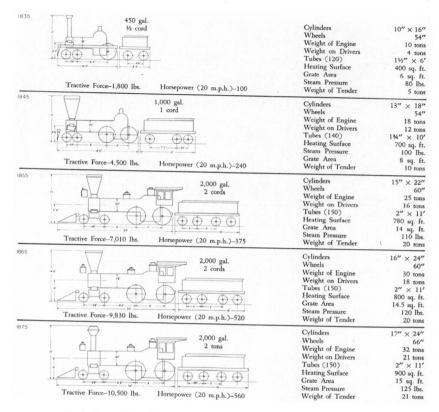

1835	450 gal.	Cylinders	10″ × 16″
	½ cord	Wheels	54″
		Weight of Engine	10 tons
		Weight on Drivers	4 tons
		Tubes (120)	1½″ × 6′
		Heating Surface	400 sq. ft.
		Grate Area	6 sq. ft.
Tractive Force–1,800 lbs.	Horsepower (20 m.p.h.)–100	Steam Pressure	80 lbs.
		Weight of Tender	5 tons
1845	1,000 gal.	Cylinders	13″ × 18″
	1 cord	Wheels	54″
		Weight of Engine	18 tons
		Weight on Drivers	12 tons
		Tubes (140)	1¾″ × 10′
		Heating Surface	700 sq. ft.
		Steam Pressure	100 lbs.
Tractive Force–4,500 lbs.	Horsepower (20 m.p.h.)–240	Grate Area	8 sq. ft.
		Weight of Tender	10 tons
1855	2,000 gal.	Cylinders	15″ × 22″
	2 cords	Wheels	60″
		Weight of Engine	25 tons
		Weight on Drivers	16 tons
		Tubes (150)	2″ × 11′
		Heating Surface	780 sq. ft.
		Grate Area	14 sq. ft.
Tractive Force–7,010 lbs.	Horsepower (20 m.p.h.)–375	Steam Pressure	110 lbs.
		Weight of Tender	20 tons
1865	2,000 gal.	Cylinders	16″ × 24″
	2 cords	Wheels	60″
		Weight of Engine	30 tons
		Weight on Drivers	18 tons
		Tubes (150)	2″ × 11′
		Heating Surface	800 sq. ft.
		Grate Area	14.5 sq. ft.
Tractive Force–9,830 lbs.	Horsepower (20 m.p.h.)–520	Steam Pressure	120 lbs.
		Weight of Tender	20 tons
1875	2,000 gal.	Cylinders	17″ × 24″
	2 tons	Wheels	66″
		Weight of Engine	32 tons
		Weight on Drivers	21 tons
		Tubes (150)	2″ × 11′
		Heating Surface	900 sq. ft.
		Grate Area	15 sq. ft.
Tractive Force–10,500 lbs.	Horsepower (20 m.p.h.)–560	Steam Pressure	125 lbs.
		Weight of Tender	21 tons

FIGURE 4.3. Evolution of American railroad locomotives from 1835 to 1875. The wheel alignments changed between 1835 and 1875 and locomotives became heavier and more powerful. *(John H. White, Jr.,* American Locomotive: An Engineering History, 1830–1880, *p. 76 (fig. 36). © 1998 by Johns Hopkins University Press. Reprinted with permission of the Johns Hopkins University Press.)*

in the rail ahead was observed from the train, it was an automatic signal for the engine crew to jump off and try to save themselves.[12]

Another safety problem lay in connecting or releasing the dangerous link-and-pin couplings between locomotives and railroad cars. This type of coupling, known to brakemen as the "Lincoln" pin, consisted of four parts: a link, a pin, a drawhead, and a drawbar.[13] The drawbar was a long, heavy, hollow metal bar. One end of the drawbar was firmly attached to the gravel car's frame, and the other end formed a concave metal shield called a drawhead with a horizontal, elongated slot at the center. Vertical holes, sometimes round and sometimes square, extended through the

FIGURE 4.4. Deformed wrought-iron rails. From the 1840s to the 1870s most of the rails in North America were made of nearly pure wrought iron (with a negligible carbon content), which had a relatively high tensile strength. These iron rails were soft and bent easily under the weight and constant pounding of the very heavy gravel trains, as can be observed on the track under the driving wheels of the locomotive "N. C. Munson." *(Photograph courtesy of the Needham Historical Society, Inc., Needham, MA.)*

center of the upper and lower parts of the drawbar behind the drawhead (see fig. 4.5).

The use of the link-and-pin coupling demanded the utmost physical ability and mental attentiveness possessed by the workman:

> He had to position himself between the cars while the engine pushed one car toward the other. As the moving car moved toward the one to which it was coupled, the trainman grasped the approaching dangling link, lifted it up, and within the second allotted him inserted it into the slot of the waiting drawhead, simultaneously dropping the pin through the drawbar of the stationary car into the incoming link and then quickly moving his hand and body out of the way of the concave drawheads.[14]

To secure a coupling, a trainman first fastened a link with a pin to one car. "Then a pin was 'cocked' at a slight angle in the other car to be coupled. As the two cars came together, the trainman guided the link into its slot. The impact of the coupling usually shook down the cocked pin, completing the coupling. If the pin did not shake down, the trainman stepped in between the cars and pounded it down with a spare pin." Often he had to walk between the two moving cars, putting one foot in-

FIGURE 4.5. Trainman in the act of coupling two gravel cars with a link and pin. To couple the two gravel cars, the trainman had to hold up the coupling link that was already pinned to the drawbar on the right side as the gravel car slowly closed in on him. The heavy wrought-iron link, approximately thirteen inches long by five inches wide, was lifted to a horizontal position and slid into the approaching slotted faceplate of the drawbar of the stationary gravel car. The trainman placed at least one foot between the rails, and a stumble could be fatal. Once the link was in the slot in the receiving drawbar, the trainman dropped the cocked coupling pin through drawbar holes and the inserted link before he quickly jumped out from between the colliding gravel cars. A sudden jolt or jerk of the train while he was connecting the link could result in the loss of fingers, a crushed hand, or worse. *(Kirsten Lindquist.)*

side the rail and the other foot outside the rail, where he could easily trip. "A man only lived long enough for one mistake."[15]

A hard jerk could break a pin or link. The links were particularly vulnerable because they were fabricated from wrought iron and only a blacksmith's weld held them together.[16] On occasion, the cars' bouncing and vibration shook an iron pin out of its slot, thus uncoupling the cars. This forced the locomotive to slow down, stop, and reverse direction so that recoupling could take place. When the trains uncoupled, additional time was required for recoupling, throwing off the train schedule. Often the uncoupled cars, still moving forward, crashed into the back of the forward part of the train as it slowed down or stopped, with damage or derailment the result.

As the locomotive was slowly backing up to couple two cars, the insertion of the pin was a matter of careful timing. Often a mistimed movement resulted in death. For example, the following coupling accident was reported on page 3 of the *Boston Weekly Transcript* for Wednesday, April 15, 1857: "Fatal Accident: We learn from the Providence Transcript that James Daggett of Seekonk, Massachusetts, a brakeman on the Boston and Providence Railroad, was so badly injured on Thursday by being jammed between two freight cars while coupling them, that he lived only a few moments."

"The uncoupling of cars was often the more dangerous job." Because of scheduling it was sometimes necessary to uncouple cars when they were in motion. The brakeman could choose either to run along between the cars and pull out the pin at the proper time, or to lie on the drawbar that held the coupling slot and pull the pin out from a prone position. There was not much room on the drawbar for a man's body and the handholds were seldom trustworthy. "If there was any miscue, or if the pins could not be pulled, the trainman could be thrown under the car."[17]

Railroad accidents were so common in the nineteenth century that only the especially grotesque of bloody accidents were reported by the press. Approximately one-fourth of railroad deaths and one-third of railroad injuries were associated with coupling.[18] In 1875 link-and-pin coupling was still being used on the majority of railroads. Automatic coupling did not become universal until about 1900.

While the locomotive power for pulling sufficiently large loads was developed by the 1830s and 1840s, the challenge of quickly loading gravel trains required more complex technical solutions. The digging of Beacon Hill gravel for early landfills and the excavations for early railroads involved large numbers of men performing slow, backbreaking labor.

Ingenious Yankee inventors would meet this challenge. Although the steam shovel was invented locally in the 1830s, for about twenty years these machines were weak and subject to numerous breakdowns. It would require the cooperation of a local railroad contractor and an inventor to produce a stronger and more reliable steam shovel—just in time for the Back Bay landfill project.

William Smith Otis, born in Pelham, Massachusetts, in 1813, conceived of his steam shovel at the age of twenty. Using various machine shops around Canton, Massachusetts, he built a working model of his machine in 1835. In 1837 it was used on the Western Railroad line between Springfield and Worcester. Otis's invention duplicated the motions of a man with a shovel. It dug up the earth, lifted it vertically in a bucket with a scooping motion, and then swung it in a horizontal arc to either side to deposit its load into a waiting wagon or train car.[19] Steam power, however, was used only for scooping and lifting the bucket of sediment. The movement of the boom to the left or to the right was controlled by two men on the ground pulling ropes attached to each side of the boom. When required, a team of horses dragged the steam shovel forward.[20]

William Smith Otis married Elizabeth Everett in Canton, Massachusetts, on June 22, 1835. Among the wedding guests was his cousin and close friend, Oliver Smith Chapman, a railroad contractor who would soon work on the construction of the Eastern Railroad and on the Boston and Albany Railroad. Otis moved to Philadelphia, where he improved his original design and persuaded Joseph Harrison, the general foreman of the locomotive firm of Barrett and Eastwick, to build a prototype for him.[21]

On February 24, 1839, Otis received a U.S. patent on his invention, which he described as a "crane-excavator for excavating and removing earth."[22] Later that same year, he died of typhoid fever in Westfield, Massachusetts, at the age of twenty-six (see fig. 4.6). During the few years following his death, only six more Otis steam shovels were produced by the newly named firm of Eastwick and Harrison, at a cost of about six thousand dollars each. There was a recession between 1837 and 1842, and Eastwick and Harrison soon closed up their locomotive shop.[23]

In January 1844 Oliver Chapman's wife died, and a little over a year later, on March 23, 1845, he married Elizabeth Otis, the widow of his cousin William Otis. The following year Chapman placed a steam shovel on the Vermont Central Railroad while he worked at Claremont, New Hampshire, and Burlington, Vermont. During this time Chapman renewed Otis's patent on the steam shovel, which gave him the right to build and sell it.[24]

In the 1850s Chapman was involved in railroad construction: on the Marietta and Cincinnati Railroad; at Jacksonville, New Jersey, on the New Jersey Central Railroad; at Girard, Pennsylvania, on the Lake Shore Railroad; and at Council Bluffs, Iowa, on the Union Pacific Railroad.[25] While in Boston, Chapman was given the loan of a desk at John Souther's Globe Locomotive Works, located at the corner of A and First Streets in South Boston. During one of these Boston visits Oliver Chapman approached John Souther about strengthening the steam shovel's numerous weak parts.

John Souther, widely recognized as a heavy-machine builder, began as an apprentice in carpentry and pattern making at the age of fourteen. Seven years later, in 1837, he was employed as a draftsman and pattern maker for sugar-mill machinery at a new foundry in Matanzas, Cuba.

FIGURE 4.6. William S. Otis and Oliver S. Chapman gravestone, Canton, Massachusetts. William Smith Otis and his cousin Oliver S. Chapman are buried at this gravesite in the Canton Town Cemetery. These men invented and improved the steam shovel that excavated sand and gravel for the Back Bay project. Elizabeth Everett, the wife of both of these gentlemen, is buried in the same cemetery plot. William Otis married Elizabeth Everett and had two children with her before he died of typhoid fever on November 13, 1839. Oliver Chapman married Otis's widow; he died of a heart attack while having his watch repaired in Boston on February 8, 1877. Elizabeth outlived both her husbands and died on January 4, 1900. *(Photographs by William A. and Anna M. Newman.)*

Two years later Souther was hired by the Hinkley and Drury Locomotive Works in Boston as a draftsman and pattern maker for the different classes of locomotives that they intended to manufacture. In this capacity he was responsible for the design of Hinkley's first locomotive. In 1846 he left Hinkley and Drury after being involved in the construction of some eighty locomotives and founded the Globe Works, later the Globe Locomotive Works, in South Boston. Here he built locomotives, stationary and portable steam engines, sugar-mill machinery, and general machinery.

(a)   (b)

FIGURE 4.7. Portraits of (a) Oliver Chapman and (b) John Souther. *(Courtesy of the Canton Historical Society and The Bostonian Society/Old State House.)*

In 1852 he went to Richmond, Virginia, and managed the locomotive shop at the Tredegar Iron Works. Because of differences with the managers in Richmond he returned to Boston in 1854.[26]

Together, Chapman and Souther worked to perfect the Otis steam shovel (see fig. 4.7). Under Chapman's direction, Souther strengthened all parts of the machine, increasing its weight by about ten tons so that it could excavate hard and compact materials. Beginning in 1859, after a production hiatus of about twenty years, John Souther's locomotive works began the production of the improved and heavier steam shovel (see fig. 4.8).[27]

There are no patents on steam shovels or their improvements in the U.S. Patent Office records between Otis's original patent of 1839[28] and Chapman's improved patent of 1867.[29] The newly improved Chapman steam shovel required only two men, one engineer and a helper, to operate the crane. It consumed about eight hundred pounds of coal in ten hours and accomplished as much work in one day as could be done by fifty to sixty laborers.[30]

In 1876 a book on American industry described the advantages of the Chapman steam shovel:

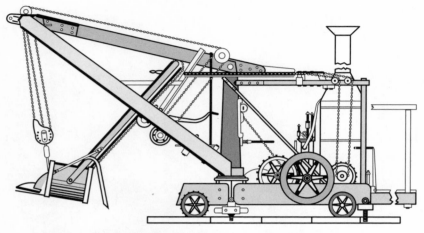

FIGURE 4.8. Schematic drawing of Otis steam shovel with Chapman's improvements. Although not patented until 1867, this type of improved, heavier steam shovel was used widely in railroad construction and gravel pit operations during the last half of the nineteenth century. The arrangement of wheels, gears, chain drives, and moving arms allowed the steam shovel to excavate in hard gravel banks and to fill a four-cubic-yard capacity gravel car with only two scoops of the shovel's bucket. *(U.S. Patent Office, patent no. 63,857, April 16, 1867. Created by Kirsten Lindquist.)*

The Excavator can be controlled and kept to work at all times, while the class of laborers who shovel on railroads are not very reliable. Generally there is much time lost by them after pay day; a strike can happen at any time and the whole work be stopped for days or even weeks; while stormy weather necessarily prevents them from working its continuance. The Excavator never loses time after pay day; it engages in no strikes, and the two men that operate it are under cover, and the machine not only scoops earth from its native bed, but deposits it just where wanted on the car, bad weather does not effect its operations. The strongest reason in favor of the Excavator however, is the great saving in expense over hand labor. One of these machines has excavated in gravel, and loaded into cars two thousand (2,000) cubic yards in one day;—but from ten hundred to twelve hundred cubic yards would be a fair day's work with the ordinary delays in making up trains for a long haul, and from three hundred to eight hundred cubic yards when working with hard material, varying with the hardness.[31]

Powerful locomotives and highly efficient steam shovels allowed rapid delivery of sand and gravel to the Back Bay, and so faster ways of un-

FIGURE 4.9. Forces on the wrought-iron rails during sand and gravel dumping. Dumping the gravel cars forced the wheels' flanges against the track away from the direction of dumping, deforming the rails and forcing them apart over time. *(Matthias N. Forney,* The Railroad Car Builder's Pictorial Dictionary, *1879, [New York: Dover, 1974], 237, figure 81.)*

loading gravel cars were required. The delay in the development of side-dumping cars, or tip cars, to transport and unload gravel was due more to the weakness of the rails than to the complicated mechanics of tipping the car's loaded gravel boxes. Side-dumping gravel cars were not practical until rolled wrought-iron rails came into general use. Even then, the action of dumping gravel on one side of the track forced the tipped gravel car outward, away from the accumulating gravel pile, regardless of how slowly and carefully the brakeman tilted the gravel box. The wheel flanges exerted a considerable force on the outside track, forcing it to bend over time even though both rails were spiked to the same ties and connected by tie rods. The result was to separate the rails further, possibly resulting in derailment (see fig. 4.9). The gravel cars used initially on the Back Bay project appear to be Nettleton dumping cars, patented in 1849.[32] These cars could be tipped to either side of the track as the situation demanded.

Even with these new technologies in place, management of the complex project would require courageous and capable contractors. The tasks ahead included finding massive gravel deposits close enough to railroads serving Boston from the south or west, obtaining all the necessary equipment, hiring and managing a large workforce, and borrowing necessary funds. Fortunately, George Goss and Norman Munson rose to the occasion as a highly effective contracting team.

CHAPTER 5

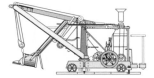

Gravel Trains and Bold Entrepreneurs

The project of filling in the Back Bay tidal mudflats was technically feasible in the mid-nineteenth century, but determined and courageous contractors were essential to make it a success. George Ordiorne had the first contracts for filling the Back Bay but he seems to have used horses and wagons, which were insufficient for the massive project. Railroad contractors fit the bill. They were a special breed of men who were accurately portrayed in the following passage from the August 1874 issue of *Harper's Magazine:*

> The railroad contractor is eminently a practical man. He is apt to be a self-made man. He is not infrequently one who commenced life with the spade, the pickaxe, and the wheelbarrow. He had greater industry or greater shrewdness than his fellows, and became the head of a gang of men. Then he took a small contract on his own account, invested luckily in real estate along the line of a projected railway, amassed a little capital, employed both capital and practical experience to good advantage and so gradually got on in the world, till now, what with capital and credit, he stands ready to undertake any work which the railroad capitalist desires undertaken.[1]

Two native New Englanders with broad experience as railroad contractors rose to the occasion: George Goss and Norman Carmine Munson. Little is known about the early life of George Goss other than that he was born in 1826 in Danville, Maine, a very small village southwest of Auburn, at the junction of the present Maine Central and Canadian National Railroads. Norman Munson was born August 15, 1820, on a small farm outside Hinesburgh, Vermont, a few miles to the south of Burlington.[2]

After completing grammar school, Munson left home to begin his railroad career. In 1833, at the age of thirteen, he worked as a superintendent of track laying on the early construction of the Boston and Worcester Railroad. Upon completion of that work in 1835, he was assigned a section of the same railroad to maintain. The following year, when work on the Eastern Railroad began, he was an overseer for a contractor. Next he became a subcontractor in the building of the Fitchburg Railroad, and then the contractor in the construction of about fifteen miles of the Feltonville branch of the Fitchburg Railroad, from South Acton to Marlborough, Massachusetts. He next laid about twenty miles of track for the Stony Brook Railroad from Groton Junction to Lowell, Massachusetts. From Lowell he went to New Hampshire, where in partnership with another contractor he built the Portsmouth and Concord Railroad. In 1848 he constructed the second track for the Fitchburg Railroad, from Concord to Fitchburg, Massachusetts, a distance of about twenty miles.[3] In 1854 Munson completed the second track on the Hudson River Railroad from Peekskill to Rhinebeck, New York, a distance of approximately fifty-one miles. He later straightened out the Philadelphia, Wilmington and Baltimore Railroad line near Havre de Grace, Maryland.[4]

It is not known when or under what circumstances Norman Munson first met George Goss. The two railroad contractors from New England probably met sometime in the 1830s on one of the New England railroad construction projects for which they were contractors, possibly during the construction of the Eastern Railroad. In 1857 Munson and Goss constructed several projects for the City of Baltimore, Maryland, including building North Avenue, a major street in the city.[5] They worked together on the Philadelphia, Wilmington and Baltimore Railroad just before getting involved in the enormous Back Bay landfill project. It was in Delaware where they may have met two important future financial backers, George Lobdell, of the Lobdell Car Wheel Company of Wilmington, Delaware, and his son-in-law, Henry S. McComb, a merchant and railroad speculator. Early in 1858 Goss and Munson began building the capacity to dig, transport, and deposit the huge quantities of "clean sand and gravel" called for in the contracts with the State and the Boston Water Power Company.

Norman C. Munson was a large, robust, energetic, self-made individual with a strong faith in the future of America (see fig. 5.1). His magnetism and courage enabled him and George Goss in 1857 to arrange contracts with the Commonwealth of Massachusetts, the City of Boston,

FIGURE 5.1. Portrait of Norman Carmine Munson. *(Reprinted with permission of the Shirley Historical Society, Shirley, Massachusetts.)*

and the Boston Water Power Company for filling the Back Bay region.[6] Some of these contracts were taken over from George Ordiorne, who may have done no work on them. All told, there were about 580 acres to be filled in the former Receiving Basin.

Needham Operations Begin in 1858

Extensive deposits of sand and gravel occurred in several communities south and west of Boston, including Auburndale (part of Newton), Canton, Dedham, Hyde Park, Islington (part of Westwood), Needham, and several other places along the Charles and Neponset River Valleys. The development of more powerful locomotives, side-dumping gravel cars, and steam shovels had solved the problems of excavating and transporting large amounts of high-quality sand and gravel over such long distances. However, the project was feasible only if extensive gravel sources were located close to a railroad line that led into the Back Bay area and permitted the heavy traffic of numerous gravel trains on its rails.

From the 1830s to the 1850s, the construction of railroads through these extensive deposits to the south and west of Boston made possible the inexpensive long-distance transport of massive amounts of sand and gravel to the Back Bay. During the 1830s the Boston and Providence and the Boston and Worcester Railroads entered Boston from the south and west and crossed near the center of the Receiving Basin. Later, on April 24, 1847, the six-mile-long Brookline Branch Line of the Boston and Worcester opened from the main line at Brookline Junction to its terminus at Brookline Village, where its right-of-way now serves as part of the Riverside Branch of the MBTA Green Line. Two years later, on May 1, 1849, a charter permitted construction of the Charles River Branch Railroad, which would extend the Brookline Branch Line westward from Brookline Village to Dover, Massachusetts.[7] These railroads and a section of the Boston and Worcester main line allowed Goss and Munson to begin filling the Back Bay in 1858.

The Charles River Branch Railroad constructed its first section from Newton Upper Falls to Brookline Village, where it connected to the rails of the Boston and Worcester's Brookline Branch Railroad. The "Lion," a small, 0-4-0 engine built by Edward Bury in England in 1835, ran from Boston out to West Newton on the Boston and Worcester main line, and then a team of horses hauled it overland to Pettee's gravel pit in Newton Upper Falls.[8] This gravel pit was located east of Pettee's foundry and machine shops, in the vicinity of today's Oak Street near the Charles River.[9] The locomotive was probably moved on Chestnut Street, the direct route over which Pettee sent his manufactured goods by wagon to the West Newton train station.[10] The locomotive "Lion" (see fig. 5.2) hauled gravel from the Newton Upper Falls gravel pit needed to build the new rail bed eastward to Brookline Village.

By 1851 the Charles River Branch Railroad had consolidated with the Charles River Railroad, retaining the name of the latter, with authority to extend the line to Woonsocket, Rhode Island. In November 1852 the new track was completed to Newton Upper Falls and operated under contract by the Boston and Worcester Railroad.[11] Passenger service began from Boston to Newton Upper Falls, a distance of six miles, on November 14, 1852.[12]

By June 1853 the Charles River Railroad opened an additional two miles of track to East Needham before the railroad ran out of money and construction halted.[13] One purpose stated for this extension into East Needham was for the "immediate access to abundant diluvial deposits of excellent gravel, for filling up the large areas of mud-flats between Brook-

FIGURE 5.2. Locomotive "Brookline," formerly the locomotive "Lion." The "Lion," an 0-4-0 locomotive built in 1835 by Edward Bury in Liverpool, England, was the first locomotive to run on the Brookline Branch Railroad. This locomotive, used in the construction of the Charles River Branch Railroad, went into the repair shop in August 1853 and came out as a 4-2-2-bicycle-type locomotive renamed "Brookline." Note the hand brake and the wooden brake shoes on the tender but no brakes on the locomotive. *(In John Gould Curtis,* History of the Town of Brookline, Massachusetts, *[Boston: Houghton Mifflin Co., 1933], figure opposite 202.)*

line and Boston, and in and bordering upon the full and empty basins formed by the Western Avenue and its branches; in order to afford opportunity to remove existing nuisances, and to convert those mud-flats into available spaces for the use and convenience of the already compressed business and population of our growing metropolis."[14] The Charles River Railroad did not transport significant amounts of sand and gravel into the Back Bay until a few years later, after 1855, after it was consolidated into the New York and Boston Railroad.[15] The Boston and Worcester Railroad took over the operation of these tracks from its inception in 1852 until April 1, 1858.[16]

After 1856, when the Back Bay plan was agreed on,[17] the State Commission prepared to start filling the key one hundred acres of the Back Bay. George Goss and Norman C. Munson took over George Ordiorne's land-filling contract with the Boston Water Power Company on December 1, 1857.[18] They seem to have had difficulty raising funds in the beginning.[19]

In August 1857 Goss and Munson signed a contract with William W. Goddard and T. Bigelow Lawrence to fill the large lot on Beacon Street that Goddard and Lawrence had purchased from the State. With these additional funds they bought or leased 145 four-wheel gravel cars and two switching engines. In addition, they purchased three main-line locomotives from the Hinkley Locomotive Works in Boston, the "General H. P. Banks," "Charles River," and "Bay State." Little is known of their wheel alignment except that the "Charles River" was a 4-4-0 American-type locomotive.[20] Munson probably purchased or leased some additional locomotives and gravel-dump cars. Used equipment was widely available because of a recession in 1857, when many of the railroad companies sold off much of their surplus rolling stock. Also, at this time foundries experienced a cutback in orders and had to sell their new locomotives at bargain prices.

Pitfalls faced the Back Bay project even with a generous amount of start-up money for buying locomotives, gravel cars, and railroad supplies. Goss and Munson's weekly payroll included the wages for the eighty men who operated the Needham gravel pit and ran the gravel trains, as well as many laborers who spread and graded the sand and gravel in the Back Bay.[21] Although the State of Massachusetts and, later, the Boston Water Power Company began by paying the contractors in land rather than cash, the land unfortunately could be converted to cash only if it was sold to the public. The contractors' cash flow required brisk land sales, which to a large extent depended on the economy. If for some reason land sales were slow, Goss and Munson were forced to mortgage their equipment to make ends meet. This situation during the early days of the filling operation generated stress between Munson, who was prone to taking risks, and the more conservative Goss.[22]

On April 1, 1858, Goss and Munson took over the entire day-to-day operations of the New York and Boston Railroad in Massachusetts from the Boston and Worcester and ran the railroad for an annual rent of $6,000. They charged the railroad for its share of operating expenses, just as the Boston and Worcester had done before them. In 1858, the operating expenses of both the Boston and Worcester Railroad and Goss and Munson were $9,097.34.[23] In addition to running their gravel trains, they provided passenger, freight, and mail service. They appear to have been excellent managers; during their first year of operating the railroad, passenger, freight, and mail volumes were increased 29, 56, and 43 percent, respectively.[24]

The New York and Boston Railroad owned the section of track from

Needham to Brookline Village, where it joined the track owned by the Boston and Worcester's Brookline Branch Railroad. Goss and Munson ran their gravel trains over both railroad lines. The managers of the Boston and Worcester Railroad Corporation were very much concerned that the increased gravel train traffic on their line would interfere with passenger and freight trains along their Brookline Branch and main line. To alleviate their concerns, Goss and Munson built a track parallel to the Boston and Worcester Railroad from Brookline Village to the Back Bay landfill site, a distance of three miles. Where the Boston and Worcester and Boston and Providence Railroads crossed in the Back Bay, Goss and Munson's track swung northeastward, parallel to the Boston and Providence.[25] Needham was the primary source of gravel for the first several years. All contemporary newspaper and magazine articles on the gravel pit and railroad operations describe the Needham period.

The first of the Needham gravel pits excavated by Goss and Munson lay some nine miles west of the Back Bay tidal mudflat on a 101-acre farm formerly owned by Hiram and Anna Story and William and Ann Cargill (see fig. 5.3).[26] This land was located west of the Charles River, north of the railroad, and south of the present Central Avenue in Needham. Today homes, commercial offices, and a park occupy this land. The farm, including a house and outbuildings, was bought by the Charles River Branch Railroad for seven thousand dollars on April 1, 1852.[27] Later, the farm was heavily mortgaged, so in 1858 Goss and Munson worked out a deal with the financially strapped railroad. They assumed the mortgage payments in exchange for the rights to all the gravel on the property.[28]

During the spring of 1858 Goss and Munson began transporting gravel from Needham to the Back Bay. The gravel sources were in eskers, kames, and kame terraces (shown earlier in fig. 1.4) that extended from the northwest to the southeast along the western side of the Charles River Valley. The tracks of the New York and Boston Railroad already cut through the gravel deposits from east to west, so temporary railroad spurs could be easily extended northwestward alongside these gravel ridges or hills.

The gravel pit operations in 1858 depended on the astounding efficiency of the new twenty-five-horsepower steam shovel, which operated on a temporary rail system adjacent to the gravel bluff. These rails closely paralleled the spur railway on which the gravel cars were pulled slowly by a locomotive. The steam shovel advanced along the gravel cut on four-foot sections of track, attached to ties, that were picked up from behind

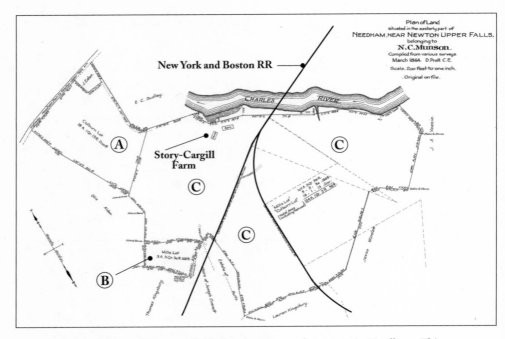

FIGURE 5.3. Map of Norman C. Munson's 1864 gravel property in Needham. This map shows Goss and Munson's early gravel pit locations in Needham. The letter designations on the map correspond with the discussions of the gravel pit operations that follow. The Story-Cargill farmhouse (left) and barn (right) appear near the Charles River in Lot C. *(Plan Book 4, Plan Number 133, March 1864, Norfolk County Registry of Deeds, Dedham Massachusetts, William P. O'Donnell, Register. All of the individual deeds are also on file at the same office.)*

the steam shovel, carried forward, and placed in the steam shovel's path. The steam shovel was pulled or pushed ahead by horses or men.

The excavation procedure was similar to slicing a log into boards at a sawmill. The initial cut extended along the full length of the gravel ridge, creating an excavation of several feet. First, the steam shovel dug into the hillside as far as its arm would reach. Then a workman or two, high up on the slope with long, stout, wooden poles, probed the bluff face, loosening the sand and gravel so that it slid down to within reach of the steam shovel's bucket. This technique made for an efficient operation because the steam shovel did not often have to be moved toward the gravel face. After excavating the gravel cut along the entire ridge, crews shifted the steam shovel and four-foot sections of track inward toward the working face of the bluff. The procedure was repeated, but now in reverse, as the steam shovel worked back along the ridge (see fig. 5.4A and 5.5B). The steam shovel moved back and forth until the entire gravel ridge was removed.

(B)

(A)

FIGURE 5.4A and B. Two photographs of an Otis-Chapman steam shovel at work in the Needham gravel pit in 1859. Photograph A, previously unpublished, is probably the best photograph of the Otis-Chapman Steam Shovel of that period. It clearly shows the small wheels that permitted it to be pushed or pulled on the four-foot-long track sections. This view also shows the heavier framework and chain drive that were innovations of Chapman and Souther. High on the esker's sand and gravel exposure is a laborer whose job was to probe the gravel face with a long pole to gener-

ate a sand slide, which brought the material within reach of the steam shovel's bucket. The men in top hats and cutaway suits suggest that this was a special occasion.

Photograph B shows the steam shovel filling the gravel cars with two scoops of sand and gravel. The small 0-4-0 switching engine viewed in the pit is slowly pushing the gravel cars forward to be loaded. This locomotive may have been one of the modified earlier engines used by the Boston and Worcester Railroad. (*Courtesy of Historic New England/SPNEA.*)

The first published account of the gravel pit operation appeared on page 1 of the *Boston Weekly Transcript* for June 9, 1858:

> It is worth a visit to Needham to witness the working of the machinery for excavating the earth. A large shovel, propelled by steam, digs away some 2500 cubic yards a day. So capacious is it, that in two dips a car is filled, containing four cubic yards of gravel. The contractors run twelve trains each day, between six in the morning and eight in the evening. During the night trains run regularly. Twenty-five cars are attached to each train.
>
> A few days since, while the excavator was performing its appointed duty, the workmen were surprised by the discovery of what is deemed to be an elephant's tooth. It was found some twenty feet below the surface, and from the nature of the material in which it was embedded, must have been washed up by an old ocean ages ago.[29]
>
> Another steam excavator of equal power with that now at work is to be built. A capital opportunity is afforded to observe these giant machines by the twelve and three o'clock trains from the Worcester depot.

A photograph of the gravel pit operation (see fig. 5.5A) was taken probably in June 1858 on the former Story-Cargill farm, north of the New York and Boston Railroad's right-of-way.[30] The occasion that prompted those dapper gentlemen shown in the photograph to view the operations in the Needham gravel pit has been lost to history. They may be officials or a group of sightseers who traveled to Needham as the result of the article quoted above. Interestingly, the etching of the same scene includes several elegantly dressed ladies.

In the gravel pit, the rails for temporary spur tracks carrying the gravel trains were spiked to the ties, and each of the sixteen-foot-long rail sections behaved as a single unit. To shift the entire spur track closer to the working face of the gravel ridge, the connection plates between adjacent track segments were probably unbolted and each section was slid or carried to its new position and rebolted.[31]

The huge scale of this project required an extensive infrastructure for the maintenance, repair, and storage of equipment. Sometime during the Needham gravel pit operation Munson leased a large building in nearby Newton Upper Falls for a machine shop and engine house, outside of which was space for storage and repairs to rolling stock.[32] Here repairs were made to the locomotives, gravel cars, and steam shovels. Theodore Hanks, of Needham, took charge of the new machinery and repair shop, which serviced all of Goss and Munson's heavy equipment.[33]

(A)

(B)

FIGURE 5.5A and B. Photograph and engraving showing dignitaries posed by a gravel train being loaded in Needham in 1858. The small, 0-4-0 switching locomotive with "Back Bay" painted on the side of its tender was one of the two switching locomotives used by Goss and Munson in the Needham gravel pit to shift gravel cars from place to place and to move them past the steam shovel during loading operations. The gravel cars, probably improved versions of the Nettleton dumping car, typically held four cubic yards of sand and gravel weighing approximately six tons. In June 1858, a mastodon or mammoth tooth was found by a workman loosening material about twenty feet below the surface of the ridge. The artist, creating the engraving from the photograph, dressed up the scene by adding the fashionable young ladies. (*Photograph: Boston Athenæum. Engraving:* Ballou's Pictorial Drawing Room Companion, *vol. 15 (1858): 209. Courtesy of the Boston Public Library/Rare Books Department.*)

The site of this combination shop and repair facility was probably in Newton Upper Falls in Otis Pettee's mill complex southwest of Mechanic Street and south of the New York and New England Railroad. The machine shop and Munson's small railroad yard appear at this site on the 1874 *Atlas of the City of Newton* (see fig. 6.11).[34] Also, Norman Munson owned a house in the Needham gravel pit very close to what is today the junction of Kearney Street and Gould Street in West Needham (see Lot C of fig. 5.3). This house, formerly the Story-Cargill farmhouse, was probably used as an office or converted into a boardinghouse for some of the workmen.

The first reference to the gravel pit operations in Needham appears in the Needham town records of December 27, 1859, which referred to a vote by the selectmen on the proposition of the "Gravel Company" to take down the hill that formed the boundary between Otis Alden's and Josiah Eaton's farms, located northwest of the railroad track and close to the present Central Avenue.[35] This esker extended through the Colburn lot (Lot A in fig. 5.3) on the property leased to George Goss on October 1, 1858, for its timber (fuel for the locomotives) and gravel deposits.[36]

FIGURE 5.6. Locomotive "N. C. Munson." This 4-4-0, American-type locomotive was purchased from the Hinkley Locomotive Works in Boston by the N. C. Munson Company in 1864. Norman C. Munson is standing to the right, next to the tender. *(Photograph courtesy of the Needham Historical Society, Inc., Needham, MA.)*

The Needham gravel pit operations began in 1858 as an arriving empty gravel train crossed the Charles River into Needham and was switched off the New York and Boston Railroad's single track onto a northward swinging spur track that paralleled an esker ridge. The engine slowly passed by a single Otis-Chapman steam shovel which would fill each car with two scoops of sand and gravel.[37] Between June 9, 1858, and April 18, 1859, Goss and Munson acquired a second steam shovel.[38]

Initially each train pulled twenty-five gravel cars.[39] By April 1859, Goss and Munson recognized the difficulty of sending as many gravel trains as the landfill required over a single track. To increase the efficiency of the operation, Goss and Munson increased the number of gravel cars to thirty-five and added more powerful locomotives to pull them.[40] The locomotives that pulled the gravel trains were larger and more powerful 4-4-0 American-type locomotive engines (see fig. 5.6); on occasion, however, the heavier gravel trains were probably pushed and pulled by less powerful engines: one locomotive was attached to the front and another one was attached to the rear of the gravel train.

❂ *Running a Gravel Train from Needham to the Back Bay in 1859: A Narrative Account*

In the early morning a powerful locomotive, pulling thirty-five empty gravel cars, crosses the wood trestle bridge over the Charles River and approaches the spur track leading into the gravel pit. The engineer signals one long blast from the steam whistle to warn the switchman that a gravel train is approaching and to switch it onto the spur track. Entering the gravel pit and steaming toward his designated waiting point, the engineer signals one short blast of the steam whistle before reducing his throttle, reversing his driving wheels, and coming to a stop. Here, the locomotive backs up very slowly to produce some slack in the link-and-pin couplings between cars. The empty gravel train is uncoupled from the large locomotive and it is coupled at each end to an 0-4-0, low-geared switching engine. Then the brakeman runs between the two cars nearest to the middle of the train and removes the coupling pin. He must act quickly to pull the pin at the exact moment when there is enough slack in the link to loosen the pin in the coupling, but before the two trains collide, possibly crushing him. This breaks the single gravel train into two smaller trains of 17 and 18 gravel cars. Switching locomotives pull each of the two smaller gravel trains apart in opposite directions.

The switching locomotives take their gravel cars onto tracks close to the working face of the esker and adjacent to the two waiting steam shovels. Each switching locomotive pushes or pulls a string of empty gravel cars very slowly past one of the two twenty-five-horsepower Otis-Chapman steam shovels. The steam shovel, its boiler and engine hissing and puffing, swings the crane and bucket through an arc of 180 degrees from the gravel bank to the dumping cars and back again. It moves with small, rapid jerks, accompanied by the loud clanging noise of its moving chain drives. The steam shovel drives its bucket into the gravel bank, scoops up a bucket of sand and gravel, and swings the bucket over the gravel car. A spring bolt releases the door at the bottom of the bucket and its contents drop, jarring the bottom of the gravel car with a weight of over a ton and a half. The procedure is immediately re-peated, so that the excavator can drop two shovels full of sand and gravel into the car before it moves out of range. Each loaded car carries approximately four cubic yards of fill. The entire train of thirty-five cars is loaded in about ten minutes.[41] After the cars are filled, the two halves of the train are recoupled and shunted to a siding. Brakemen un-couple the switching locomotives from the string of thirty-five gravel cars, and the switching locomotive engineers await the arrival of the next empty gravel train.

Preparing for the return trip to the Back Bay, a powerful 4-4-0 American-type locomotive (see fig. 5.6) backs slowly to the end of the recoupled string of full cars with three short steam whistle blasts and a searing cloud of steam. The brakeman walks up briskly behind the lo-comotive and lifts the attached link to a horizontal position, at the same time guiding it toward the slot in the parked gravel car as the lo-comotive reaches the waiting train. With his other hand he quickly drops a pin into the slot through the link in the stationary car before leaping out of harm's way. The engineer waits for a signal from the brakeman that the coupling is complete and then orders the fireman to stoke the firebox.

With two long blasts from the steam whistle the gravel train slowly begins its return trip to the Back Bay. The long, heavy train slowly moves ahead in a series of successive, sharp jolts and loud clanks as the cars pull apart—slowly at first and then increasingly faster. As the train reaches the New York and Boston main-line track, the fireman slowly builds up a full head of steam. This task, hot and arduous even in the winter, requires the firebox to be regulated at a roaring two thousand degrees Fahrenheit. Occasionally, as the train gains speed, acrid wood smoke fills the air and flows into the cab, choking the engineer and fireman unless they tie bandannas over their faces. Any boiler leaks noticed by the fireman on the inbound trip can be plugged by shoveling a bushel of horse manure into the water-filled boiler.[42] The fibrous material of partially digested straw contained in the horse manure is carried into any rivetted seams, which going in from the inside is forced into the seam by the leaking pressure, thus sealing it. In England porridge was placed into the boiler on the basis of the same principle.[43]

Once the boiler pressure has increased sufficiently, the engineer pushes the throttle forward for maximum power. The huffing of the large locomotive gradually picks up speed as the train heads eastward toward Newton, Brookline, and Boston (see fig. 5.7). It is a noisy ride: heavy gravel cars bang against each other and bounce along on uneven tracks, and the wheels clack as they slam into each joint between the thirty-foot sections of iron rails. The gravel trains are the heaviest trains on the railroad and, consequently, inflict the most damage to the rails. The train's speed is limited to twelve miles per hour to minimize the damage to the rail joints.[44]

The gravel train surges forward on level ground, soon crossing the Charles River into Newton and passing the small Newton Upper Falls Railroad Station. Accelerating slowly, the train reaches maximum speed and crosses a straight stretch of track paralleling the main road from Needham to Newton.[45] The train begins to labor uphill into Newton Highlands toward the crossing of Walnut Street as the engineer lays on more power to keep his speed up.[46] Continuing northeastward, the locomotive pulls its string of thirty-five loaded gravel cars past Crystal Lake and Newton Centre (see fig. 5.7). The engineer concentrates on watching the rails ahead, looking for obstructions on the track or breaks in the rails caused by the heavy pounding of the wheels, which are especially dangerous in winter when the wrought-iron rails are cold and brittle.

A mile or so farther on, the inbound gravel train pulls into a siding

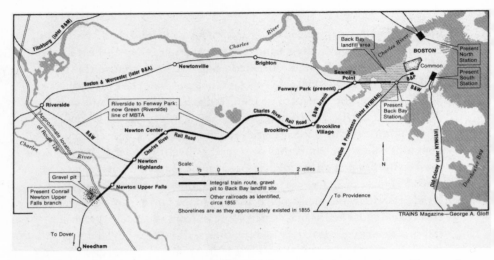

FIGURE 5.7. Gravel train route from the Needham gravel pits to the Back Bay. The gravel trains left the Needham pit, crossed the Charles River, passed Newton Upper Falls, and rolled through Newton Highlands, Newton Centre, Brookline, and Brookline Village on the tracks of the New York and Boston Railroad. From Brookline Village to Boston the right of way was owned by the Boston and Worcester Railroad, which did not permit the passage of gravel trains. Goss and Munson were forced to lay three miles of their own track on the north side of the Boston and Worcester Railroad right-of-way into Boston. (*Tom Nelligan, "Mr. Kneiling Meet Messrs. Goss and Munson," Trains 37, no. 12, [October 1977]: 30. Reproduced with the permission of Kalmbach Publishing Company.*)

and an outbound passenger train rushes past. A series of double-ended sidings between the gravel pit and Brookline Village permits heavy traffic on the single track. After Brookline Village, where Goss and Munson's own track paralleling the Boston and Worcester begins, the gravel train passes an outbound passenger train. The busy line now handles about twenty-five gravel trains every twenty-four hours.[47]

The engineer and brakeman are vigilant in case the vibrations shake an iron pin out of its slot or a hard jolt shocks the coupling between two cars of the heavy train and breaks a wrought-iron link. They are aware of the dangers and difficulties when either of these problems causes gravel cars to uncouple from a train. The engineer must be ready to slow down, stop, and reverse direction for recoupling if some of the gravel cars are rolling to a stop or gaining speed going downhill, either toward or away from his train. Sometimes it is

FIGURE 5.8. A nineteenth-century gravel train passing through Newton. *(Newton History Museum at The Jackson Homestead, Newton, Massachusetts.)*

necessary to increase the locomotive's speed to avoid having the un-coupled cars, gaining speed, crash into the forward part of the train, which would result in damage or derailment. Even at the slow speed of five miles per hour, colliding gravel cars can be badly damaged. Since recoupling and derailments take additional time, the engineer fears the risk of throwing his train off its very tight schedule.

In Brookline Village the train is switched to the separate track built by Goss and Munson for the exclusive use of their gravel trains. From here on, there will be no passenger or freight trains on their track, but the crew <u>must</u> still <u>must</u> watch for off-schedule gravel trains. As the train nears the signalman controlling the crossing at the busy junction with the main line of the Boston and Worcester Railroad, near today's Fenway Park, the engineer slows the gravel train. From this point on the train runs on an embankment and trestles crossing several deeper channels in the Back Bay, first crossing the Full Basin west of Gravelly

Point, where a few decrepit mill buildings still stand. About halfway across the terribly polluted Receiving Basin, with its nauseating stench, the train swings to the northeast to run parallel to the Boston and Providence track.

Not long after moving onto the Boston and Providence right-of-way, the engineer slows the heavy gravel train as it nears the spur tracks leading into the area being filled just west of Arlington Street. The manager of the filling process decides which track is ready for another trainload of sand and gravel, how far down the track the train should be stopped, and on which side the fill should be dumped. Arriving at the dumping site along the selected spur rail, the gravel train is secured by blocks placed under some of the wheels. Then the brakeman uncouples the locomotive and tender from the string of thirty-five gravel cars. The engine moves forward slowly to have its boiler refilled from a large water tank standing on a high platform supported by pilings. Wood or coal can also be supplied to the tender if it is needed. By the time the locomotive is ready, the gravel cars have been emptied and are ready to be recoupled to the locomotive and tender. On a signal from a signalman, the empty gravel train begins its return trip to the Needham gravel pit.

Dangers on the Gravel Trains

The lack of safety features and the inherently dangerous nature of the work on gravel trains resulted in the death or maiming of many trainmen. "By the late 1880s it was estimated that one thousand trainmen a year were killed and another four thousand to five thousand injured" in railroad accidents across the United States.[48]

Five or six deaths occurred on Goss and Munson's gravel trains during their first year of operation. An accident that may have resulted from the lack of effective brakes was reported by the *Boston Herald* soon after the project began, on Friday May 14, 1858: "A man named William Reynolds, employed in constructing the new branch track from Needham to this city, which is to be built for the purpose of filling up the back bay, was run over and instantly killed by a locomotive and some twenty-five gravel cars, near Longwood, in Brookline, Wednesday evening. He resided on the Mill Dam."

Another accidental death was reported on the Boston and Worcester track by the *Boston Herald* about ten weeks later: "Saturday noon, a man named Patrick Regan, while attempting to jump from a gravel train that was in motion on the Back Bay lands, was thrown upon the track and his skull fractured. He was carried to the office of Dr. George H. Gay, No. 75 Boylston Street, and from thence to the hospital where he died in about half an hour. He was a stranger in Boston and was thirty-eight years of age. He was employed on the Back Bay improvements.[49] A similar accident resulting in the death of a gravel train worker was reported on the same railroad on October 21, 1859."[50]

Brakes on some of Munson's locomotive tenders consisted of hand-operated wheels attached to iron rods that forced wood or metal shoes against two or more wheels of the tender. Often the vertical wrought-iron brake rod on the tender contained varying amounts of slag, which weakened the rod at specific points. This rod occasionally snapped as the brakeman attempted to apply more and more pressure to the brake wheel; the brakeman could be thrown off balance and sometimes pitched beneath the wheels of the forward-moving gravel cars. Such an incident was described by the *Boston Daily Traveller* on Wednesday, April 27, 1859, on page 4:

> Fatal Railroad Accident—John McGee, a brakeman upon the Back Bay Gravel Train, while the cars were coming with a load to the city, at ten o'clock last night, was thrown from the train while applying the brakes, by a sudden giving way of a rod, run over, and horribly mangled. When reached he was dead. He was forty years of age, and resided in Newton Upper Falls, where he leaves a wife and four children. This is the fifth or sixth death that has occurred upon this train within a year past.

In spite of being extremely dangerous for railroad workers, the fast and efficient technology for loading and running the gravel trains allowed Goss and Munson to dump up to eight hundred carloads of gravel in the Back Bay every workday.

Unloading and Spreading Out Gravel

Efficient machinery and innovative procedures were required to prevent huge piles of gravel from accumulating beside the tracks and bringing the operation to a grinding halt; grading and preparing land were slow operations done with horses and laborers. In addition, very soft ground underlay some sections of the Back Bay, so innovative solutions were required to prevent the loaded gravel trains from sinking.

A great deal of information about the filling procedures can be deduced from several lines of evidence. The engineering firm of Fuller and Whitney compiled very detailed composite maps of the Back Bay landfill area for 1851, 1861, 1871, and 1881, which allow accurate interpretations of the use of railroad spur tracks and the stages of the landfill process.[51] A photograph of the Back Bay, probably taken in 1859, shows three railroad spurs and a gravel train unloading on one of them. For more than a century engineers and geologists have studied the Back Bay silts, peat, glacial drift, and Boston blue clay (discussed in chapter 1). They have identified the locations of the softest parts of the former tidal mudflat, which affected the contractors' ability to run heavy gravel trains into the area. Published accounts detail how similar problems of swampy terrains and weak soils were solved by railroad companies in other parts of the country, using techniques available to Goss and Munson. Finally, two detailed dioramas of the Back Bay landfill in progress suggest probable techniques that were not mentioned in contemporary accounts of the Back Bay project, but were used elsewhere.

The filling procedures used by Goss and Munson early in the project are revealed in the pattern of newly filled land shown on the Fuller and Whitney 1861 Back Bay map.[52] Four separate areas of the Back Bay were filled simultaneously (see fig. 5.9).

Two or more spur tracks splayed northward and southward from the Boston and Providence Railroad right-of-way just east of its junction with the Boston and Worcester. This operation filled the area roughly bounded today by Clarendon, Stuart, Arlington, and Boylston Streets ("a" in fig. 5.9). Spur tracks immediately north of the Boston and Worcester allowed the filling of a triangle of land adjacent to the railroad between today's Clarendon and Berkeley Streets ("b" in fig. 5.9). A third small and irregularly shaped area was filled using a spur track that left the Boston and Worcester rails and swung southward to cross the Boston and Providence Railroad on a new embankment near today's Dartmouth Street ("c" in fig. 5.9). Near the present Columbus Avenue the spur tracks splayed out in several directions to allow the filling of areas along the existing shoreline.

The 1861 Fuller and Whitney map shows the landfill in the Back Bay proper ("e" in fig. 5.9) extending westward beyond the present Clarendon Street. The first spur tracks left the Boston & Providence Railroad's right-of-way near the multiple tracks entering its railroad station and

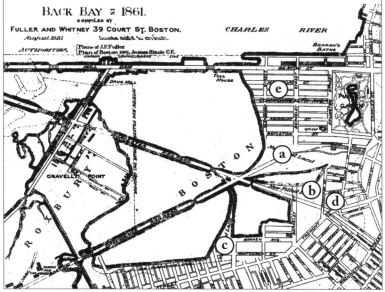

FIGURE 5.9. The 1861 Fuller and Whitney map of newly filled areas in the Back Bay. The letters a, b, c, and e identify four separate areas that were being filled simultaneously by Munson in 1861. *(Fuller and Whitney,* Back Bay in 1861 *[Boston: Fuller and Whitney, 1881]. Courtesy of The Bostonian Society/Old State House.)*

swung north along the line of present-day Arlington Street, about fifty yards west of the 1858 shoreline. Later, as the filling progressed, spur tracks entered the Back Bay from points farther to the west. An 1859 photograph (see fig. 5.10) provides more precise information on the locations of spur tracks used by Goss and Munson to dump sand and gravel in this section of the Back Bay.

Where the marsh surface was firm, railroad embankments extended spur tracks into the Back Bay from the railroad's main line. After the gravel trains dumped their loads from the contractors' spur tracks, horse-drawn, two-wheeled dump carts transported sand and gravel forward to extend railroad embankments for new spur tracks. Grading the surfaces of the embankments was accomplished by horse-drawn scoops that filled the depressions and horse-drawn scrapers (graders) that leveled and smoothed these surfaces (see fig. 5.10). The rail-laying crew ✓ moved ahead on a newly constructed embankment so that side-dumping gravel cars could be pushed by a locomotive to the end of the track.

(A)

(B)

FIGURE 5.10A and B. Gravel train being unloaded in the Back Bay, probably in 1859. Fig. 5.10A is part of the only known photograph of a gravel train being unloaded in the Back Bay. The line of trees shown is just east of Arlington Street as it was being constructed. There are three spur tracks from which dumping is being done. One track is just behind the trees with mounds of gravel lying in front of it. The second spur track, running diagonally between the other two tracks, is occupied by the train being unloaded. The third spur track, parallel to the first, is at the outer edge of the filled area and has another row of sand and gravel mounds along it. With dumping along three spur tracks at a time, the filling material could be shifted and graded much more efficiently.

In the close-up view in fig. 5.10B, most of the gravel cars on the right end of the train are being dumped away from the camera. Soon the car bodies will return to their nor-

There workmen tipped the cars, dumping the sand and gravel and forming mounds on either side of the railroad embankment. The railroad embankments shown in figure 5.10 were probably built in this manner during the preceding year.

This view is a small part of a panoramic photograph that encompasses the Public Garden and most of the Back Bay (see fig. 5.10). It was taken from the roof of a building at the northeast corner of Beacon and Charles Streets, probably in the summer of 1859, approximately a year after the filling began. This is the only known photograph showing a train in the act of unloading gravel in the Back Bay. The filling has not been completed as far as Berkeley Street and no finished buildings show in this view, as was the case in 1859.

It is very clear from the photograph that gravel was being dumped from at least three tracks simultaneously to speed up the process. Recently dumped sand and gravel is seen along the nearest track, which runs on the line of today's Arlington Street, perhaps fifty yards west of the Public Garden at the time. A moderately deep depression remains between the filling material and the temporary road with its double line of trees along the edge of the Public Garden. At the edge of the unfilled, polluted marsh, a line of gravel piles can be seen clearly at or near the location of today's Berkeley Street. The spur track on which the train sits branches off the third track near the left edge of the view and runs diagonally to join the first track to the right, near where Commonwealth Avenue will reach Arlington Street (see fig. 5.11).

According to a Boston Water Power Company document, "The mode of filling used by the contractor was to lay railroad tracks and to extend them upon the land" where "the streets were to be constructed; and as one part of the street was finished, to remove them to another, and so from place to place until the whole was completed."[53] The specifications of the contracts required that the elevation of streets be eighteen feet above mean low tide, or Boston City Base,[54] the level of the Mill Dam. Men used horse-drawn scoops and scrapers to grade the streets under construction. The rest of the landfill area would be at the elevation of twelve feet. House lots were filled to a level six feet lower than the streets to avoid wasting sand and gravel where basements would be located.

----

mal position so the train can return to Needham for more sand and gravel. Just to the right of the tall wooden structure, a man wearing a white shirt is standing in the last car. *(Courtesy of the Bostonian Society/Old State House.)*

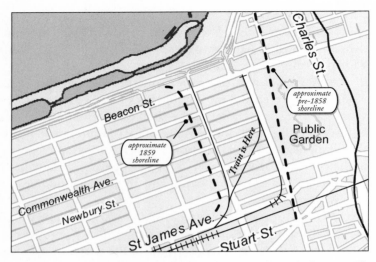

FIGURE 5.11. Map of the approximate spur track alignment shown in fig. 5.10A. The photograph in fig. 5.10A, along with confirmation from an early newspaper account, allows us to create this map of the spur track alignment that was probably used to fill the Back Bay during the first year of the project. Tracks are on embankments that follow the lines of Arlington and Berkeley Streets. A third track connects these two tracks, starting near the intersection of Berkeley Street and the main line of the Boston and Providence Railroad. This diagonal track joins the track on the future Arlington Street near the future Commonwealth Avenue. *(Spur track alignment interpreted by Wilfred E. Holton.)*

Viewed from above, the filling area would have resembled a huge waffle until buildings were added (see figs. 5.12 and 5.13).

Using at least three tracks at a time was necessary because sand and gravel could be brought in and dumped at the rate of thirty-five carloads every forty-five minutes, much faster than men with horse-drawn equipment could remove the material and prepare the surface of the filled area. By using three tracks and dumping cars that could deposit their loads on either side of a track, the operation could create up to six rows of gravel piles. Crews could remove any or all of these piles at the same time to clear spaces for the next trains to deposit their loads. Since each horse-drawn cart when fully loaded held a little over 1.2 cubic yards of fill, laborers wielding shovels filled approximately 115 cartloads to clear away the gravel dumped from one thirty-five-car gravel train.

The land-filling process was accelerated by laying the spur tracks close enough together for the horse-drawn equipment to move the newly dumped gravel efficiently. The plan of spur tracks shown in fig. 5.11 in-

FIGURE 5.12. Photograph of Jubilee Hall. This photograph shows the massive exhibit building of 1869 near Copley Square. It is clear that only the streets have been built up close to the level of the Mill Dam; vacant lots lie considerably below street level. Sewer or water pipes are being laid beneath the street. *(Courtesy of The Bostonian Society/Old State House.)*

dicates that the three spur tracks lay about a hundred yards apart at their widest points of separation. We assume that the same technology of using three or more tracks simultaneously was employed throughout the Back Bay landfill project.

The gravel train shown in fig. 5.10, with no locomotive attached, is being unloaded on a track running diagonally between the lines of today's Berkeley and Arlington Streets. Eight or nine gravel cars on the train are being tipped away from the camera. Probably only one or two cars could be emptied at a time because of the limited number of trainmen.[55]

Adjacent spur tracks could not be very far apart because of the enormous stresses on the horses pulling the dumping carts. The trick of using these gravel carts was to balance the approximately fourteen-hundred-pound load evenly across the cart's axle so it could be tipped easily at the landfill site. The horse was harnessed with an extra-wide supporting bellyband to the delicately balanced cart because on uneven terrain the heavy load caused the cart and attached shafts to tip forcefully up or down. If the shafts tipped up, the wide bellyband harness connected to the shafts could lift the horse completely off the ground. If the shafts tipped

FIGURE 5.13. View of Commonwealth Avenue. This photograph, apparently taken from the church tower at the corner of Clarendon Street and Commonwealth Avenue, shows the view to the west in 1872. Most houses have been completed in the block between Clarendon and Dartmouth Streets. The corner lots at Dartmouth Street lie six feet below the street level, illustrating the waffle pattern that was created when the middles of residential blocks were left unfilled. Building construction had yet to occur on Commonwealth Avenue west of Exeter Street. (*Boston Athenæum.*)

down, the harness forced the horse down into the ground. Dumping carts were hard on horses and many probably died during this project.

Moving numerous loads of sand and gravel to the appropriate places on the landfill required a high degree of organization and strict cost controls. The filling project may have been organized like the smaller operation of filling a section of St. Louis, Missouri, in the late nineteenth century. Each cart driver would have his load measured before driving his cart, as directed, to the section of the landfill where sand and gravel were needed. Immediately after tipping the cart's bed and emptying its contents, he would proceed to a ticket boy who handed him a ticket that certified the delivery of a full load. Carts and their drivers had numbers that were recorded when the timekeeper tallied tickets at the end of each day.

Drivers were paid either by the load or for the day's work when a certain number of tickets were accumulated. A man brought buckets of water for the horses and ice water for the drivers as needed. A walking foreman kept the work moving and enforced strict rules against smoking and drinking. After only one warning, a second transgression of the rules caused a worker to be discharged from the job.[56]

It appears that a locomotive is about to be connected to the right end of the train in fig. 5.10. The last gravel car on the right end of the train has been emptied and returned to its horizontal position. A man wearing dark pants and a white shirt is standing stock-still inside the back part of that car, directly over the coupling. Soon, in fact, the remaining tipped gravel boxes on the last gravel cars will be lowered and the train will steam off. There is a nearly identical photograph with the train missing, taken a few minutes later, as can be determined by the changing shadows on the Charles Street sidewalk.[57] The empty train will be backed out to the contractors' track and the locomotive will pull it westward back to the Needham gravel pits.

The firmness of the mudflat and its ability to support the heavy weight of gravel trains, particularly when the trains were in motion, varied from place to place within the Back Bay and depended on both the thickness and composition of the underlying soils. The strength of soils depends on the thickness of the underlying silt, peat, clay, and till layers (see chapter 1) and on the moisture content and compactness of each layer. The sinking of the soil surface resulting from settling or water loss (or both) is called subsidence. Some of those areas prone to rapid subsidence were saturated sediments in old discharge channels, such as the mouths of the Muddy River and Stony Brook. In other places there were thick, spongy layers of organic silts and peat.[58]

Soft sections of the mudflat surface presented major problems to the contractors' heavy gravel trains. Goss and Munson must have realized early on that those thick, spongy areas of the tidal mudflat would not support the weight of the swaying and jolting gravel trains, and they must have planned accordingly. The typical American-type locomotive and tender in 1855 was about forty-seven feet long and weighed about forty-five tons. Fully loaded, it carried two thousand gallons of water and two cords of wood, bringing its total weight to about seventy tons. A locomotive pounding along on an uneven temporary track would increase the effective weight of the train and thus accelerate the rate of subsidence.

Slow subsidence was common throughout the filling of the Back Bay and into the twentieth century. Two examples of serious landfill problems arose because of soft underlying soils. A Boston Water Power Company subsidence repair estimate, dated February 10, 1858, refers to placing 578 cubic feet of earth on top of the mud pushed up on the north side of Avenue III (Warren Avenue) and west of Street B (Clarendon Street) in today's South End neighborhood.[59] In 1862 the State Commission required Munson to refill a section between Berkeley and Clarendon Streets "a second time to grade 12" and paid him about $17,800 for the additional fill required.[60] The marshy ground under the Back Bay led to settling of the fill in various places, which required remedial work. The State Commission noted in its minutes: "Voted that the contractors fill up the depression on Newbury Street and in the lots north of it forthwith. Mr. Munson being present agreed to fill according to the vote at once."[61]

As the spur track embankments projected farther and farther out into the mudflat toward the Mill Dam (Beacon Street), the organic silts and peats became thicker, softer, and more susceptible to subsidence, particularly in the former tidal estuary drainage channels. These silts and peats would flow away in all directions from beneath a heavy gravel train pounding down on the surface of the mudflat. Probably Goss and Munson controlled the subsidence problem for supporting their tracks by attaching the rails to ten-foot-long ties that that were twelve inches wide and set only two or three inches apart.[62] The contractors may have planked their rail bed for a short distance when they encountered occasional soft spots beneath their rail spurs. They first laid a layer of planks crosswise and then placed a second layer diagonally over them. Workmen then spiked the rails to ties, laid them on the planking, and filled the intervening spaces with gravel.

When the soil was particularly soft over a large area, a wooden railroad trestle (like the one seen in fig. 5.14) may have been the best solution for the more serious subsidence problems. Piles driven into the firm blue clay below, close together in two rows and connected by crosspieces to form a low railroad trestle, would prevent or reduce sinking along a spur track subjected to heavy traffic.[63] After trestle construction, the trains could as easily cross the deep tidal channels as they could the gently undulating upper surface of the soft, sandy silts overlaid by salt marsh peat. One of four dioramas exhibited in the former New England Financial Building, at 501 Boylston Street, clearly shows dumping cars unloading gravel from a trestle on Berkeley Street, parallel to the Mill Dam. These dioramas were said to be accurate "right down to the halters on the horses"[64]; the creators of the dioramas, Sarah Annette Rockwell and Henry H. Brooks, may have had an unknown source of information on a trestle system used during the Back Bay landfill. A low railroad trestle system provided an ideal way to deliver sand and gravel to the unstable portions of the Back Bay tidal marsh. As the gravel train reached some predetermined point on the trestle track, the side-dumping cars would pour out their sand and gravel in either direction, as needed. The falling sand and gravel would flow around the trestle's supporting timbers, eventually burying them. The trestles then remained buried beneath the newly constructed streets. As more and more fill was dumped off the trestle, mounds of sand and gravel would accumulate in continuous ridges on both sides of the tracks; the sand and gravel would be transported to predetermined locations between the tracks by horse-drawn carts and horse-drawn scoops.

Filling the Back Bay began in 1858 at the edge of the Public Garden, and continued westward to reach Massachusetts Avenue by 1870. Before building construction took place, sections of the expanding land area resembled a dusty desert or a waffle of mud-filled depressions, depending on the season and weather conditions. The sand and gravel dried out entirely between periods of wet weather. Then winds sweeping across open expanses of the Charles River and the Back Bay created dust storms, which were a serious problem for residents of the new houses and for people in nearby sections of Boston. On April 21, 1860, the *Boston Sunday Evening Gazette* reported choking clouds of dust that "have doubtless done more injury than three times the expense of a good coating of green grass would have cost."

Officials contracted for covering dry areas with loam and planting grass, and for watering down the surface, to reduce the dust problem on the newly filled vacant land. Both solutions were tried in spring 1860. The Minute Books of the State Commission first mention spreading loam on December 17, 1859: "Consultation with Mr. Goss (Contractor). Mr. Goss says that he can furnish loam but it would cost about 15 cents pr. yd. more than gravel." Three days later the Minute Books recorded that the advisability of planting grass seed on newly filled lots was considered. Almost three months later, on March 7, 1860, the Minute Books noted: "Voted that the Contractors be directed to fill one train of (the usual number of) gravel cars with loam and deposit the same where re-

Fig. 5.14. Diorama showing gravel cars unloading, a wooden railroad trestle next to a pile driver, and horse-drawn equipment grading the new fill. The Public Garden and the Boston Common are visible in the distance. The wooden railroad trestle is near the line of today's Arlington Street. The pile driver is extending the trestle northward toward the Mill Dam. The men and horses working in the foreground are near the diagonal track (see fig. 5.11) near present-day Berkeley Street. The lobby dioramas were commissioned by the New England Life Insurance Company at 501 Boylston Street. (*The models were created by Mrs. S. Annette Rockwell of the former Pitman Studio in Cambridge, and the backgrounds were*

quired on the Back Bay." Then on April 25 the commissioners ordered that the loam be spread immediately.

The Minute Books on May 1, 1860, reported: "Engaged Michael Gormley to sow grass seed on the Back Bay $1.50 for self and $1.25 for man." On the same day Gormley was given "an order on Curtis and Cobb for whatever seed he required for planting the Bay lands." The grass grew well and on September 27, 1861, "John Murphy applied for permission to cut the grass on flats in the Back Bay," probably to use it as hay for animals.

The commission also considered wetting down the Back Bay to allay the dust; it wrote to the mayor and aldermen of the City of Boston on April 16, 1860, requesting "the use of one of the Steam Fire Engines belonging to the City for the purpose of laying the dust on the new filling in the Empty Basin." This request was denied and on April 30, 1860, the commission "applied to the Cochituate Water Board for permission to use water for sprinkling the Back Bay."[65] This permission was granted the next day, and a private contractor carried out the watering at a cost of two hundred dollars. Apparently the experiment was unsuccessful because the commission ordered the watering to stop on the same day.[66]

After sections were filled, the six-foot depressions left intentionally between the streets, for later construction of buildings, tended to collect water in rainy periods and fill with mud. On February 18, 1861, the Minute Books of the State Commission referred to "a letter from Mrs. J. D. Bates complaining of the state of walking from her house to Beacon Street." The commissioners immediately ordered the clerk to assess the problem and a plank sidewalk "was ordered to be commenced at once."

The filling of the Back Bay had a serious environmental impact on the adjacent Church Street District (Bay Village area), a low-lying neighborhood near today's Theater District and Park Square. Bay Village, built on the shoreline of the Back Bay tidal marsh in the 1820s, lay south of Boston Common and the new Public Garden ("D" in fig. 5.10). When the eastern end of the former Back Bay tidal marsh was filled, the new, higher surface on a thick layer of sand and gravel raised the water table about two and a half feet in Bay Village. The rising waters caused backups of sewage and groundwater into the basements and streets of Bay Village, and the property owners and the City faced two options. One choice was to raze the buildings, fill the land to a higher level, and re-

painted by Mr. Henry H. Brooks. Courtesy of CBRE/Whittier Partners, 501 Boylston Street, Boston. Photographed by Bruce Hamilton.)

build. The alternative, which they chose, was to jack up hundreds of row houses and a church, and to place them on new foundations supported by cribbing before filling in around them. The "Church Street Improvement" in 1868 raised whole blocks of buildings twelve to sixteen feet and thereby overcame constant flooding. The backyards were left considerably lower to save filling material. Part of the sand and gravel came from Fort Hill, which was being leveled north of South Station.[67]

The filling of the Back Bay progressed very rapidly in 1858 and 1859. The partnership of George Goss and Norman Munson was very successfully managing the complex project, operating steam shovels and trains twenty-four hours a day, six days a week. Munson was the entrepreneurial risk taker in the partnership, and this created much stress for George Goss.

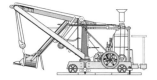

CHAPTER 6

A Shocking Development
Fails to Derail the Project

Late in 1859 the partnership of George Goss and Norman Munson was strong financially and making rapid progress. A little over a year into their enterprise, their rolling stock, railroad equipment, and track were valued at $150,000 and they owed about $50,000. The partners had about $12,000 in cash reserves and they had sold all the land received from the State in payment for their work. Beginning on April 1, 1860, they were to receive their pay in cash from the state treasury. In addition, Goss and Munson had recently signed a contract with the Boston Water Power Company to fill up the flats west of Tremont Street and they were to be paid in cash. The partnership was never in a more favorable financial position than in early 1860.[1]

The filling project was large and complicated, so from the beginning Goss and Munson were forced to borrow and mortgage equipment and land from time to time in order to have enough cash to meet payrolls and other expenses. During the early years of the project, the partners received two-fifths of the house lots they filled for the Boston Water Power Company and the City of Boston.[2] This land payment procedure often created cash flow problems for the contractors because, early on, their operating funds, including payrolls, depended entirely on their sale of land. With rapid sales of house lots, Goss and Munson reaped ample profits. Land sales fluctuated from month to month and from year to year; when the sales declined and selling prices dropped, they experienced a financial crunch. Again and again Goss and Munson fell behind on the tax payments on their newly acquired properties.[3]

Goss and Munson borrowed to cover operating expenses through short-term mortgaging and remortgaging of their rolling stock, construction equipment, and land. For example, on July 26, 1858, they mortgaged all their locomotives and gravel cars to the Commonwealth of Massachusetts. Again, in August 1858, they mortgaged one of their locomotives to the Boston Water Power Company for $2500, and later they mortgaged their locomotive "Commonwealth" to the same company for $2500. By January 1859 Goss and Munson had mortgaged their two steam shovels to J. F. Gilman for $4500, and by April 1859 they remortgaged all their locomotive engines to J. H. Loud for $19,000.[4] These mortage loans had to be repaid with interest.

By November 1859 Goss and Munson had filled twenty-five of the approximately one hundred acres of the badly polluted Receiving Basin for the Commonwealth, meeting all the requirements of their contract to the satisfaction of the commissioners. This was much faster progress than had been predicted at the beginning. The contractors' financial position seemed quite strong, and their mortgages for the purpose of borrowing money served as security to various parties for the faithful performance of filling in the Back Bay lands.[5] George Goss and Norman Munson seemed to be on very good terms as business partners into late 1859.

A Mysterious Disappearance

A shocking and unexpected development occurred late in the fall of 1859, when George Goss abruptly disappeared from Boston, abandoning his work and his business partner. At the time, Goss's whereabouts was unknown even to his own family. Munson was caught completely off guard by Goss's sudden disappearance. Because Goss left Boston without warning, some people, including creditors, suspected suspicious circumstances. Munson, apparently unaware of Goss's whereabouts for a short time and uncertain about the financial position of their partnership, continued to fulfill their Back Bay contracts.[6]

The situation became clearer over time, and by March 1860 it was known that George Goss was in poor health and had left the Boston area to recuperate.[7] It was reported later that his illness was the result of his concern and anxiety about the large enterprise that he and Munson had undertaken.[8] Goss apparently had a nervous breakdown caused by the financial stresses associated with carrying out the Back Bay landfill project and, possibly, other contracts. Goss may also have been troubled by Munson's habits of taking financial risks and attempting to carry out several large projects at the same time.

We do know that Goss did not steal from the partnership and that the business relationship between the partners was reestablished a month or two after Goss disappeared. In December 1859 Goss appointed Munson as his personal representative with power of attorney to represent him in all financial dealings and legal matters with respect to the Back Bay and other business.[9] Later in the same month Goss transferred to Munson some eleven joint contracts for filling the Back Bay. These included contracts for filling with George Ordiorne of Boston, the State Commissioners on the Back Bay, the Boston Water Power Company, and T. B. Lawrence and W. W. Goddard (who had bought the first group of lots from the State on Beacon Street and had to have them filled themselves). Other contracts transferred from Goss included the right to lay and use a railroad track along the Boston and Worcester Railroad's right-of-way, the use of the New York and Boston Railroad Company's track from Needham to Brookline Village, and the use of all the New York and Boston Railroad's locomotive engines and gravel cars.[10] George Goss apparently never returned to Massachusetts.

After Goss's sudden disappearance, Norman Munson continued to carry out the gravel pit operations in Needham at a rapid pace. Munson took over Goss's deed and promissory notes on the Colburn lot and paid them off completely on March 21, 1864.[11] As the gravel ridges were being cut down and removed from Goss's formerly leased property, Munson purchased a small parcel of adjoining land to the east containing about 145 square rods for $250 in March 1860.[12] Three years later, after the gravel was removed and the land was of little value, Munson sold this plot to Ezra C. Dudley for $25.[13]

By June of 1860, George Goss worked as a contractor and lived with his family in El Dorado County, California.[14] He may have stayed in California ten years[15] and by the 1870s he was General Superintendant of the Bingham Canyon and Camp Floyd Railroad in Utah.[16] Goss worked in Utah into the 1890s as co-owner of a gilsonite mine near Ashley, Utah,[17] and vice president of the Pleasant Valley Coal Company.[18] Goss, who never became a Mormon, died at Salt Lake City in 1904 at the age of seventy-eight.[19]

Munson Stays the Course

When George Goss left suddenly, Norman C. Munson continued the Back Bay landfill project without interruption. As Munson depleted the gravel reserves on the former Story-Cargill farm and Goss's lease, he shifted his operations southeastward. The gravel was never entirely removed from the gravel pits immediately to the west and north of the New York and New England Railroad right-of-way. This is because it was far more cost-effective to remove gravel from the high, steep-sided, and elongated eskers, kames, and kame terraces than it was to excavate the thinner patches of gravel between the high ridges. Much more heavy labor would be required to constantly shift track and equipment to obtain the same volume of gravel from thinner deposits. Also, the water table may have been significantly higher at the time, which would have reduced the depth to which gravel could be extracted economically. Several photographs taken in the 1890s show a high gravel ridge just outside the Fuller lot eastern boundary north of the Kendrick Street Bridge (see fig. 6.1). Steep gravel bluffs at former gravel pits may have resulted when the edge of a lot owned or leased by Munson was reached.

In July 1860 Munson extended his gravel landholdings by buying the 102-acre Stephen Fuller lot for $3,285.[20] This property (lot D in fig.6.2), is today bounded approximately by Kendrick Street on the south and Greendale Street and Route 128 (I-95) on the west. Most of this property is now within the New England Industrial Center, which includes the site of today's Coca-Cola Company bottling plant near the intersection of Kendrick Street and Route 128.

In this case, transporting sand and gravel off his property required Munson to construct and use spur rails across adjacent properties on leased rights-of-way. In November and December 1860 Munson leased a curving strip of land about two rods (thirty three feet) wide and about twenty-seven hundred feet long from four abutting landowners to run his gravel trains from his new gravel pit on the Fuller lot to the New York and Boston main line. Part of the rail spur extended into the present-day Route 128 Exit 19 cloverleaf. Fortunately, a surveyed map and profile along the railroad right-of-way that led to Munson's newly acquired lands is preserved in one of his leases.[21]

A comparison of the 1861 topography along Munson's branch railway (see fig. 6.2) to today's shows it to be similar to the profiles of the present gravel ridges located south of Kendrick Street.[22] In the depicted 1861 profile the vertical scale is sixteen times greater than the horizontal scale, making it easy to see the relief of the landscape at that time. It can be assumed that the same kinds of eskers, kames, and kame terraces were found in Munson's new gravel pit north of the public road leading to Kendrick's Bridge.

FIGURE 6.1. Partially preserved gravel ridges on the border of Munson's Fuller lot near the Kendrick Street Bridge over the Charles River, 1890s. Partially excavated eskers or kames can be seen in this photograph taken during the construction of water wells and filter basins in the Newton Water Lands adjacent to Munson's former gravel pit in Needham. The site of these gravel ridges is thought to be in today's New England Industrial Park, between Fourth Avenue and the Charles River and about five hundred yards northwest of Kendrick Street, just to the east of land parcel D at X in fig. 6.2. The gravel load in the cart was delicately balanced over the single axle for ease in dumping and the drivers generally walked beside the loaded carts. *(Newton History Museum at The Jackson Homestead, Newton, Massachusetts.)*

The topography of Needham's gravel lands has been altered drastically since Munson's time. Hills were removed and swamps filled in because of extensive gravel pit operations followed by urbanization. Both the Circumferential Highway, constructed in 1933, and Route 128, constructed in 1955, cut through a portion of the old Story-Cargill farm and Munson's other gravel pit properties. These two periods of highway construction reactivated and expanded the dimensions of existing Needham gravel pits. Only very small segments of the formerly extensive esker system remain in Needham.

By January 1861 Goss's name was dropped from the company's letterhead and in its place appeared "N. C. Munson & Company. The new excavation site at this time was situated south of the railroad tracks in an esker that was fifty feet high and extended over about a hundred acres. Approximately fifty acres of the new hill had been removed in about four months. O. S. Chapman and Company operated and maintained

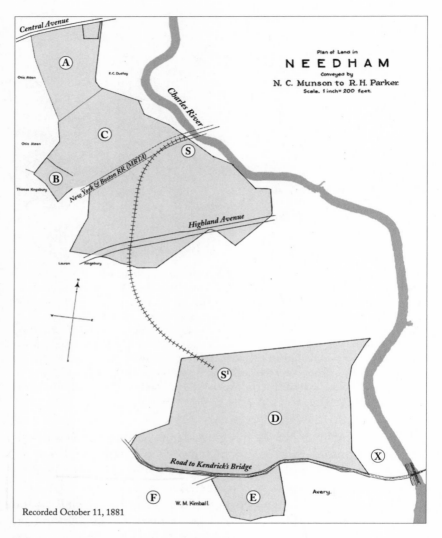

Plan of Land in

N E E D H A M

Conveyed by

N. C. Munson to R. H. Parker.

Scale. 1 inch= 200 feet.

Central Avenue

A

Otis Alden

E.C. Dudley

Charles River

C

Otis Alden

S

B

Thomas Kingsbury

New York & Boston RR (MBTA)

Highland Avenue

Lauron Kingsbury

N
W E
S

S¹

D

X

Road to Kendrick's Bridge

F

W. M. Kimball.

E

Avery.

Recorded October 11, 1881

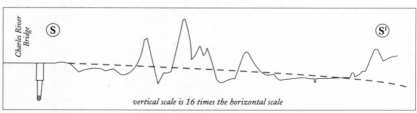

Charles River Bridge

S

S¹

vertical scale is 16 times the horizontal scale

the two steam shovels excavating the gravel. Every six weeks a cut was excavated parallel to the axis of the esker and extending from one end to the other. Laborers worked day and night, with a break only on Sundays and St. Patrick's Day. As soon as one twelve-hour shift had completed its day's work, a second shift took over.[23]

Munson continued to fulfill contracts with the State and the Boston Water Power Company. During 1862 Munson delivered 106,472 gravel cars, or 472,380 cubic yards, of Needham sand and gravel to Boston Water Power Company lands.[24] During this time Munson may have established a new partnership for operating the gravel trains. For example, in August 1861 and again in November 1861, there were bills for the repair of the locomotive "Uncle Tom," made out to Whitney and Munson.[25]

About the same time as the Boston Water Power Company mudflats south of the Mill Dam were being filled, the Mill Corporation mudflats north of the Mill Dam were also being filled. As early as 1822 the Mill Corporation had been authorized to widen the Mill Dam from fifty to one hundred feet to permit the building of wharves, storehouses, and other buildings on the dam, and in 1824 the width was increased again, to two hundred feet.[26] The Mill Corporation had constructed a seawall two hundred feet north of the dam as far west as what was is now Clarendon Street by the mid-1840s, and the flats between the Mill Dam and the seawall were filled with mud (see fig. 6.3).[27]

In exchange for the mudflats north of the Mill Dam granted in 1854, the "Boston and Roxbury Mill Corporation was to continue the seawall to the Brookline shore (now Kenmore Square) and fill the flats intervening according to the plans of the state. The Boston and Roxbury Mill Corporation was also to release its rights both to all of its territory south of the Mill Dam and to charging tolls on the Mill Dam Road (now Beacon Street) after May 1, 1863."[28]

Few pre-1850s records relating to the filling north of the Mill Dam have survived. In 1859, the Boston and Roxbury Mill Corporation signed

---

FIGURE 6.2. Map of Munson's total land holdings in Needham showing a rail spur and its topographic profile extending into the Fuller lot, 1881. The topographic profile "ss" extending along Munson's railroad spur has a vertical scale sixteen times greater than the horizontal scale, permitting an exaggerated cross-sectional view of the several parallel north-to-south trending eskers that once existed in this area. (*Map of land in Needham conveyed by N. C. Munson to R. H. Parker, recorded October 11, 1881, no. 329, Norfolk County Registry of Deeds, Dedham Massachusetts; Land of Norman C. Munson, vol. 294, 144, Norfolk County Registry of Deeds, William P. O'Donnell, Register. Created by Kirsten Lindquist.*)

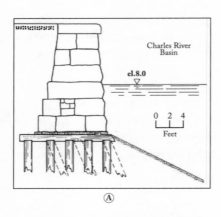
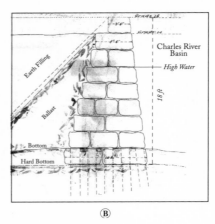

FIGURE 6.3A and B. Cross-section plans of Charles River seawalls. Similarly designed seawalls were constructed along the south side of the Charles River in the 1860s. Piles were
driven through the estuary silts and into the underlying blue clay and cut off at the lowest tide level, provided that they were more than ten inches in diameter. For the section
of seawall built in the 1860s behind the Union Boat Club and other buildings along
Brimmer Street, a solid multilayered plank platform was built onto the piles, and the
drystone granite seawall was constructed directly on the wooden platform (A).

Another style of seawall construction placed the granite blocks forming the seawalls
directly onto the underlying piles. Each of the granite blocks was placed on a minimum
of three piles and arranged in such a way that gaps separating the individual blocks were
not continuous longitudinally nor laterally across the wall. This type of seawall paralleled the Mill Dam (B) for its entire length.

Headers—granite blocks five to six feet long that extended through the seawall—
were placed every twelve to fifteen feet between the stretchers in each rock course and
offset above and below by one half of the distance between the headers.

The typical width of the Charles River seawall ranges from ten to twelve feet at the
base narrowing upward to about four feet at the top, and the height of the wall generally
varied from fourteen to sixteen feet, though at the western margin of the Boston and
Roxbury Mill Corporation land the height is eighteen feet. The other face of the seawall
is battered or sloped backward and curved upward slightly. The batter or slope of the
dressed exterior wall, on average, was one-and-a-half inches per foot rise, and the top of
the seawall was capped with granite split headers, four feet in length, six inches or more
in thickness and of variable width.

The space directly behind the seawall is often filled with ballast that consists of an assortment of mixed sized stones similar to beach or river gravel. The gravelly ballast helps
in supporting the wall and it helps prevent seepage of the river mud fill through the dry-
wall, with no mortar between the stones. *(A. Charles River Basin Commission, "Existing Wall,
Boston Marginal Conduit 2: Details of Masonry," Record Plan Sheet no. 2, May 21, 1910. Courtesy DCR
Plans Library. B. "Notice, Comm. Of Mass. To Griggs et al.," August 15 and 28, 1872, Lib. 1160, fol. 121,
Suffolk County Courthouse, Boston. Map provided courtesy of the Suffolk Registry of Deeds.)*

an agreement with two East Boston contractors, Timothy Corcoran and John Lynch, to fill a section of mudflats with mud dredged from the Charles River, topped with four feet of "upland earth." This project filled the space between the Mill Dam and the existing seawall, and the seawall was extended westward another 250 feet.[29]

> In June 1860 the Boston and Roxbury Mill Corporation contracted with Lewis Broad of Natick and Robert Rhoades of Neponset to fill the next 500 feet, beginning 304 feet west of Clarendon Street, and to build an additional 450 feet of seawall, a contract that led to difficulties when Broad sold out his part of the agreement to Rhodes [sic] and the latter demanded more time to complete the work. Rhoades apparently obtained some of his fill from Brookline uplands, since in December 1860 he was reported to be digging away at the old Revolutionary War fort at Sewall's Point.[30]

In July 1862 the Boston and Roxbury Mill Corporation "made an agreement with Dalrymple and Lennon . . . to fill the last two hundred feet of mudflats remaining east of the [Mill Dam's] sluice gates and to build another two hundred feet of seawall. This time the top layer of gravel fill had to be only three feet thick except next to the seawall, where a strip thirty-two feet wide was to be filled entirely by gravel, presumably to help support wall.[31]

On April 28, 1863, Norman C. Munson signed an agreement with the Mill Corporation to continue the filling north of the dam, extending westward from near the east end of the Mill Dam wharf to the wharf at Danforth's Store, a section about 1,775 feet long and 190 feet wide, except for a small portion opposite the Mill Dam wharf that was less than 100 feet wide. This time the entire fill was to be "clean earth or gravel" and brought up to level 14 (14 feet above Boston Base). For this fill he was to be paid forty-nine cents per cubic yard.[32] Unlike previous the Mill Corporation agreements, Munson's contract was for filling only. The contracts for driving the piles to support the new section of seawall went to the Boynton Brothers and to Ross and Lord, contractors from Providence, Rhode Island, and Ipswich, Massachusetts, respectively.[33] A seawall constructed by the Mill Corporation was to be completed 50 feet in advance of Munson's filling. The material was to be put in at a rate of 25,000 yards per month, if required, and brought up to a level not to exceed level 17, the height of the roadway at the top of the Mill Dam.[34]

The location of the Mill Corporation flats north of the Mill Dam presented certain logistical problems in their filling. The use of gravel trains along the north side of the Mill Dam was impracticable for two obvious reasons. Gravel trains could not approach the Mill Corporation flats from the east because the construction of residential buildings had kept pace with the filling, so gravel trains had no access. The gravel trains could not approach from the west because a branch line would have to extend from the main line near Sewall's Point and down the north side of the Mill Dam on a trestle to the dumping site. The only practical way to bring in sand and gravel fill to the Mill Corporation flats was by scows, large, flat-bottomed boats. The slow rate of filling by the earlier contractors suggests that the mud and gravel fill was obtained from the bed of the Charles River or from a bluff immediately adjacent to the Charles River. Empty scows would be towed out into the Charles River at high tide and then lowered to the exposed riverbed by the falling tide. River mud, blue clay, or gravel would be hand-loaded into the scows and then refloated at high tide. This was a labor-intensive technique used earlier in the filling of South Bay.[35]

Munson's operation in 1863 was more efficient. His rate of filling of 25,000 cubic feet of sand and gravel per month was much higher than those of his predecessors. It is highly likely that he obtained his gravel along the Charles River in Brighton or Watertown, where a large gravel ridge was breached by the Charles River.[36] In Brighton, the ridge extended between Market and North Beacon Streets and in Watertown it occurred east of the Watertown Arsenal.

Munson probably owned or leased several scows and a steam tug to transport them from the gravel banks of Brighton some five and one-half miles down the Charles River to the Mill Dam wharf or some designated point along the seawall west of the wharf. It is likely that the following procedure was followed. At the Brighton gravel pit Munson would have had several small, empty wooden boxes loaded on flatbed railroad cars. Rails were extended from the banks of the Charles River to the working face of the gravel pit, where gravel was loaded, possibly by steam shovel, into the empty boxes. A team of horses pulled the flat cars to the edge of the Charles River, where the filled gravel boxes were lifted off the flat cars and placed onto the scows by a horse-powered derrick (see fig. 6.4).[37] After being towed to the Mill Dam wharf by a steam tug, the gravel boxes were offloaded from the scow by a second derrick at the wharf and the gravel was poured out of the boxes into large piles. Subsequently, the gravel was loaded onto dump carts and transported to the filling site.

FIGURE 6.4. 1882 photograph of dredges, scows, and gravel boxes in the Back Bay fens. This rare photograph shows both the loading and dumping of gravel boxes on scows. The steam dredge boat shown in the photograph was invented by John Souther, who modified an Otis-Chapman steam shovel and attached it to a barge. Gravel boxes are being filled on the larger scow. On the distant scow a gravel box is being dumped into shallow water.

Norman Munson probably loaded similar gravel-filled boxes on scows by derricks at along the Charles River in Brighton and unloaded them by derrick at the Mill Dam Wharf in the Back Bay. This was a far more efficient system than the traditional method of hand loading and unloading the sand and gravel onto and off of scows. *(From Eighth Annual Report of Boston Park Commission for 1882, City Document no. 20 (1883), opposite page 12. Trustees of the Boston Park Commission. Courtesy of the Boston Public Library/Rare Books Department.)*

In June 1863 Norman Munson negotiated with the Town of Needham to remove the sand and gravel hill between his land and Kendrick's Bridge, and, in return, to build a "good and substantial" road (now Kendrick Street) to the bridge. It was to be built to the satisfaction of the selectmen and presented to the town of Needham free of charge. The Needham selectmen accepted this proposal after Norman Munson gave a bond. Munson removed the gravel but was slow in completing the new road. The town petitioned the selectmen to request Munson (and if necessary to force him) to complete the public road through his gravel pit to Kendrick's Bridge.[38] Needham politicians discussed Munson's bond as late as 1873.[39]

In July 1863 Munson leased the gravel rights to about twelve acres and five rods of land owned by Jonathan Avery (east of lot E in fig. 6.2) on the south side of Kendrick Street for $2,411.25 and began to remove gravel from that site. According to the agreement, the material removed from the Avery property could not extend below the level of the adjacent meadow, and the land would be left in a graded condition.[40]

Early in 1864 Norman Munson controlled every aspect of the Back Bay landfill operations. He owned all the locomotives and gravel cars transporting the gravel, and he maintained and repaired that portion of the tracks on which his cars ran. In the spring of that year Munson ran 175 gravel cars and eight locomotives. Two switching locomotives were kept in the Needham gravel pit. The average daily run into the Back Bay consisted of thirty gravel trains, each containing more than thirty cars.[41] On the basis of an interview with Norman C. Munson, Myron Munson wrote in 1895 that at the height of the landfill operations Munson had fourteen locomotives, 225 gravel cars, and twenty-five miles of track.[42]

The filling procedure in the Back Bay remained essentially the same as it was in 1859 and 1860, continuing westward from the earlier fill sites. Railroad spurs ran north of the Boston and Worcester and Boston and Providence Railroads into the Back Bay. The main rail spur probably followed a route that swung northward along what is now Dartmouth Street, with secondary rail spurs swinging eastward toward Clarendon Street and others westward toward Exeter Street (see fig. 6.6).

Munson's many investments and operations became profitable beginning in October 1862. He had obtained high prices for the house lots in the Back Bay that he had received as payment for filling work. Also, he invested $150,000 in New York and Boston Railroad bonds at an average price of $45 per share; within a year they were selling at $75 per share. That investment gave him control of the board of directors and made him president of the New York and Boston Railroad, over which he ran his gravel trains. Munson's estimated worth in April 1864 was between $200,000 and $300,000.[43]

In March 1864 Munson purchased the original Story-Cargill farm, which was at one time owned by the Charles River Branch Railroad Company and comprised all the Hiram T. Story and Mills land as well as the lot formerly leased by George Goss.[44] That was the last of Munson's individual purchases in Needham (lots A, B, and C in fig. 5.3).

It is unclear exactly when or why Munson's management of the New York and Boston Railroad came to an end. According to Karr, Munson gave up his control in 1863,[45] but the incomplete collection of New York and Boston Railroad contracts does not support this interpretation.

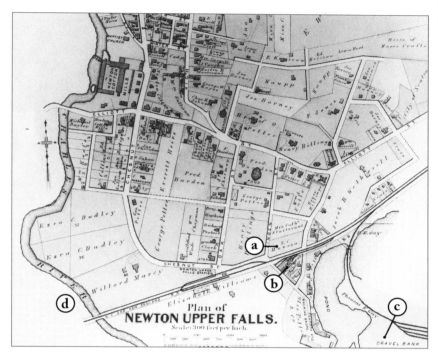

FIGURE 6.5. Map showing the location of Munson's machine and repair shops and Phineas E. Gay's gravel bank in Newton Upper Falls. Part of the Newton Upper Falls map showing: (a) the location of N. C. Munson's rail siding for storing locomotives and gravel cars, (b) his leased repair facility and machine shop, (c) Phineas E. Gay's Gravel Bank, (d) and Goss and Munson's 1859 Gravel Pit. ("Plan of Newton Upper Falls," Atlas of the City of Newton *[Middlesex County, Mass.: G. M. Hopkins and Company, 1874], pl. K.; Newton History Museum at the Jackson Homestead, Newton, Massachusetts.)*

More likely, Munson lost control of the Massachusetts branch of the New York and Boston Railroad following its amalgamation into the Boston, Hartford and Erie Railroad in 1864.[46] It seems reasonable that all the high-level managerial positions of the New York and Boston Railroad would have been filled by personnel of the Boston, Hartford and Erie Railroad following their takeover.

Following Munson's departure, the management of the Massachusetts branch of the Boston, Hartford and Erie Railroad appears to have been taken over by Edward Crane. In December 1864 Crane was submitting bills to the New York and Boston Railroad Accounting Department for expenses in maintaining their rolling stock and for paying labor

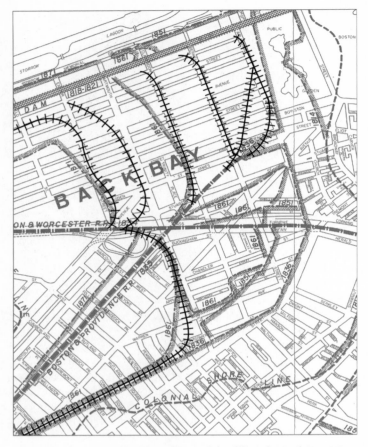

FIGURE 6.6. Probable spur-track alignments used for filling the Back Bay. We were able to draw the probable alignments of spur tracks because of the shape of the new lands shown on the map. *(Map compiled by Harl P. Aldrich, Jr., "Back Bay Boston, Part 1," Journal of the Boston Society of Civil Engineers Section/ASCE 57, no. 1 (January, 1970): 4. Reprinted with permission of Boston Society of Civil Engineers Section/ASCE, Civil Engineering Practice, Journal of BSCES. Probable rail spur positions interpreted by Wilfred E. Holton.)*

costs.[47] The transition of the railroad's management from Munson to Crane took place between June and August 1864.

That August Norman Munson "sold out his Back Bay contract and equipment to Edward Crane and others" connected with the Boston, Hartford and Erie Railroad for $500,000, with a down payment of $100,000 and installments of $10,000 per month for forty months, with interest.[48] Edward Crane and his associates, however, did not or could not keep up with the mortgage payments and the property reverted back to Munson, who resold it in July 1865 to the newly formed American Railroad Construction and Transportation Company, of which he was president.[49] Having purchased Munson's former gravel pit properties back from Crane, the American Railroad Construction and Transportation Company must have arrived at some agreement with the Boston, Hartford, and Erie Railroad and expanded its Needham gravel pit properties. On November 4, 1865, it bought the Kimball lot,[50] located south of the public road over Kendrick's Bridge and west of land that Munson leased from Avery in 1863 (lot E in fig. 6.2).[51]

Munson continued to dabble boldly in new business ventures. By May 1870 the Harbor Improvement Company was formed and incorporated with Munson as president and Henry Edgerton as treasurer.[52] This was a huge project to build wharves and warehouse facilities on the South Boston waterfront. The following year Munson formed yet another company, the American Railroad Construction and Land Company, in the city of Boston, with his brother, Silas, D. N. Stanton, and others; they had $600,000 in capital and the power to contract for building or equipping railroads, for filling flats, and for constructing wharves and seawalls.[53]

By the mid-1860s Norman C. Munson's business projects were strong, in spite of the loss of his partner and his key position with the New York and Boston Railroad. After removing large amounts of gravel from the land that he owned or leased in Needham, Munson faced the challenge of locating huge new gravel pits to fulfill his contracts to fill more Back Bay land for the State and the Boston Water Power Company. As before, the gravel deposits had to be near direct railroad connections, which could provide cost-effective transportation to the landfill sites in Boston. Munson probably searched for other sources of fill in Needham and in other towns along the Boston and Worcester Railroad. The other possibility was to use gravel from kames, kame terraces, and eskers in the Neponset River Valley south of Boston, along the Boston and Providence Railroad main line.

Gravel from Canton, Dedham, Hyde Park, and Westwood

The Needham gravel pits were the first source of Munson's Back Bay gravel, but they were by no means the only gravel pits he excavated or the last gravel sources for the Back Bay landfill. As early as 1867 or 1868 Munson was shifting his active gravel pit operations away from Needham, and by December 1870 a large part of Munson's gravel train operation into the

Back Bay was being run on the Boston and Providence line.[54] Munson obtained sand and gravel from Hyde Park, Dedham, Canton, and probably other sources along the Boston and Providence line for at least seven years. He found large, high-banked gravel pits close to major railroads leading to Boston and excavated all the sand and gravel that he could remove profitably with his steam shovels. When the excavation of sand and gravel was no longer profitable, Munson moved on to the next source.

The filling of the State's lands in the Back Bay was mostly completed by 1865, and all the Boston Water Power Company's lands were filled south of the Boston and Providence Railroad.[55] Approximately 75 percent of the former Receiving Basin was filled by 1871 (see fig. 6.7).

Munson had lost control of the Massachusetts section of the New York and Boston Railroad following its amalgamation with the Boston, Hartford and Erie Railroad in December 1865.[56] He still owned Needham gravel pits and apparently there was still a large amount of gravel in them. Now, he had to negotiate with the new owners for the right to run his gravel trains on their track to Brookline Village, where it joined Munson's track parallel to the Boston and Worcester Railroad's main line leading into Boston. Perhaps the increased cost of using the Boston, Hartford and Erie's rails was more than Munson was willing to pay. The Boston and Providence line provided a less complicated route, a straight shot into the Boston Water Power Company flats south of that railroad in the Back Bay; it minimized the disruption of rail traffic and offered gentler grades than the Needham route. Whatever the case, Munson decided to shift most of his gravel train operations to the Boston and Providence line in the late 1860s or early 1870s. The rate of filling in the Back Bay did not diminish during this period. The amount of sand and gravel available at several sites along the Boston and Providence line was extensive, perhaps exceeding that in the Needham pits.

Filling the Back Bay was just one of the many projects that Munson was completing simultaneously. For example, in 1865, he left his brother, Silas, in charge of the Back Bay landfill operation, while he was constructing a section of railroad for the Boston, Hartford and Erie Railroad. In 1866 Munson founded a large cotton mill on the Catacunemaug River in Shirley, Massachusetts, where he lived.[57] By September 1868 the firm of Munson and Edgerton Manufacturing was producing horseshoe nails, also in Shirley.[58]

A major turning point in the filling of the Back Bay lands occurred on May 4, 1865, when the Massachusetts Commission on Public Lands met

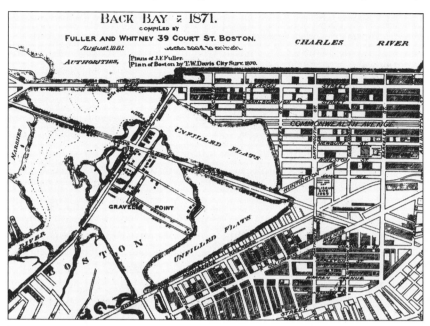

FIGURE 6.7. Fuller and Whitney map of the Back Bay in 1871. The filling of the State's land in the Back Bay was nearly complete in the winter of 1868, and all of the lands had been filled south of the Boston and Providence Railroad. This map shows that approximately 75 percent of the former Receiving Basin had been filled at this time. *(Courtesy of The Bostonian Society/Old State House.)*

to discuss, with Norman Munson and others, discontinuing the sluice-ways and allowing the Boston and Roxbury Mill Corporation to fill them up at the earliest possible time.[59] Three weeks later Mr. Henck, the commission's engineer, recommended closing the sluices near Exeter Street on the Mill Dam (see fig. 6.10), which had been used for empty-ing the Receiving Basin. This required opening a new sluice through the Cross Dam at Commonwealth Avenue to allow the water in the unfilled section of the Receiving Basin to drain through the Full Basin and out into the Charles River at low tide.[60]

In May 1863 Norman C. Munson had signed a contract with the Boston Water Power Company[61] to fill a portion of the flats between Common-wealth Avenue and Beacon Street, extending from near Fairfield Street to the Cross Dam, an area that probably crossed the main drainage channel leading to the emptying sluices (compare figs. 6.9 and 6.10). Earlier, Munson had constructed a trestle for his gravel trains that probably crossed the main channel near Clarendon Street. Now he wanted to bridge the channel at Commonwealth Avenue near its present junction with Exeter Street to complete his contract with the Boston Water Power Company.[62] The State Commission denied Munson's request to build a bridge at that time and noted that in light of the June 9, 1861, indenture, the Boston Water Power Company had surrendered its right to control the flow of water through the Receiving Basin.[63] This denial is hard to understand in light of the State's interest in the filling project.

Until 1866 water accumulating in the remaining part of the Receiving Basin was allowed to drain through the sluices in the Mill Dam near Exeter Street. As the filling encroached on the sluices, a controversy arose over blocking them. In January 1866 the Boston Water Power Company objected to continuing the filling process before the channels of the sluices were blocked.[64] The State Commissioners decided to keep the Mill Dam sluices open and hired Munson to repair them the following month so that the drainage out of the Receiving Basin would be maintained. He placed approximately 850 yards of gravel at the base of the emptying sluice under the Mill Dam, and he submitted a bill to the commissioners for $408. In September of the same year Munson was authorized by the commissioners to build a bridge and fill in the west side of the drainage channel leading to the Receiving Basin's emptying sluices. He agreed to assume all responsibility and liability for any damages due to changes in water level in the Receiving Basin.[65]

Nathan Matthews, president of the Boston Water Power Company, appeared before the Massachusetts Commission on Public Lands on June 4, 1867, and urged for the second time that the commissioners allow the filling of the sluices in the Receiving Basin. Again, they denied Matthews permission to have Munson fill the sluices and make the filling continuous.[66] Unfortunately, the open drainage channel discharging water and sewage through the Mill Dam separated the newly filled land of the Boston Water Power Company from the elegant neighborhood east of Exeter Street. It was smelly, polluted, and an eyesore.

In June 1867 and again in November of the same year, the Commissioners on Public Lands informed Nathan Matthews that the timbers covering the sluices in the Mill Dam were, and had been for a long time, decayed and in a dangerous condition. The commissioners requested Matthews to have the Boston Water Power Company repair them immediately.[67] Finally, sometime before 1870, the Boston Water Power Company was permitted to build new sluices through the Cross Dam (see fig. 6.7) and to close the old emptying sluices in the Mill Dam near Exeter Street.

In addition to his numerous construction projects, <u>Munson was constantly wheeling and dealing in real estate.</u> Some of his holdings were in the Back Bay, but much of his real estate was outside Boston along various railroad right-of-ways. For example, in 1857 Munson built his own house on Center Road in Shirley, Massachusetts, on a lot adjacent to property of the Fitchburg Railroad. He probably developed an interest in this site when he was a contractor building the Fitchburg Railroad from Boston to Marlborough between 1848 and 1855.[68] In 1868 he purchased eight house lots on Winter Hill in Somerville for $20,000.[69] Munson was at this time very successful. His overall worth in 1867 was $150,000.[70] In September 1868 his profit from the Back Bay project alone was estimated at $500,000 to $750,000.[71] Munson's rapidly expanding business enterprises apparently required him to seek larger and larger offices. Between 1861 and 1865 the address of Munson's Boston headquarters changed from 25 Phoenix Building to 22 Congress Street and then in 1866 to 13 Studio Building.[72]

Norman C. Munson, as president of the recently formed American Construction and Land Company, signed contracts with the Boston, Hartford and Erie Railroad in 1867 and again in 1869 for filling the South Boston mudflats with dredged clay from Boston Harbor and for building seawalls in South Boston.[73] In 1867 Munson was an equal partner in filling the Church Street district of Boston.[74] In October 1867 Munson signed a contract with the Boston, Hartford and Erie Railroad to build a twenty-six-mile section of their railroad from Mechanicsville to Willimantic in Connecticut.[75] Construction began on the railroad in December 1869, at the same time he was filling in the Back Bay. He had nearly completed this construction project in 1870 when the railroad company failed—owing him about $873,000 for labor and material.[76] He sued the Boston, Hartford and Erie Railroad for his money, but there is no record of his receiving any compensation for his claims. Shortly afterward the Boston, Hartford and Erie Railroad went bankrupt and was subsequently restructured as the New York and New England Railroad in 1873.[77]

In spite of his financial reversals, Munson returned to railroad construction in 1870 and began laying eight miles of railroad for the Middlesex Central Railroad in Massachusetts; he later laid forty miles of track for the Montpelier and Wells River Railroad in Vermont.[78] At this time Munson was still filling in the tidal marshlands, but the gravel was being transported into the Back Bay on the tracks of the Boston and Providence Railroad. During the following year, 1871, Munson transported additional sand and gravel into the Back Bay from ridges or "banks" along the Charles River in Brighton on the Boston and Albany Railroad, formerly the Boston and Worcester Railroad.[79]

Munson suffered heavy financial losses in the Boston, Hartford and Erie Railroad failure,[80] but he was resilient. In November 1870 he signed a new contract with the Boston Water Power Company to fill in the Crafts and Hathaway tidal mudflat located between the Boston and Providence and the Boston and Albany Railroads (see fig. 3.9). This area, about 1,300,000 square feet, was to be filled to the city grades, and the rest of the land was to be filled to within seven feet of the height of the street surface. Munson agreed to fill at least 300,000 square feet of the Crafts and Hathaway lot by May 5, 1871, and to complete the entire job by November 5, 1872. The filling was to be continuous until the entire section was completely filled.[81]

In December 1870 Munson was running gravel cars into the Back Bay on the Boston and Providence Railroad and later, in October 1871 on the Boston and Albany Railroad (see Table 6.1). Although large volumes of sand and gravel were being brought into the Back Bay, the Boston Water Power Company did not complete its three contracts on time with the City, the Trustees of the Huntington Avenue Lands, and the Trustees of the Boylston Street Lands.[82] Part of the reason that the company failed to fulfill its contracts was its dispute with Nathan Matthews, who stepped down as president in 1869 and had not paid the amounts due on the land that the Boston Water Power Company had mortgaged to finance the filling.[83]

While Munson's claims against the Boston, Hartford and Erie Railroad were pending in 1871, he began the construction of the Massachusetts Central Railroad from Boston to Northhampton, Massachusetts, a distance of 117 miles. For this job he took his construction crews of Irish and Italian laborers and four of his locomotives to make up his construction trains. These were numbered 6, 7, 10, and 11, and named the "Bay State," "Charles River," "Wayland," and "N. C. Munson," respectively.[84] By December 1871 Munson was once again worth half a million dollars.[85]

Apparently, Munson's first gravel pit along the Boston and Providence Railroad line was in Hyde Park, about seven miles from the Back Bay. It is likely that Munson bought the rights to excavate sand and gravel on

TABLE 6.1. Numbers of Carloads of Gravel for Filling of the Back Bay for the Boston Water Power Company Delivered by Norman C. Munson by Month from Each Railroad, 1871 and 1872

Year	Month	Boston & Providence RR	Boston & Albany RR
1871	January	3,367	
	February	2,932	
	March	5,061	
	April	4,158	
	May	3,656	
	June	9,221	
	July	9,257	
	August	10,587	
	September	10,635	
	October	10,764	352
	November	10,300	3,948
	December	10,646	2,297
1872	January	10,882	5,057
	February	10,616	5,473
	March	9,665	5,745
	April	10,957	9,106
	May	12,572	11,917
	June	6,342	9,055
	July	9,052	14,500
	August	12,090	13,712
	September	12,044	10,587
	October	11,731	13,315
	November	10,824	11,401
	December	9,441	9,509

Source: "Boston Water Power Company N.C. Munson Accounts," Boston Water Power Company, May 1, 1873, case 4, Harvard Business School Baker Library Archive.

land owned by the Boston and Providence Railroad or other landowners. His sand and gravel operations were well established in this area within a few years.

Munson developed somewhat complex business partnerships in Hyde Park and Dedham for carrying out his operations. On March 26, 1872, he and his new associate, Edward Thompson of Boston, together bought land in both Dedham and Hyde Park for $35,000.[86] The plan for the Hyde Park property suggests that it was bought for the purpose of maintaining and repairing locomotives and gravel cars as well as for storing equipment (see fig. 6.9). The Dedham land was a twenty-six-acre lot with

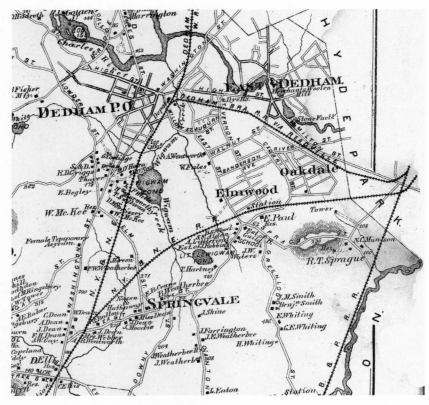

FIGURE 6.8. Map showing N. C. Munson's gravel property along Sprague Street in West Dedham, Massachusetts, in 1875. Munson purchased twenty-six acres of sand and gravel land along Sprague Street and adjacent to the Boston and Providence Railroad in West Dedham, Massachusetts to supply fill for his Back Bay landfill contracts. (*West Dedham section of the* Atlas of Norfolk County, Massachusetts, from Recent and Actual Surveys and Records under Supervision of W. A. Sherman, *Pub. [New York: Comstock and Cline, 1876], printed by H. J. Toudy and Co. Courtesy of Canton Historical Society.*)

a house, close to the Boston and Providence line that contained abundant sand and gravel deposits (see fig. 6.8). It was probably connected to the main line of the Boston and Providence Railroad by a short spur line. The Munson and Thompson partnership did not hold up. In December 1873 Munson bought out Thompson's share in both the Dedham and the Hyde Park properties.[87]

Soon after establishing a base of operation in Hyde Park and Dedham, Munson began to extract sand and gravel from Canton, about five miles

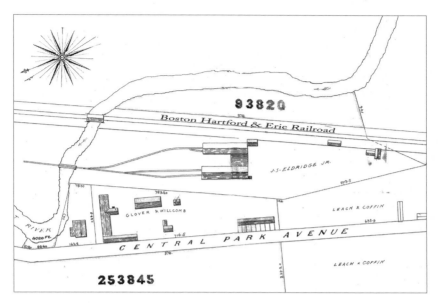

FIGURE 6.9. Plan of Munson's Hyde Park repair facility formerly owned by J. S. Eldridge, Jr. The Hyde Park repair facility was used to repair and service Munson's locomotives and gravel cars, which were used to fill the Back Bay and were from the Boston and Providence Railroad. On the site were two service sheds that were probably connected by a storage facility. Two sets of tracks, extending the length of the building, were used to house rolling stock brought in on a spur track. *(Refer to Norfolk County Courthouse Deed, Lib. 425, fol. 227; Norfolk County Registry of Deeds, William P. O'Donnell, Register.)*

to the south. Munson must at first have leased the land or bought the sand and gravel outright, as there is no record for his buying the property. The first evidence of his new base of operations was in 1871, when he built a house for his workers in the Canton gravel pit.[88] Munson's Canton operation appears to have been quite extensive. The large sand and gravel deposit that included Pillion Hill (see fig. 6.10) can be located today just east of where Route I-95 crosses over the M.B.T.A. track in Canton.[89] Pillion Hill before its removal resembled: "the easy cushion attached to the back of a good man's saddle, on which our grandmothers used to balance their lovely forms . . . We presumed that this hill resembled a pillion, but it was not the writer's good fortune to see it before that Canton invention, the steam excavator—some times called the 'Steam Paddy'—had accomplished its fell purpose."[90]

An inspector for the Boston Water Power Company at the Back Bay

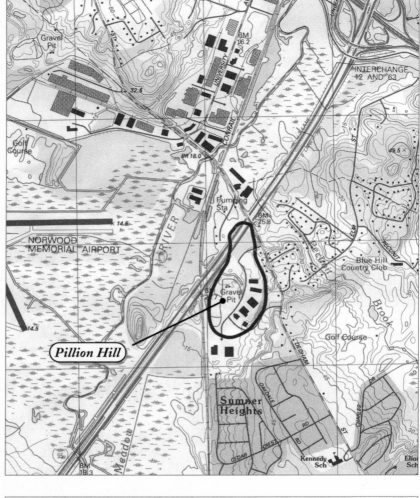

FIGURE 6.10. Map showing Munson's Canton gravel pit and the location of Pillion Hill. Pillion Hill in Canton was one of Norman C. Munson's gravel sources in the 1870s. It was located where the words "Gravel Pit" appear in the center of the pit outline. Munson either purchased volumes of gravel outright or leased the rights to the gravel on the property. There is no record of the exact boundaries of Munson's nineteenth-century gravel pit operation in Canton. *(U.S.G.S. Topographic Map Norwood Quadrangle, 1958, 1:24,000.)*

landfill site reported that Munson's gravel trains on the Boston and Albany Railroad were more than full and there were twenty-two, twenty-three, and twenty-four cars to a train.[91] In March 1872 the gravel cars on the Boston and Providence Railroad for the Boston Water Power Company were, on average, three to seven inches short of being full and consisted of forty-one, forty-two, and forty-three cars to a train. The question of the fullness of the cars was probably due to the nature of the sand and gravel that was being loaded onto the railroad cars and the distance that the cars traveled before arriving at the landfill site. The larger the mix of sand and gravel sizes from the gravel banks, the more settling occurred during transit to the landfill. And the farther the fill had to travel, the more settling was likely to occur because of jostling as the trains bumped along the tracks.

By 1871 most of the filling of the State's lands (shown earlier in fig. 3.6), bounded on the west by a jagged line between Exeter and Fairfield Streets and on the south by Providence Street, was finished. The State did not fill the small remaining area in the early 1870s because the adjacent Boston Water Power Company flats were not yet filled and Munson did not start on them until 1872. In 1876 the State's filling was complete.[92]

In 1871 Norman Munson signed a contract with the Boston City Council for $300,000 to construct within two years, and grade with "good clean sand" to an elevation not less than eighteen feet above mean low water, the following new streets and avenues in Boston: "Commonwealth Avenue, two-hundred feet wide from its present termination to its junction with the proposed extension of West Chester Park Street [now Massachusetts Avenue]; Huntington Avenue one-hundred feet wide from Boylston Street to Camden Street [now Gainsborough Street] and West Chester Park Street from the Boston and Providence Railroad to Beacon Street."[93]

Included in the agreement was the construction of a sufficiently high grade to carry the new roadways over the Boston and Providence Railroad and the Boston and Albany Railroad by means of bridges. Munson agreed to pay for all damages caused by the erosion of sand and gravel from the raised streets and sidewalks into the adjacent lots. This slope erosion posed a serious problem to the lower building lots because they lay six feet below the streets and sidewalks. Furthermore, Munson was to maintain the newly constructed streets six feet above the level of the building lots without the use of any retaining walls or bulkheads to support the sides of the roads.[94]

"In 1872, however, [Norman Munson] assigned the receipts from the city contract to the Boston Water Power Company because he evidently owed the corporation money, and the Boston Water Power Company then became responsible for this filling."[95] It is not clear what prompted this action. He may have been over-extended and have owed the corporation money. While filling the Back Bay in 1872, Munson was deeply involved in constructing the Central Massachusetts Railroad and had signed an agreement with J. R. Smith of Springfield, Massachusetts, to erect a masonry-supported truss structure some fourteen hundred feet long across the Connecticut River. The bridge was to be completed on or before September 1, 1873.[96] By June 1873 Munson had large contracts and had made money rapidly; his estimated worth was almost a million dollars.[97]

In the 1870s the Boston Water Power Company experienced severe financial problems. Part of the problem was that Nathan Matthews, its president from 1860 to 1869, had obtained large amounts of company land at lower than market value prices. In the 1870s the company, while continuing to sell individual lots, began selling large tracts of unfilled mudflats; included in the price was the filling of the land. In 1871 almost forty acres of mudflats bounded now by the Southwest Corridor Park, Camden Street, Huntington Avenue, and the Massachusetts Turnpike were sold to the trustees of what became known as the Huntington Avenue Lands. A year later, in 1872, the Boston Water Power Company sold another segment of mudflats, between Boylston and Newbury Streets and extending west of Exeter Street, to the trustees of what became known as the Boylston Street lands. In each case the Boston Water Power Company agreed to fill the land to grade 12 and the streets to grade 18.[98]

Also in 1872 the Mill Corporation signed an agreement with William Woolley of East Boston to fill the mudflats between the Mill Dam and the recently constructed seawall from Gloucester Street to the Cross Dam. These flats were to be filled with mud or gravel that had been dredged from the bed of the Charles River and brought to the site in scows. The dredge was basically an Otis-Chapman steam shovel attached to a barge, following a design by John Souther. Woolley was to be paid the equivalent of fifty cents per cubic yard for the dredged fill, which was comparable to the price for the gravel transported by Munson's gravel trains. This suggests that Woolley transported and unloaded the dredged fill from dump boxes, thus reducing his costs (see fig. 6.4).[99]

The round of filling activity continued at least until 1876 for both the Boston Water Power Company and the City of Boston after Munson shifted at least part of his gravel operations to Dedham, Canton, and Westwood along the Boston and Providence Railroad.[100] After Munson left Needham, Phineas E. Gay, a Boston contractor, filled several small sections in the Back Bay beginning in 1872. Using Otis-Chapman steam shovels, Gay excavated a large sand and gravel bank at Newton Upper Falls (see fig. 6.5) and ran gravel trains into Boston for two or three years.[101] Other fill was supplied by the Boston and Albany Railroad, which brought it from Auburndale in Newton near today's Riverside Station. Souther's ✔ New England Dredging Company supplied clay and sand from the bed of the Charles River for Back Bay landfill using a modified Otis-Chapman steam shovel attached to a barge.

The Huntington Avenue Lands and the city streets were finally completed in 1875.[102] The Huntington Avenue Lands, known as the St. Botolph district, after the street that was laid out between Huntington Avenue and the Boston and Providence Railroad, was ready for sale in 1879. "Meanwhile, in 1874 the BPW [Boston Water Power Company] signed a contract with Munson to fill the Boylston Street Lands, and in subsequent years Munson worked on filling this area as well as the one just south of the Boston and Albany tracks."[103]

Apparently, Munson was not involved in Back Bay landfill activities from 1876 to the time of his sudden death, on May 16, 1885. By this time the Back Bay was filled except for small areas in lower Roxbury. Munson's obituary in the *Boston Evening Transcript* on May 18, 1885, read:

> Mr. Norman C. Munson died suddenly at his office, corner of State and Devonshire Streets, Saturday of angina pectoris. Mr. Munson was widely known in connection with railroad enterprises. He was born in Poultney, Vermont [*sic*] about sixty-five years ago, and spent his early days on a farm. He came to Boston when quite a young man, and went to work upon the Boston & Worcester Railroad as superintendent of track-laying. When the Fitchburg Railroad was building he took a contract to do the work, and took up residence at Shirley, where he has since resided. He did a great deal for the town. He built the town hall, an elegant gateway for the cemetery, and laid out a park. His next large operation was the building of the second track of the Hudson River Railroad. Upon its completion he went to Baltimore and engaged in some large work for the city, in company with a man named Goss, the firm name being Munson & Goss. After a year both came to Boston and took a large contract for filling in the Back Bay, for the State, City and Boston Water Power Company. Mr. Goss was interested in this contract, but after a short time his courage

failed him and he sold out to Mr. Munson, who put all his means into it. He prosecuted the work with vigor from 1859 to 1873. At one time it was estimated that he was worth $3,000,000, but by unfortunate land speculation and the misfortunes of the Massachusetts Central Railroad it was greatly lessened. Mr. Munson was president of the Norfolk County Railroad, which was merged into the old Hartford & Erie. He put money into it, and when Governor Claflin vetoed the bill giving the road State aid the road was owing him $1,040,000, vouchers for which are now in the Massachusetts State House. It was a very severe blow to Mr. Munson, but did not discourage him. In 1873 he had a large amount of money in the Massachusetts Central Railroad. When the panic occurred, Jay Cooke, who was the banker who was to dispose of the bonds, was unable to do so, and Mr. Munson's operations on the railroad and the Back Bay came to a sudden close. He struggled until 1876, when he found it was impossible for him to continue, and he went into bankruptcy. In 1879 he reorganized the Massachusetts Central Railroad and began the work of construction in 1880, and continued until the failure of Charles A. Sweet & Co., bankers. The deceased was one of the most active business men in Boston, and at the time of his death was engaged in building the Florida Southern Railroad.

In 1883 the Boston Water Power Company was still involved in "filling the area south of the Boston and Albany tracks between West Chester Park (Massachusetts Avenue) and Dalton Street and did not finish filling the area east of Massachusetts Avenue until later in the decade."[104] Thus was completed the filling of the Back Bay's Receiving Basin, forming the areas now known as the Back Bay, the Prudential Center, and the St. Botolph district, as well as a large part of the South End.[105]

The Boston Embankment

The last segment of land to be filled in the Back Bay involved the tidal mudflats immediately north of the Mill Corporation's land along the Charles River. A narrow strip of land, called the Boston Embankment, was created on the Boston side of the Charles River during the construction of the Charles River Dam between 1907 and 1910. The one-hundred-foot-wide swath of new filling for the Boston Embankment between Berkeley Street and Charlesgate West was north of the Mill Corporation's seawall, which had been built in the 1860s and 1870s.

Haglund tells us that construction of this early-twentieth-century seawall differed from the traditional method. The usual technique was to
drive wooden piles into the underlying silts, and to construct a wooden
platform on top of the piles. Finally, the seawall was constructed of large,
rough-cut granite blocks atop the wooden platform, with the new seawall advancing in front of the filling area. In 1907 the filling for the construction of the embankment was under way before the piles were driven
for the seawall. Also, instead of the bulk of the seawall being granite
blocks, it was concrete with granite only for the capstones.[106]

A large portion of the fill used in the embankment was dredged from
the Charles River. A small amount of the material was probably transported to the site by horse-drawn tipcarts. "Work was delayed by plans to
construct a subway under the embankment, which were later dropped,
but by 1909 the park was sufficiently ready to be topped with loam
brought by scows from Squantum."[107] At the same time that the Boston
Embankment was under construction, the Boston Marginal Conduit (described in chapter 7) was built under entire length of the embankment.[108]

In 1928 the legislature approved a new commission to consider developing parks, playgrounds, beaches, and promenades along the Charles
River and to make the basin much more attractive for water-related activities. "At about the same time Helen Storrow submitted plans for a
huge boathouse along the river to promote the sport of rowing in the
greater Boston schools." She donated one million dollars to the project
in honor of her deceased husband, James Jackson Storrow, a former
mayor of Boston. This was the beginning of the transformation of the
Boston Embankment (now known as the Esplanade).[109]

The Esplanade and Storrow Drive

The stabilizing of the water level in the Charles River Basin and the creation of the Boston Embankment did not substantially increase the recreational use of the Charles River Basin or the Esplanade. "Wind-driven
waves bouncing off the seawall created a chop that made the basin too
rough for small boats and the section of the embankment along Back
Bay was too narrow for boathouses. Finally, in 1929 a state commission
recommended widening what had come to be known as the Esplanade
to remedy some of the deficiencies." In the Back Bay section, plans called
for doubling the width of the Esplanade, to about 230 feet, and building

a dike 240 feet from shore, between Exeter and Fairfield Streets, to form a lagoon for skating and canoeing.[110]

Work began on widening the Esplanade late in 1931. According to Seasholes, "Most of the fill was sucked from the bottom of the river by a huge hydraulic dredge and then pumped through as much as a half mile of pipe to the locations being filled." During the summer of 1932, "Beacon Street and Bay State Road residents made many complaints about the noise of the dredging operation and the smell of the material being deposited." By design, the river's edge was gently sloped along the Boston side to minimize the problems with waves that characterized previous seawalls. The project was mostly complete by 1934.[111]

The widening of the Esplanade in the 1930s was achieved because a proposal for the construction of a highway down its center from the Longfellow Bridge to the Cottage Farm (Boston University) Bridge generated a tremendous number of protests. In addition, Helen Storrow privately opposed the plan and she was financing some of the Esplanade's recreational improvements with her million-dollar gift. "Opened in 1935, the new park was formally dedicated as the Storrow Memorial Embankment the following year."[112]

After Helen Storrow passed away in 1944, the Esplanade "highway proposal was revived as a means of dealing with Boston's traffic problems and, in spite of enormous opposition, was finally rammed through the legislature." Ironically, the new highway was named the James J. Storrow Memorial Drive.[113]

CHAPTER 7

Environmental Problems and Zoning

Groundwater Levels in the Back Bay

Before the construction of the Mill Dam, the Back Bay area was a typical tidal mudflat, drained by two branching tidewater channels. The surface of the water table[1] in this mudflat was probably at mean tide level in Boston Harbor, or at an elevation of 5.65 feet BCB.[2]

Following the construction of the Mill Dam, most of the water was drained out of the Receiving Basin during every low tide. As the tide began to rise in the lower Charles River Estuary, the sluice gates were closed in the Mill Dam, preventing tidal flow into the Receiving Basin. The Receiving Basin then dried out because the water table dropped to levels below the mean tide level, and terrible pollution resulted, as described in chapter 2. Later there was a wind-blown dust problem for the new Back Bay residents, after sections of the land had been filled and lay vacant.

As the Back Bay was filled, loosely packed sand and gravel fill, averaging about fifteen feet thick but in some places as much as thirty feet thick,[3] provided the necessary pore space to store enormous quantities of groundwater. Even after the Mill Dam's initial purpose was discontinued, it still acted as an impervious barrier to groundwater flow in both directions between the Receiving Basin and the Charles River. In 1878, after much of the filling east of Massachusetts Avenue was complete, the water table had risen about two feet, to 7.7-feet BCB.[4] The water table in the Back Bay was lowered overall because the Mill Dam remained under Beacon Street, preventing Charles River water from moving southward into the Back Bay and replenishing its groundwater.

Other factors raised the water table in the Back Bay. During and after the filling, rainwater and melted snow seeped down into the sand and gravel fill, raising the water table. Also, leaking water mains extending across the Back Bay have raised the water table near the mains. By the end of the nineteenth century, the water table in the Back Bay rose slowly to approximately 8.0 feet BCB.[5]

As we saw in chapter 1, the irregular solid rock surface beneath much of the Back Bay is 50 to 150 feet below the present surface. The rock surface is overlain by an assortment of different soils that reflect different phases of the Back Bay's history. These soils are completely saturated throughout their thickness, but it is only the sand and gravel fill on top and the layers lying directly under it that were of importance to the construction of town houses in the latter part of the nineteenth century.

Preparing the Land Surface

A great deal of preparation for the construction of buildings and utilities was required after the filling of the Back Bay with sand and gravel. Grading created the higher areas for streets and left the middles of blocks at a lower level, ready for the construction of foundations and cellars.

The difficult packing and grading of the new land was done entirely with human and animal power. Two of the four small dioramas in the lobby of the former New England Financial building at 501 Boylston Street (one of which was shown in fig. 5.14) depict aspects of filling and construction in the Back Bay. Men are shown using small tip-carts, scoops, and scrapers pulled by horses to move sand and gravel from long piles left by the trains. This method filled open spaces between the temporary tracks and graded the finished land according to specific requirements of the State and the Boston Water Power Company.

Proper grading of the land surface required repeated surveying to establish the levels of fill needed in specific areas. "Grade stakes" marked the levels or grades of fill needed as the project continued. On March 23, 1860, Norman C. Munson asked the commissioners to have grade stakes set on Commonwealth Avenue immediately, and the commission ordered its engineer to have it done.[6] The placing of grade stakes was a continuing issue as the filling pushed forward on several fronts at once.

Subsidence Problems after Filling

The original filling and grading resulted in rough contours, and newly filled streets often settled. The investigator of the case of Munson's lawsuit against the City of Boston, over subsidence of streets in 1875, found four reasons for the grades of the streets to drop after filling: rapid sinking because of the underlying soft ground; gradual settling over a stretch of several years; rain washing away banks sloping down into house lots; and wind blowing away sand and gravel from the surface. The investigator concluded that the contractor should be required to add fill at his expense only if there was immediate and rapid settling. If there was a gradual settling over a period of years, the contractor should not be responsible for additional filling.[7]

The marshy ground under the Back Bay caused settling of the fill in various places, particularly over the former drainage channels of the tidal mudflat. These areas required extensive remedial work. For example, in 1860 the commission voted to have the contractors fill up a depression in Newbury Street and in the lots north of it. Munson agreed to complete the filling at once.[8]

Grading and Finishing the Streets

Grading the streets required great attention to detail to assure good drainage into the gutters and down to drains at the corners. The Minute Books of the Boston aldermen in 1859 stated that the grades on the streets "should rise from the junctions of the streets towards the middle of each block of house lots at a rate of not less than nine inches in the hundred feet"[9] There also had to be a humping effect in the cross section of each street so that water would drain toward the gutters along the curbs. A better quality of fill than the common type of material was needed to support streets and alleys on the new land. The State Commission ordered the contractors to finish the surface of the streets and alleys with "good clean gravel instead of sand to the depth of at least 18 inches."[10] The Back Bay streets were not paved until later.

Curbstones had to be placed around the blocks to complete the streets before the house lots could be sold. On December 14, 1859, the commission's engineer, Mr. Henck, submitted an estimate of the lengths and types of curbstones needed up to that point on Arlington Street, Berkeley Street,

Marlborough Street, Commonwealth Avenue, Newbury Street, and Boylston Street. These three blocks required 6,098 feet of straight granite curbstones and 198 feet of curved ones for the corners.[11]

As the filling proceeded, the commissioners realized that gaps were left in front of new buildings where the level of fill in the middle of a block was a few feet lower than the level of the street. On May 4, 1860, the commissioners agreed to provide enough gravel without charge to fill the spaces in front of the houses. The gravel would be delivered along the contractors' temporary track at convenient places; moving it to its destination would be the expense of the new homeowners.

Commonwealth Avenue, designed as the elegant centerpiece of the Back Bay, demanded special treatment to make it as attractive as possible. In July 1860 the commission recorded a vote calling for curbstones to be "placed about the Park in the centre of Commonwealth Avenue between Arlington & Berkeley Streets and the space within covered with loam; with a gravel walk in the centre."[12]

Streets had to be much higher to reach bridges over railroads. Boston required in 1861 that all the streets and avenues at railroad crossings and approaches be as high as necessary to accommodate to the heights of the bridges.[13]

Sewers and Drainage of the Back Bay

We have seen that, through 1850, sewers were emptying directly into the Back Bay from outfalls along the shoreline, which made the former tidal marsh a badly polluted basin. When filling began following the Tripartite Indenture of 1856, wooden sewers were extended through the new land to the nearest shorelines. These wooden sewers were cheap and easy to build. The basements of buildings lying just a few feet above the low-tide level in the filled land, however, made it very difficult to build and maintain effective sewers.

Before the major filling began, in 1854, wooden sewers three feet wide and four feet high were built along the Mill Dam, extending a few blocks west of Arlington Street and running through the north wall of the Mill Dam to empty into the Charles River (see fig. 7.1). White pine planks five or six inches thick and a foot wide were used in their construction. The sewers, having a very gradual downward slope of only 1.1 feet for every 300 to 500 feet of horizontal distance, ran between the side streets where

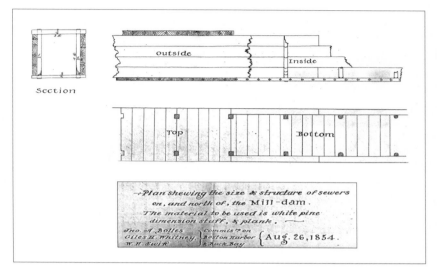

FIGURE 7.1. Wooden sewers on the Mill Dam in 1854. This early wooden sewer on the Mill Dam served houses that were built on the Corporation's two-hundred-foot-wide filled area north of the Mill Dam before the Receiving Basin was filled. The sewer was built of heavy white pine planks with double-thick walls. The top of the sewer was six inches thick, and the bottom was only three inches thick because the top had to support the weight of the overlying fill and the streets above the sewer. Five-or-six-inch-thick planks formed the sides, and four-inch square braces provided strength inside the side walls. The inside dimension of this sewer was four feet high and three feet wide. *(Assignment Way to Pratt, August 26, 1854, Lib. 675, fol. 134, 135, Suffolk County Court House, Boston, Massachusetts. Map provided courtesy of Suffolk Registry of Deeds.)*

north- and south-running sewers emptied into the Charles River Estuary under the new strip of land created by the Boston and Roxbury Mill Corporation.[14]

The Tripartite Indenture of 1856 called for two main sewers to drain from the new Back Bay land into the Charles River Estuary through the old emptying sluices between today's Dartmouth and Exeter Streets.[15] These new, brick sewers would collect the flows from the wooden sewers under most streets. They were to be constructed in sections by the three parties to the Indenture, but they were never built. Instead, more wooden sewers were built as streets were filled by the contractors and buildings began to be erected on them.

In 1864, over six years after filling began on the State's and the Boston Water Power Company's land, a new agreement was signed to construct main sewers. The State agreed to replace its wooden sewer under Berkeley Street with a new sewer "in bricks and cement in a good substantial and workmanlike manner, equal in capacity to a sewer of six feet in diameter" to empty into the Charles River Estuary. The Commonwealth would also build an identical sewer under Dedham Street (now Dartmouth Street) from the Boston and Worcester Railroad near today's Back Bay Station to the Charles River. The 1864 agreement required the City of Boston to build three brick sewers outside the State's land to carry sewage to outfalls in the Charles River or in the South Bay, to the south of the Neck.[16] The old sewers had to be dug up so new brickwork sewers could be built. In building the new sewers, the State agreed to provide substantial tidal gates for emptying into the Charles River and to connect with lateral sewers.

The State could drain its lands into the new sewers, but the City of Boston would charge new property owners for connecting to the system and would be responsible for repairing, cleaning, and relaying the sewers. The Boston Water Power Company would pay the City of Boston fifty thousand dollars but not be responsible for building any sewers.

The Back Bay land surface was barely above the water table and, consequently, the new, larger brick sewers had to extend below the water table to drain into the Charles River Estuary or into the South Bay. The sewers had only slight downward slopes, which in effect reduced the outward flow of noxious sewage. The basement floors in the new Back Bay houses lay below the level of high tide, only about five feet above the low-tide mark. House drains extended down from the basements into sewers lying at lower elevations under the streets. These early sewers were constructed on top of eight- to twelve-inch diameter underdrains designed to collect groundwater during construction (see figure 7.3).[17] These underdrains probably remain functional today, and many of the early sewers make up a maze of underground channels of which little is known.[18]

During periods of exceptionally high tides and strong east winds, the waters of Boston Harbor sometimes rose to levels considerably above mean high tide. There are records of tides as high as fifteen feet above low tide.[19] When such conditions prevailed, the sewers could back up into the basements of houses. It was therefore impossible to place the dining room or any other main room in the basement. Kitchens, however, were generally situated there, although they too were occasionally removed to the safer heights of the first floor. This problem explains why the main entrance in the early days was never situated in the basement, although modern alteration has frequently located it there. The first-floor kitchens are generally found in houses designed by Snell and Gregerson (for example, 145 Marlborough Street and 177 Commonwealth Avenue). Bainbridge Bunting noted, "Because of these factors, the Back Bay architect was prevented from using the so-called 'English basement' which was popular in both New York and Boston's New South End."[20] The unsatisfactory and unsanitary drainage conditions continued until 1884, when Boston completed its present divergent sewer system, which drains the lowest Back Bay basements at all times and which pumps the sewage into the outer harbor at Deer Island.

The early, low-level sewers could not drain into the Charles River or South Bay except near low tide twice each day, and tide gates were built at their mouths to prevent tidal water from backing up into them. As a result, "these tide-gates also shut in the sewage, which accumulates behind them, along the whole length of the sewer, as in a cesspool." This put large amounts of stagnant sewage under the Back Bay streets for most of each day and night, and, because the sewers had no currents at those times, solid waste material was deposited and remained in the bottoms of them. The sewers had been made large enough to allow for storage capacity and ventilation was inadequate; the stinking air was compressed in them and forced through the connecting pipes to the new houses. Further exacerbating the situation was the fact that when the sewers were emptied through open tide gates near the times of low tide, large amounts of sewage flowed out into shallow bays just as the incoming tide came to push the sewage back toward the shore "to form deposits upon the flats and shores around the city."[21]

Sewers continued to empty into the Charles River for decades, making the Beacon Street side of the Back Bay very unpleasant at low tide. The Charles River was tidal up to Watertown until 1910, when the Charles River Dam created the basin. Factories, slaughterhouses, and residences dumped raw sewage that accumulated. Twice-daily tides provided some flushing, carrying sewage and other debris out into Boston Harbor, but in shallow areas polluted material sank to the riverbed and created a nearly constant problem.

The public health hazards created by these inadequate sewers were of great concern in the years after the Back Bay landfill project began. In 1870 the consulting physicians of Boston submitted a report urging a better system for disposing of sewage. The State Board of Health annual reports from 1868 to 1874 echoed those concerns. In 1872 the state legislature authorized the City of Boston to appoint a commission to investigate the problem of dumping sewage into the Charles River and South Bay, and to recommend a solution. The City finally acted in 1875 and the commission recommended late in that year that a system of intercepting sewers be combined with a pumping station that would release the sewage well out into the harbor.[22]

The worst pollution could not be reduced until new sewers intercepted older ones. Until that was done, combined sewers carried both storm water from the streets and sewage from buildings into the river at Beaver (at the base of Beacon Hill), Berkeley, Dartmouth, Fairfield, and Hereford Streets. The much-needed West Side Interceptor sewer (see fig. 7.2) was so long in coming because of its expense and the technical challenges that had to be met. This sewer, part of the Boston main drainage system, was constructed between 1877 and 1884.[23]

The West Side Interceptor gathered the flows from all the old sewers that had emptied into the Charles River; east of the Neck, the East Side Interceptor prevented continuing pollution of the South Bay in the same way. The two new interceptor sewers combined and carried all the sewage to the Calf Pasture Pumping Station on Columbia Point in Dorchester. From there the sewage was pumped to Moon Island in Boston Harbor, where it was released into the harbor on outgoing tides.[24]

Because the new sewers had to flow downslope to the Calf Pasture Pumping Station, the sewage was pumped up thirty-five feet there before it flowed in a tunnel to Moon Island, off Squantum Head in Quincy. A reservoir at Moon Island held the sewage until the first two hours of each outgoing tide, when it was released to be carried as far as possible into the outer harbor.[25] It should be noted that the new sewer outfall, releasing all the untreated sewage of a metropolitan district covering fifty-eight square miles, including nine square miles of low-lying land, was located close to Long Island, where the City operated an almshouse and a hospital.

The Boston Marginal Conduit was constructed in 1910 as part of the project constructing the new dam and lock on the Charles River, which turned the tidal estuary into a basin with a constant water level that is maintained today. The Marginal Conduit collected flow from Stony Brook and mixed sewage and storm water overflows from the West Side Interceptor, which formerly discharged wastes into the Charles River. The Marginal Conduit collected so much sewage that it had to be very large, a horseshoe-shaped, reinforced concrete structure seventy-six inches wide and ninety-two inches high (see fig. 7.3).[26]

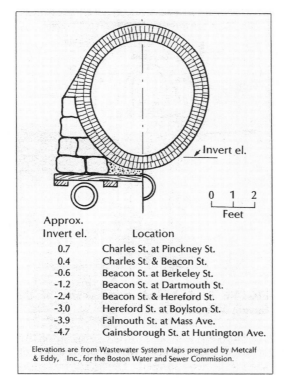

Approx. Invert el.	Location
0.7	Charles St. at Pinckney St.
0.4	Charles St. & Beacon St.
-0.6	Beacon St. at Berkeley St.
-1.2	Beacon St. at Dartmouth St.
-2.4	Beacon St. & Hereford St.
-3.0	Hereford St. at Boylston St.
-3.9	Falmouth St. at Mass Ave.
-4.7	Gainsborough St. at Huntington Ave.

Elevations are from Wastewater System Maps prepared by Metcalf & Eddy, Inc., for the Boston Water and Sewer Commission.

FIGURE 7.2. Cross section of the West Side Interceptor. The West Side Interceptor sewer ran parallel to the Charles River to collect the flows from sewers that previously had emptied directly into the Charles River by cutting them off near their ends. The inside dimensions of this egg-shaped brick sewer were about six feet high by five feet wide. The cross section shows a part of the sewer in soft ground, which required a wooden platform for extra support. In areas with solid ground, no wood or stone was required. The twelve-inch-diameter underdrain pipe that is shown was for draining water from the excavation during the period of construction. The underdrains are still in place, and they probably contribute to drawing down the water table in places. *(Harl P. Aldrich, Jr., and James Lambrechts, "Back Bay Boston, Part II: Groundwater Levels," Civil Engineering Practice: Journal of the Boston Society of Civil Engineers Section/ASCE 2 (1986): 39. Reprinted with permission of the Boston Society of Civil Engineers Section/ASCE, Civil Engineering Practice, Journal of BSCES.)*

The present system of sewers in the Back Bay was built between 1910 and 1912, after the Charles River Dam was completed. There are two separate sewers under each street, including a thirty-inch-diameter storm sewer for the water from the street.[27]

There is, however, a continuing but largely hidden pollution problem

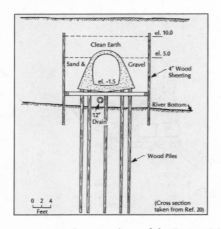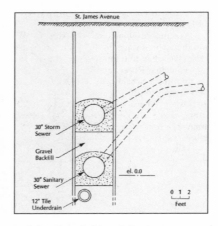

FIGURE 7.3. Cross sections of the Boston Marginal Conduit (left) and the St. James Avenue sewer (right). The Boston Marginal Conduit ran along the edge of the Charles River, just north of the sea wall that now runs next to Storrow Drive. The conduit was built with thick concrete walls and was supported by a wooden platform and wood piles. The St. James Avenue sewer used two thirty-inch-diameter pipes encased in concrete to separate storm water from the streets, carried in the top pipe, from sewage carried in the sanitary sewer at the bottom. Both diagrams show twelve-inch-diameter underdrain pipes, required during construction and left in place. *(Harl P. Aldrich, Jr., and James Lambrechts, "Back Bay Boston, Part II: Groundwater Levels," Civil Engineering Practice: Journal of the Boston Society of Civil Engineers Section/ASCE 2 (1986): 40. Reprinted with permission of the Boston Society of Civil Engineers Section/ASCE, Civil Engineering Practice, Journal of BSCES.)*

in some parts of the Back Bay. The groundwater moving through the underlying sand and gravel contains large amounts of dissolved hydrogen sulfide. Upon escaping the water, this gas "has been offensive to passersby and injurious to the health of those working in it." This gas, derived from organic wastes buried under the landfill material in the former tidal marsh, is particularly destructive to metal.[28]

Driving Piles and Laying Foundations

Supporting heavy brick and stone buildings on soft, filled land presents a difficult engineering challenge. In the nineteenth century the solution was to drive untreated wood piles into the ground through the landfill sediment and underlying organic soils to reach firmer layers of sands and gravels or the oxidized zone of the blue clay. The upper ends of the piles were cut off below the water table level to prevent rotting. The piles were tree trunks with all branches removed and their slender tops cut off. Most of the piles are spruce trees measuring about twelve inches in diameter at the butt end and between twenty and forty feet long. Trenches were dug below the average level of high tide under each building foundation and the piles were driven in them. Along the foundation walls, each pair of piles was topped with a granite leveling block that was hollowed out on the bottom to fit over each pile.[29] It was common practice to cut off wood piles at an average tide level of 5 feet BCB. After the Back Bay was filled and through the remainder of the nineteenth century, the water table in the Back Bay was at an elevation of approximately 8 feet BCB, sufficiently high to keep the piles from rotting.

Bunting shows two row houses in the Back Bay that are supported by about 270 piles under the foundation walls that surround each house under its outside walls and cross the foundation under major bearing walls (see fig. 7.4).[30] The piles are about one and a half to thee feet apart between their centers, placed to maximize the friction on their sides.[31] With 270 piles under a house and between thirty-six and forty-two houses in each block that has no church or other institution, the total number of piles per block would range from 9,720 to 11,340. With more than eighteen blocks in the State's portion of the Back Bay alone, that means there are probably between 175,000 and 204,000 tree trunks supporting the residential buildings. Consider the large, dense, inverted "forest" of spruce trees buried in the ground below the Back Bay neighborhood: how many acres of forests were logged bare to provide the huge number of trees needed for the construction of buildings in this new Boston neighborhood over a period of about forty years? Our only clue to the source of the piles is a quote from the 1896 *Encyclopaedia Brittanica* about filling the Back Bay: "Whole forests from the State of Maine . . . [had] been put to service in . . . furnishing pilings and solid foundations."[32] There were a number of wholesalers in Boston selling piles at that time.[33]

Churches and other institutions in the Back Bay were large, heavy buildings that required many piles to prevent them from sinking, tipping, or cracking because of the soft ground under their foundations. For example, Trinity Church in Copley Square is a massive structure of neo-Romanesque design with a large central tower that weighs an estimated 9,500 tons. The tower is supported by four square groups of piles that underlie pyramid-shaped granite pedestals. With about 700 piles

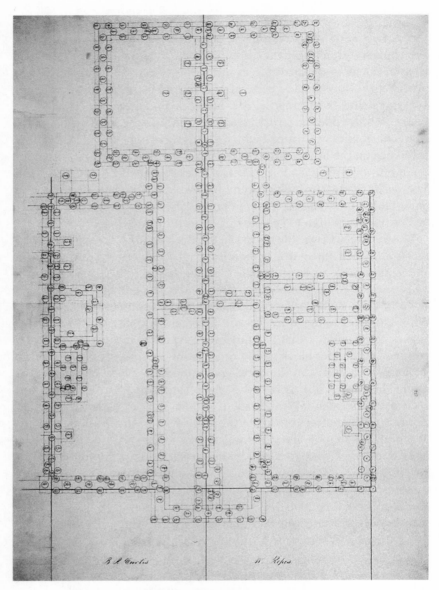

FIGURE 7.4. Pile arrangements for two Back Bay houses. This diagram shows the plan of piles supporting 91 and 92 Beacon Street. Each of the houses requires about 270 piles under the outside foundation walls and under the bearing walls inside the house. The piles averaged about thirty feet in length and extended into the blue clay beneath the filling material. Other houses in the Back Bay may have required more or fewer piles to support their foundations. *(Boston Athenæum.)*

under each of the corner columns, the tower alone requires about 2,800 piles. The entire building has over 4,500 piles under its foundation (see fig. 7.5). The church has settled nearly a foot since its construction. Because keeping the piles damp is essential to preventing the church from sustaining structural damage, the foundation was designed with a waterway around the piles that would allow someone in a small boat to check the water level frequently. Now there is system of automatic sensors to check the water level, and water can be pumped in if it drops to dangerous levels. When the new John Hancock Tower was built in the next block around 1970, the drawing down of the water table and shifts caused by driving long steel and concrete piles down to bedrock caused serious damage to the foundation of Trinity Church.

The firm blue clay stratum that lies a few feet below the landfill's sand and gravel in most places is very important for supporting the piles under Back Bay buildings. An engineering book on foundations states that it is best "when the piles are driven through soft material to or into a stratum of firm or practically unyielding material."[34] Spruce is one of the preferred types of wood for piles, and research has shown that timber cut in the winter and early spring was significantly less strong than that cut in the other months of the year. Piles were carefully selected because their strength would be reduced by defects such as decay, splits, twisted grain, bends, large knots, or holes.[35]

Driving the piles to support the Back Bay buildings was a huge undertaking: so many piles were needed in such a short period of time. When the filling of the Back Bay proper began in the 1850s, a derrick was brought into place on each building site that was high enough to hold a new pile between two "leads"—tall, parallel timbers that guided the pile vertically. Between the leads above the new pile, a heavy weight was lifted by a system of ropes and pulleys. When the weight was a good distance above the pile it was dropped onto the butt end of the pile, driving it some distance into the ground. The weight had to be lifted and dropped over and over until the pile was driven far enough and it was tightly held in the ground by friction so it would provide maximum holding power for supporting the building's foundation.[36] The resistance to penetration depended on the type of material beneath the pile.

Around 1845 an important technological advance was made when steam engines were attached to the same "drop-hammer" type of pile driver, which had been operated by hand. With a lot more power, a steam pile driver could lift and drop the weight much faster, driving each

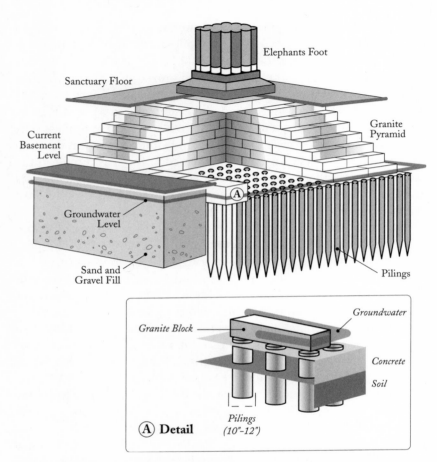

FIGURE 7.5. The pilings and granite pyramidal structure supporting one corner column of the Trinity Church. About 700 piles driven into a square of thirty-five feet on each side support the corners of the Trinity Church tower, which weighs about nineteen million pounds. The piles were cut off at five feet above mean low tide, below groundwater level, with their top sections encased in concrete and capped with large granite blocks. This drawing shows the pyramidal granite pedestal cut away to reveal the tops of the piles. Each granite pyramid is seventeen feet high and seven feet square at the top. The granite blocks in the pyramids are about two feet high and between four and eight feet long. The elephant-foot column base atop each pyramid in the church sanctuary supports one corner of the massive tower. As of 2005, the stone pyramids can be viewed in the church's Undercroft. (*Redrawn from a* Boston Globe *illustration. Created by Kirsten Lindquist. Republished with the permission of Globe Newspaper Company, Inc., from the July 25th edition of* The Boston Globe, *©2004.*)

pile in less time. Steam power could also be used to lift the next pile into place and begin driving it. Pile drivers made a lot of noise and shook the ground nearby.[37]

Piles did not always penetrate easily into the Back Bay in a way that gave them maximum holding power. If soft mud and peat underlay a section of fill, piles would not hold tight because there was little friction surrounding them. Sometimes there were buried rocks or old piles from preexisting buildings that made it impossible to drive piles. Occasionally, "brooming" occurred when a pile hit a hard layer or other obstruction and its tip split in several directions; the pile seemed to be penetrating into the ground, but instead its lower end was distorted like a broom, splaying outward and providing very little support.[38]

A problem associated with the Back Bay subsidence is the downdrag on piles due to settlement of the surrounding soil. This downdrag increases the load on the pile, which in turn increases the settlement of the pile and can result in pile failure. All buildings in the Back Bay that are supported by piles driven through the fill and organic soils and into the blue clay will experience negative friction or drag loads when the ground surrounding the piles settles. Buildings may settle as a result. The potential adverse effects are most pronounced for wood piles, which derive their support by skin friction in the blue clay. Although significant drawdown undoubtedly developed in the nineteenth century from the compression of organic soils under the weight of the overlying fill, and from the temporary lowering of the water table, this is not likely to be a serious concern in the future.

Details of the pile supports of a larger building in the Back Bay are available for the Rogers Building of the Massachusetts Institute of Technology, which stood on Boylston Street between Berkeley and Clarendon Streets. The four-story brick structure was completed in the mid-1860s next door to the earlier Museum of Natural History (now Louis Boston, a clothing store). By 1898 serious cracks opened both outside and inside the Rogers Building's double brick walls. Detailed diagrams were made of the piles and stone foundations when they were excavated to determine what measures were needed to shore up the building.

Double rows of foundation piles under the Rogers Building, cut off about 3.5 feet below the normal water table, had 6 feet of heavy granite foundation walls on top of them. Diagrams show that the tops of the piles were between 1.4 and 2.2 feet apart at their centers along the side walls, with the crosswise pairs driven closer to 1 foot apart.[39] Where a column

2 feet 8 inches square was supported, five piles were driven close together under a square capstone. Notations on the diagrams indicate that "the Piles are in all probability 26 to 28 feet long and about 8 in. diam. at the point." Under a large, rectangular pedestal, piles were driven in three rows of ten, spaced less than 2 feet apart. In the area around this pedestal, there is a note that "on digging June 18' 98 to expose top of piles—water was struck about 2.5 feet below the cellar bottom." Since the piles' tops were about 3.5 feet below the water table level, it is clear that they were not drying out. Extensive work was required to strengthen the foundation of the Rogers Building; 20-inch I beams were used above the lowest layers of granite foundation blocks. The old wooden piles seem to have been left in place and not augmented with additional new piles.

The Boston Public Library in Copley Square, built between 1888 and 1895, rests on at least 4,000 piles. A photograph dated October 26, 1888, shows a steam-powered pile driver at work on the Boylston Street side of the excavation.[40] Very detailed records of the pile foundation were kept and saved, including the length of each pile and the diameter at its butt and tip, the "elevation of the hammer" when it was dropped, and the "sinkage," that is, the distance the pile penetrated on the last blow of the hammer.[41] The piles under the Boston Public Library ranged from 25 to 31 feet long, with butt ends between 10 and 12 inches in diameter. Difficulty arose during driving of some piles, and in some places trenches had to be excavated to remove sand and gravel before piles could be driven.

Leakage into the new sewers that lay below the water table began to draw down the water table and create problems in the nineteenth century. Just after the West Side Interceptor was completed, observation wells showed water levels in the Back Bay were unchanged. Within ten years, however, in 1894, in some areas the groundwater level had fallen to about five feet above mean low tide because of leaking sewers.[42] There already was a warning: piles supporting buildings could rot if the water table dropped further.[43]

The St. James Avenue sewer, parallel to Beacon Street near the middle of the Back Bay, has been a source of groundwater table drawdown since about 1930, when it was investigated as a result of concern for the foundations of Trinity Church and the Boston Public Library. The installation of a dam in the sewer caused the nearby groundwater to return to acceptable levels, but the dam requires periodic maintenance. When the St. James Avenue sewer dam does not function properly, the groundwater level falls.

Leaky pipes, particularly water mains, can be significant localized sources of raised groundwater levels. Cotton and Delaney in 1975 provided groundwater contours that indicated several elevated areas where water levels were as much as five to ten feet above surrounding areas.[44] The overall contribution to the water table from leaking water mains may be about equal to that from precipitation. Cotton and Delaney reported that the Boston Water Department data from the early 1940s indicated that water main leakage would have provided an equivalent recharge of 0.73 million gallons per day per square mile. This amount is approximately equal to the recharge from fifty inches of precipitation per year, assuming a 30 percent infiltration rate for rain and melted snow. Storm and sanitary sewers located above the groundwater table can also leak and contribute to groundwater. Because they are not under pressure, their effect is probably minor.

Damage to Piles Caused by Dropping Water Tables

Most of the nineteenth-century public, commercial, and residential buildings in the Back Bay are constructed on untreated wooden piles, and their condition remains a serious concern. Piles have behaved satisfactorily for centuries when they are completely submerged below the water table at all times. Decay of untreated wood piles may occur if they are exposed to air in a moist environment, particularly when they are exposed to alternating periods of wetting and drying. These conditions occur when the water table fluctuates above and below the top of the pile.[45]

If the groundwater level drops below the tops of the piles, conditions may be favorable for fungus growth and insect attack. A greatly increased supply of air, combined with moisture and moderated temperatures, is conducive to the growth of fungi. Wood borer grubs, termites, and other insects may attack the exposed wood. The butts of piles that are surrounded by fill, in particular sand and gravel as well as ashes and cinders, are more prone to rotting than are piles that are embedded in organic silt and other, more impervious soils. When the water table drops, the fine-grained soils remain saturated for a time, thus protecting the piles from immediate deterioration.

Through the past hundred years, the city of Boston has periodically experienced the problem of local rising and falling of the water table and deterioration of untreated timber piles. The water table began to rise after

1880 as the porous and pervious 15- to 30-foot-thick landfill began to store rainwater and snowmelt. From 1880 to 1910, after the filling was completed, the groundwater level rose to an elevation of 5.8 feet BCB at the Charles River and to 8 feet BCB or more in the interior of the Back Bay.[46]

Leakage into sewers from the water table is a serious and continuing problem in the Back Bay. In 1929 the Boston Public Library underwent an extensive repair of pilings at a cost of five hundred thousand dollars. The building was crumbling and sinking because the lowered water table caused many of its more than four thousand piles to rot and become useless for supporting the heavy weight above them. An investigation showed that "the tops of some piles were completely gone and others were very badly decayed so that about 40% of the area of the building's underpinning had to be rebuilt." The decayed pile tops had to be cut off and replaced with concrete to support the large stone building.[47] The area in which the piles were most affected was near the deep sewer laid in 1912 under St. James Avenue.

In the mid-1980s seventeen homes were condemned and vacated on Brimmer Street at the base of Beacon Hill on land filled around 1840. About three hundred more homes were watched very carefully. The foundations were failing because of rotten piles under them, and it was feared that nearly every attached brick building might come down. The city engineer, John Sullivan, Jr., said, "At least we are fairly certain that leaks in sewer walls have been siphoning away groundwater." The immediate solution for saving threatened buildings was to cut off the rotten tops of piles, hold up the structure with screw jacks placed on top of the piles, and later pour concrete around the jacks to provide solid support. Leaks found by examination inside sewers were repaired, and the groundwater levels seemed to be rising. Monitoring wells were put in place to provide warnings when sewers might be leaking and to prevent additional damage to buildings.[48]

Current loss of groundwater, and the resulting lowered water levels in the Back Bay, occurs primarily from leakage into sewers and drains, leakage through walls and floors of subway tunnels, underpasses, building foundations, and other structures below the water table, and by pumping from sumps. In addition, water levels may be lowered temporarily by pumping from excavations in order to facilitate construction.

The underdrains built under the sewers to drain excavations at the time of their construction, and the presence of many old and forgotten drains and sewers that crossed or went under the sewers, provide channels that conduct water for long distances underground before they reach an outlet at a sufficiently low elevation. This could cause groundwater levels to drop, rotting the piles. Also, it was the practice of the city to make connections between such old drains and sewers because some of the older buildings were believed to be connected to them.[49]

Foundations under High-Rise Structures

After the turn of the twentieth century, improvements in building materials, structural design, and construction technology permitted the building of larger, taller, and heavier buildings. This new generation of high-rise buildings demanded innovations in foundation design. Wooden pilings, successfully used in the construction of nineteenth-century buildings, were not suitable for high-rise structures built on the unstable soils of the Back Bay.

One of the first of the heavier Back Bay buildings was the Liberty Mutual Insurance Company building on Berkeley Street constructed between 1936 and 1937. The foundation of this building consists of belled piers or "Gow" caissons, which were introduced after 1900.[50] These new foundations were similar in purpose to wooden pile foundations, but their design and installation employed a different technology. The caissons were constructed by auguring a cylindrical hole and slowly inserting a steel casing to keep the hole open during the drilling process. Smaller, telescoping steel casings were extended along the sides of the hole until the bottom of the excavation was reached. There, a reaming tool was used to enlarge the base of the drilled shaft, giving it a bell-shaped profile. Once completed, the excavation was filled with concrete as the telescoping steel casings were slowly withdrawn. The Gow caissons beneath the New England Mutual building are supported by the oxidized surface of the blue clay (see fig. 7.6).

The compacted concrete pile, or pressure-injected footing (see fig. 7.6), is another pile type that is successfully used in the Back Bay. The underground parking garage in the Christian Science Church complex in the Back Bay is supported on this type of foundation.[51] Constructing this type of pile begins with a heavy steel tube placed over the sand and gravel surface where it is to be driven. The lower end of the tube is filled with about three feet of gravel. A heavy drop hammer operating within the tube "compacts the aggregate gravel into a solid plug which then penetrates the soil and takes the steel tube down with it."[52] After the desired depth is reached, one or more batches of very dry concrete mix of

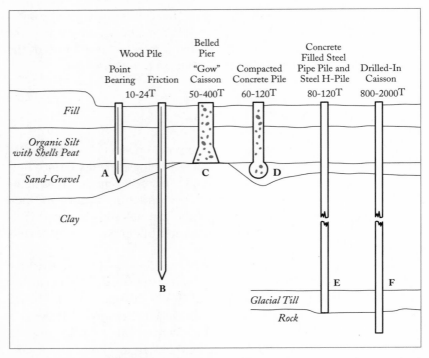

FIGURE 7.6. Common foundation types used in Boston's Back Bay with the typical safe load for each type given in tons (T). Untreated wooden piles support most nineteenth-century buildings in the Back Bay (A and B). The belled pier or "Gow" caisson (C) was introduced in the twentieth century and was used in the construction of the Liberty Mutual Insurance Company Building on Berkeley Street in the 1930s. The compacted concrete pile (D) was used later in the construction of the Christian Science Church's underground garage. Heavy buildings require foundations extending down to solid rock: the John Hancock Tower is supported by steel H-piles (E), and drilled-in caisson foundations (F) are used to support the Prudential Center. *(Reprinted, with permission, from "Preserving the Foundations of Older Buildings: The Importance of Groundwater Levels," Technology and Conservation, Summer 1979 issue, 33. Kirsten Lindquist.)*

five cubic yards each, placed in the tube, are driven out at the base of the tube by the drop hammer and into the walls of the borehole, forming an expanded bulb of gravel mixed with dry concrete (see fig. 7.6). Filling the caisson with fresh concrete and adding steel reinforcing rods completes the construction of the compacted concrete pile.[53]

Another solution for heavy building construction on unstable subsoils is the floating foundation, which was first used in the New England Life

Insurance Company building on Boylston Street. According to one account: "The foundation excavation was entirely confined to the fill and underlying estuarine deposits. The weight of the soil excavated for the foundation was nicely balanced against the total weight of the building, less the buoyancy forces acting on the submerged basement, that is, that part of the basement falling below the water table. The basement structure itself was a water-tight box and acted in the manner of a ship's hull, while the building simulated the ship's superstructure."[54]

Very tall and heavy buildings, such as the fifty-two-story office building at the Prudential Center and the sixty-story John Hancock Tower, required foundations that extended down to solid rock. The Prudential Center office tower is supported by thirty-inch-diameter steel caissons that extend down about 120 feet to 180 feet to the Cambridge mudstone. The soil column that collected in the steel pipe was removed with compressed air.[55] When the solid rock surface was reached, a twenty-nine-inch-diameter hole was drilled sixteen to twenty-five feet into the rock. A heavy steel H-section beam was welded or bolted together and lowered into the empty caisson until it extended from the bottom of the drilled hole to the top of the caisson. The space between the H-section beam and the steel caisson was filled with fresh concrete.[56] The foundation of the John Hancock Tower consists of about three thousand steel H-section beams in concrete-filled caissons that extend down to the lower glacial drift or to the Cambridge mudstone surface.

Subsidence and Reasons for This Phenomenon

The primary reasons for subsidence in the Back Bay are the removal of groundwater and the compaction and lateral spreading of the soil because of loading. We have already discussed the removal of groundwater by leakage into sewers, subway tunnels, and basements, which results in compaction. The second type of subsidence occurred as a heavy layer of sand and gravel fill of variable thickness was placed on top of the saturated peat, silts, and clays of the Back Bay mudflat. As the fill was dumped, the underlying saturated sediments were slowly squeezed together, so the pore water was forced laterally out of the underlying mudflats and away from the site of active dumping.

There is no detailed record as to how much subsidence by compaction took place during the nineteenth-century filling operation. It would have varied depending on the weight, and hence the thickness, of the overlying fill and the thickness and nature of the underlying peat, silt, and clay. The sand and gravel fill that was placed on top of the estuary sediment "averages 15 feet in thickness and increases up to 30 feet in places."[57] During the construction of the Boylston Street subway in 1914, pockets of peat two to four feet thick, were discovered below the silt between Massachusetts Avenue and Hereford Street, and at Exeter Street. "Another extensive body of peat occurs between Arlington and Charles Streets, where it attains a great depth."[58]

Peat is the most compressible of the Back Bay soils because of its very high porosity and weak skeletal structure. Peat compacted by a nineteenth-century layer of fill, observed in a buried peat bog during the excavation for the Boston Common Garage, was found to have been reduced to about 25 percent of its original thickness.[59] Therefore, among other factors, the amount of subsidence of the underlying peat depends on the original thickness of the peat and the weight of the overlying fill.

After the initial rapid settlement, subsidence probably continued at a much slower pace in the Back Bay. The high tower of the New Old South Church, resting on spruce piles in Copley Square, settled unevenly in the soft ground until its top was approximately thirty-six inches off vertical after about fifty years. That tower had to be taken down in 1931 and it was rebuilt at a slightly reduced size on a better foundation in 1940.[60] The curb at the southeast corner of Dartmouth Street and Huntington Avenue settled nearly half a foot in a nine-year span. A block away, the six-foot brick sewer in Dartmouth Street at Boylston Street was found to have subsided two feet lower than the proper grade within a period of thirty-four years. In the early twentieth century, the curb between Clarendon and Fairfield Streets underwent settlement of three or four inches during a ten-year period. At the same time, the general subsidence of the ground around Copley Square seemed to be progressing at a rate of about five inches in ten years.[61]

The Earthquake Threat in Boston and Potentials
for Earthquake Damage in the Back Bay

The Boston area has experienced a number of moderate to strong earthquakes over time, and there will probably be more in the future. Eastern Massachusetts was shaken by moderately strong earthquakes in 1638,

1727, 1742, and 1755.[62] The 1638 earthquake, believed to have originated in central New Hampshire, was significantly greater than the 1755 Cape Ann earthquake.[63] It was felt in all new European settlements in southern New England.[64] The 1727 earthquake, probably centered between the modern city of Amesbury, Massachusetts, and the old Newbury town center, was a strong earthquake that "cracked some chimneys, collapsed a few cellar walls, and threw down several stone walls in Newbury, Massachusetts, and some nearby communities. . . . In Boston the earthquake was felt strongly but no damage was reported."[65] The 1744 earthquake was smaller than the 1727 earthquake but was strongly felt in northeastern Massachusetts and noted by people as far away as central Massachusetts and southern Rhode Island. The epicenter of the 1744 earthquake is believed to have been offshore of Cape Ann.[66]

The most damaging earthquake to affect the Boston area was the earthquake of November 18, 1755. The epicenter[67] of this earthquake was probably located about twenty-four miles east of Cape Ann and fifty miles offshore of Boston[68] because these places are where the greatest damage occurred, and sailors on a ship about 210 nautical miles east of Massachusetts also felt the earthquake. "The shock was felt so strongly that those on board believed the ship had run aground."[69] The 1755 earthquake occurred at about 4:30 in the morning, waking residents throughout New England. John Hyde of Boston described his experiences during the earthquake:

> "I was awakened by the shaking of my bed, and of the house; the cause whereof I immediately concluded could be nothing but an earthquake, having experienced one before. The trembling . . . increasing I soon got out of bed and went towards the window on the other side of the chamber . . . about the time that I got about halfway across the room, which might be six or seven seconds from my first awaking, the shaking was a little abated; . . . instantaneously the shock came on with a redoubled violence, and loud noise . . . the whole house rocking and cracking to such a degree, that I concluded that it must soon fall, or be racked to pieces."[70]

During this earthquake the wooden buildings on the compacted glacial drift of the Boston peninsula swayed back and forth, but they sustained no serious damage because they were flexible. The brick houses and brick chimneys, however, were very rigid structures and did not yield to the swaying motions of the ground. Consequently, the gabled ends of some brick buildings came down and many were cracked.[71] Numerous chimneys were snapped off at the roofline and collapsed into piles of rubble alongside the buildings. Other snapped chimneys simply rotated slightly without collapsing, or they collapsed and fell onto the roofs of the buildings, causing considerable damage.

The major damage in Boston from the 1755 earthquake appears to have occurred along the waterfront, where the filled-in ground near the harbor probably amplified the ground motions as it was shaken. Here the streets were almost covered by bricks that had fallen from the buildings. Fortunately, there were no deaths probably because it occurred at night when most people were home and presumably asleep. If the quake had occurred in the daytime, almost certainly there would have been some loss of life from falling bricks.[72]

Numerous smaller earthquakes have been felt in eastern Massachusetts since the major earthquake of 1755, but little significant damage has been reported. The shaking caused by a 1925 earthquake centered in Quebec was most severe in areas of the nineteenth-century landfill, and some Boston buildings were evacuated for fear of structural failure. In other buildings the earthquake went unnoticed.[73] The most recent earthquake of note in the Cape Ann area occurred off the Massachusetts coast near Marblehead in October 1963. This earthquake "caused great consternation through the Boston area," but there was little if any damage to buildings. "There was some mention of great shaking motions in the Back Bay."[74]

The cause of the earthquakes in the northeastern United States is not clearly understood. Usually, earthquakes are caused by the sudden relief of stresses that have built up within the earth. The earthquake vibrations radiate out from the point of an abrupt rock fracture and travel rapidly through the earth. A new fracture resulting in the offset of opposing rock slabs is called a fault. Thus far, the search to identify the specific faults that created the historic New England earthquakes has been unsuccessful. There are numerous ancient faults scattered throughout northeastern North America, but researchers have yet to discover any recent movement that has occurred on any of these faults that could be responsible for the recent earthquakes close to Boston.

A very serious concern is what would happen if an earthquake occurred today in Boston's Back Bay with the same or greater seismic intensity as the 1755 earthquake.[75] Today's Boston is much different from the Boston of 1755. In 1755 the town of Boston occupied a small patch of land at the end of a narrow neck. It was characterized by a small population living on the compacted glacial till that underlies the original Boston, except around the harbor area, where some warehouses and wharves had been constructed on filled-in land. The Back Bay at that time was part of the Charles River Estuary and there were no man-made structures on it. A few houses were constructed of brick or stone, but most of the buildings were of wood with brick chimneys. The buildings were relatively small, two or sometimes three stories in height.

Since the 1755 earthquake, the city has greatly expanded to accommodate a rapidly increasing population. The fact that sand, gravel, and other fill were simply dumped and spread out onto the mudflats of the nineteenth-century Back Bay is a concern should the Boston area experience an earthquake similar in intensity. John Ebel and Kathleen Hart studied many newspaper articles from the earlier half of the twentieth century that documented people's experiences in selected earthquakes.[76] According to the reports, observers in Boston landfill areas, including the Back Bay, experienced ground shaking significantly greater than was experienced on solid ground in Boston. In a study by Haley and Aldridge, it appears that the landfill areas of Boston and vicinity are at the greatest risk for serious damage in future earthquakes owing to the local amplification of ground shaking on soft ground.[77]

Another problem with the loosely packed landfill areas is that during an earthquake the shaking compacts the fill. This is analogous to filling up a bucket with sand and shaking it. The material assumes a more dense arrangement as sand grains move closer together and decrease the volume: the ground subsided about two feet by compaction of landfill sediment during the 1906 San Francisco earthquake. Because the fill is not homogeneous, the amount of settling may vary from place to place. This could cause some parts of roads, railroads, sewer lines, and water mains to settle more in one part than in other parts, which could result in severe damage to structures.[78] There is no evidence of settlement during the 1755 earthquake. However, if the earthquake shaking in Boston is strong enough in the future, then settlement might occur.

Associated with compaction is liquefaction, which often occurs during earthquakes in loosely packed sediment that is close to or below the water table. The earthquake's violent shaking jostles the soil particles, thus increasing the pressure on the water between the sediment grains, forcing them apart and transforming the once firm ground into a slurry of sandy mud. Several regions of artificial fill within the downtown Boston area are susceptible to liquefaction. The stability of the filled land during a strong earthquake is highly variable, so some of its regions may experience more damage than others due to liquefaction.[79]

Most of the outside bearing walls of nineteenth and early twentieth-century buildings in Boston's Back Bay are mortared stone or brick structures. Floor joists are often supported by the external bearing walls. Many Boston buildings of this period have large bolts extending out from the floor joists through the exterior bearing walls and secured with large, fancy washers and nuts. The very rigid brick and stone buildings will not flex in a strong earthquake. Instead, they will crumble and collapse. Of particular danger are the decorative cornices, cemented in place by mortar, that would fall under a minimum amount of shaking. Considering all the modification to the original landscape in the Boston area, the potential exists that a strong earthquake near Boston could cause extensive damage because of ground-shaking amplification or liquefaction in the filled areas.

In 1981 a seismic-risk analysis subcommittee of seismologists and engineers completed a study for the Massachusetts Civil Defense Agency and recommended that an earthquake loss analysis study be conducted for the metropolitan Boston area. A loss study was commissioned by the Massachusetts Emergency Management Agency and completed in 1990. It stated that an earthquake similar to the 1755 Cape Ann earthquake would cause about four to five billion dollars in damage in the Greater Boston area (that is, within Route 128). In all the earthquake scenarios, the estimated number of deaths and injuries would be in the hundreds and thousands, respectively.[80] "The damage would likely be greater in areas of landfill and to unreinforced buildings of brick or other masonry construction. Furthermore, such an earthquake would probably severely impair the operation of medical facilities, emergency public facilities, schools, and telecommunications.[81] The areas of greatest damage would include the Back Bay, much of Cambridge, South Boston, Logan Airport, and parts of Winthrop, Lynn, and Everett.

Massachusetts adopted seismic requirements in its state code for most new structures in 1975, and in 1993 it became the first state east of the Rockies to impose its code on existing structures when certain additions or modifications are made.[82] This leaves the older buildings in Boston's Back Bay very vulnerable to severe damage from future earthquakes. However, these buildings are vulnerable only if they are not refurbished. One important aspect of these codes is that as buildings in the Back Bay are upgraded or replaced, there will be a gradual increase in the general earthquake resistance of the Back Bay building stock as a whole. "This then leaves the question of whether the next damaging earthquake will wait until all of the unsafe buildings have been replaced."[83]

Strict Enforcement of Zoning Regulations

Strict zoning ensured the preservation of the Back Bay as a wealthy neighborhood. Mercantile uses were prohibited, except on Boylston and Newbury Streets. In that way, most of the wealthy families living in the neighborhood would have appropriate goods and services nearby but live on quiet streets separated from the hustle and bustle of business areas. There were residential units above the stores on Newbury and Boylston Streets and, remarkably, many families on those streets were listed in the "Blue Book" of members of society up to the 1920s. Commercial stables with many horses and strong smells were restricted to a short stretch of Newbury Street west of Fairfield Street, well away from the best mansions. "Industrial" and "mechanical" businesses were altogether prohibited in the Back Bay.[84]

Zoning regulations imposed and enforced by the State specified types of building materials, building heights, distances that buildings were to be set back from the sidewalks, the nature of projections from buildings, and more. The State saw the enforcement of zoning regulations as an important step in maintaining the exclusive nature of the neighborhood. No wooden buildings were allowed, but the mixture of brick and stone homes resulted from the preferences of architects and the families who hired them to design their town houses. The changes in architectural tastes over a period of several decades can be seen in the different building styles as one proceeds block by block from east to west.

An 1884 State Commission report summed up the importance of enforcing strong zoning regulations: "The intention was, and the result has been to make the Back Bay an especially attractive place for residence." The report discussed the importance of wide avenues, park areas, height restrictions, and preventing the obstruction of residents' light and views.[85]

Bunting discusses the establishment of the City Building Department in 1871 to survey and inspect buildings, with new laws passed in 1871, 1872, and 1873 that "regulated every phase of building from the driving of the pile foundations to the construction of heating ducts and roofs."[86] Many of the restrictions related to fire safety or were designed to assure buildings would be structurally sound. Other regulations affected the appearance of buildings. Party walls between row houses, two walls separating adjacent buildings, had to extend thirty inches above the roofs. Mansard roofs could not be more than one story high, cornices had to be covered with noncombustible material, and so on.[87]

The 1872 "Report of the Inspector of Buildings" described serious considerations in the construction of new buildings. The thickness of brick walls was seen as a problem because the standard thickness for buildings above three stories had been reduced from twelve inches to eight inches over the preceding thirty years. By 1870 some people claimed that four inches was thick enough.[88] The 1872 report also emphasized the fire hazard posed by "Mansard or French roofs," which were attractive but extremely dangerous because they were finished and ornamented with wood and fire could easily jump from one building to another. The building inspector recommended using iron instead of wood on these roofs, at only a slightly higher cost.[89]

Private stables in the Back Bay were the focus of much controversy, and legal cases challenging them reached the Massachusetts Supreme Judicial Court. The legislature and commissioners acted inconsistently on the matter of private stables from the start, although the standard form of deed for house lots stated that buildings "shall not, in any event, be used for a stable." In about twenty of the early deeds, however, the words "except a private stable" were added. Then, when land began to be sold at public auction in 1860, the deeds prohibited stables but the auction catalogues added a note: "It is understood that the Commonwealth will not enforce the stipulation and agreement of the deed, that buildings erected on the Back Bay *shall not, in any event, be used as a stable,* in such manner as to prevent the erection and use of private stables by gentlemen as appurtenances to their own dwelling houses: *provided,* such stables are so constructed and used as not to be justly offensive to the occupants of the surrounding buildings."[90]

Soon some purchasers of house lots objected strongly when they learned that neighbors had deeds that did not prohibit stables while theirs did. A homeowner on Marlborough Street protested to the commissioners when Sam Hooper, a congressman and merchant, built a stable behind his mansion on three house lots at the corner of Commonwealth Avenue and Berkeley Street. It was claimed that the stable was an eyesore and large amounts of manure were piled beside the alley behind Hooper's mansion. The commissioners ruled that Hooper's deed allowed a private stable.[91]

Owners of house lots that were originally sold at auction sometimes objected to stables near their homes because they were unaware of the stipulation in the auction catalogue that the State would not enforce the prohibition of stables. When lots were resold, only the deed ruling out all private stables was in evidence. Then the new owners sometimes found that neighbors had been allowed to build private stables as additions to their homes. This inconsistency resulted in bitter complaints and lawsuits.

The State moved strongly against "projections" when bay windows, porches, or building cornices extended too far toward sidewalks, or even into alleys. Complex formulas governed allowable designs, and several lawsuits ended with building owners being required to remove improper projections.[92] Two cases of zoning violations late in the development process demonstrated the State's seriousness in preventing building practices that were not allowed by the zoning regulations for its portion of the Back Bay. These cases involved two large institutions, a well-located hotel and an exclusive men's club.

The Hotel Kensington was built at the corner of Boylston and Exeter Streets on a lot that extended back 112 feet from Boylston Street to a 16 foot-wide passageway that is now called an alley. The deed extended to the hotel the ownership of half the passageway and said that it was "to be kept open and maintained by the abutters in common."[93] The hotel owners built bay windows starting eight feet above the ground and extending upward to the top of the building. The owners contended that the bay windows would not obstruct passage along the ground level or block vehicles used to make deliveries or remove garbage.[94]

The State claimed that the bay windows behind the Hotel Kensington were not allowed, and the case went to court. The State argued that alleys must be kept open for their full width for light and views, that no obstructions could be created, and that the attorney general could enforce stipulations in the deeds. The hotel's owners filed several appeals after the judgment went against them. The final decision of the Supreme Judicial Court came down in December 1885: the hotel would have to remove the bay windows from the back of the building, and the work had to be completed by July 1886.[95]

The case of the Algonquin Club on Commonwealth Avenue involved a zoning violation in which "the club proceeded to project the whole basement story five feet beyond the front wall of the main building."[96] The deed allowed only bay windows, projecting out at no more than a forty-five degree angle and covering no more than seven-tenths of the lot width, to extend closer than twenty feet from the curb.[97] The Algonquin Club constructed a projection along the full eighty-two-foot length of the facade, forming a terrace for the second floor, even after receiving a notice from the Board of Harbor and Land Commissioners.[98] The at-

torney general filed a bill of complaint with the Supreme Judicial Court
in June 1888, which was followed by repeated conferences and hearings
about removing the unauthorized projections.[99]

The decision of the court in the Algonquin Club case supported the
board's position that the zoning restrictions legitimately preserved the
light and air for abutting properties while providing a broad avenue with
a width of two hundred feet and nearly clear setbacks of twenty feet behind each curb.[100] The court ordered that the extension on the ground
level be removed completely, although smaller projections would be allowed if the State agreed.[101] In this case, the court noted the danger of
making an exception and setting a precedent. The court also fully justi-
fied the State's right to enforce zoning regulations for the improvement
of land, even if elite organizations wanted to have exceptions made.[102]

Unrealized Land Plans and Schemes for the Back Bay

By 1869 the State Commissioners had completed the filling of approximately one hundred acres of ideally located land in the Back Bay. About
two-thirds of the State's land had been sold, including all the blocks between Arlington and Dartmouth Streets lying north of Newbury Street.
On the south side of Beacon Street, all the lots had been sold to the
middle of the block between Exeter and Fairfield Streets, almost to the
end of the State's land. All the land on Marlborough Street had been sold
as far as Exeter Street, and all the Commonwealth Avenue lots had been
sold into the block between Dartmouth and Exeter Streets. The state
treasury had benefited greatly and the commissioners were poised to sell
more land in 1870 and 1871. And so the State was facing the termination
of a very successful and remunerative development.

The State considered how it could add to the size of the Back Bay and
increase its profit from the sale of land. The State's only option was to fill
more of the Charles River, which was under its control because the Tripartite Indenture of 1856 had granted the right to fill the rest of the Receiving Basin to the Boston Water Power Company. If the "Commissioners' Line" could be moved into the river, more land could be filled
behind it.

In 1869, before the beginning of a serious depression that would crip-
ple America's economy and cause the commissioners to hold Back Bay
land off the market, the State Legislature optimistically expected that the

(a)   (b)

FIGURE 7.7. The Algonquin Club before and after the court decision. The Algonquin Club built its new clubhouse at 217 Commonwealth Avenue in 1887 with a projection along the entire front at ground level, as shown at the left (a). That projection was not allowed by the zoning regulations and the club had to rebuild the bottom floor with projections in the front for the door and bay windows, as shown at the right (b). *(Courtesy of The Bostonian Society/Old State House.)*

demand for Back Bay land would continue to be high. In that year the Massachusetts House of Representatives looked for a way to develop more land in a valuable location adjacent to the Back Bay. A plan was prepared by E. E. Hewins (see fig. 7.8) for a committee of the House of Representatives in June 1869. If carried out, this plan would have added about twenty-five residential blocks—approximately doubling the number of blocks of houses in the existing State's land. The "Flat of Beacon Hill" would also have been widened considerably. In addition, a wide strip of parkland would have stretched alongside the Charles River.

This 1869 plan is most striking for the change it would have made to the Charles River Estuary. From the line of Hereford Street, at Back Street near the former start of the Cross Dam, a new seawall would jut northward more than four blocks. This would have been about the same distance added as that from Beacon to Boylston Streets. The Charles River Estuary would have been narrowed abruptly by about two-thirds, continuing as a slim channel from Hereford Street to beyond the West Boston Bridge (the present site of the Longfellow Bridge). The tidal flow into and out of the Charles River would have been greatly reduced, limiting its cleansing action, and much pollution would probably have collected

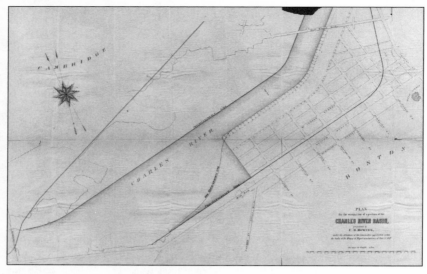

FIGURE 7.8. Plan for expanding the Back Bay into the Charles River Basin, 1869. After filling was nearly complete for the approximately one hundred acres of state land in the Back Bay, the State Commissioners developed a bold new plan. This map shows a proposed extension of the filling that would reach about two-thirds of the way across the remaining Charles River estuary. Three more blocks of housing and a wide park along the river would run from Hereford Street on the west to Charles Street (Longfellow) Bridge. This development would probably have reduced the value of property in the original filled area. The extension of the landfill area was not done. *(Courtesy of the State Library of Massachusetts.)*

in the sharp angle west of Hereford Street. And the later Massachusetts Avenue Bridge would have been only a block west of the parallel seawall at Hereford Street.

We have not learned why the 1869 plan was not pushed forward. If the change had been made, there would have been negative consequences. In addition to the danger of increased pollution, hindsight tells us that the land would not have sold quickly because of the depression in the early 1870s. With much new land standing vacant, the attractiveness of the original plan of the Back Bay would have been greatly reduced, and property values decreased. And the rich families that had already built mansions in the Back Bay would suddenly have lived farther from the Charles River, which would have reduced the attractiveness of their locations.

Epilogue

The Back Bay today is an outstanding Boston neighborhood largely because it was carefully planned and attracted wealthy families who built elegant mansions almost 150 years ago. Brick and stone residential buildings on tree-lined streets still give the Back Bay its distinctive character, which is widely recognized and respected.

The Back Bay is known today for its parks, hotels, exclusive shops, classic Victorian architecture, and modern office towers. This neighborhood is primarily an upscale residential neighborhood with attractive and very expensive apartments and condominiums. Commonwealth Avenue remains the most distinctive street in Boston. Thriving retail areas lie along the south side of the residentially zoned blocks. Small, more expensive shops and art galleries are located on Newbury Street. Boylston Street, the parallel commercial street, has more chain stores mixed in with office buildings. Two large and modern urban malls, Copley Place and the Prudential Center, draw throngs of shoppers to the southern edge of the Back Bay. Business offices in modern and renovated buildings hold tens of thousands of professional and clerical workers who contribute to the economy of the neighborhood.

The Back Bay today contributes to Boston's tourist, convention, and business industries. At least half the top-ranked hotels in Boston are located in the neighborhood and attract large numbers of affluent visitors. Many of the city's most highly rated restaurants are also in the Back Bay, in hotels and in popular shopping districts. Small and medium-size conventions often use the Hynes Convention Center, adjacent to the Prudential Center.

The Back Bay today contributes to the social and cultural life of Boston in very significant ways. The French Library and the Goethe Institute are venerable institutions committed to preserving European cultures and languages. Several private clubs continue to have active schedules of activities and draw their memberships from the whole metropolitan area. Historic Protestant churches maintain active religious and social service programs in the Back Bay. The Christian Science Church complex occupies an impressive site near the southwest corner of the area. Only Saint Cecelia's Church, between the Prudential Center and Massachusetts Avenue, serves the Catholic population; there are no Jewish synagogues. The Boston Public Library in Copley Square, the first free public library in the United States, is a center for research, and an active program of educational lectures and other events is held in its Rabb Auditorium. Just outside the original Receiving Basin, Symphony Hall and three music colleges are clustered near Massachusetts Avenue; they play central roles in Boston's cultural life.

The Commonwealth Avenue Mall and the Charles River Esplanade provide attractive parkland. These areas of green space and water in the heart of a great city add to the Back Bay's image and attract many people for relaxation. Summertime concerts on the Esplanade and in Copley Square are popular, crowned by the famous and very popular Fourth of July Boston Pops concerts. The Charles River, formerly a tidal estuary, has been cleaned to a great degree, so it is more attractive than ever for rowing, sailing, and even sailboarding, which often dumps participants into the water.

The current success of the Back Bay derives largely from factors stemming from the planning and development work done in the nineteenth century. The location continues to be very popular—close to workplaces in the downtown and to Back Bay businesses, near restaurants and theaters, and adjacent to Beacon Hill, the Public Garden, and Boston Common. The construction of nineteenth-century mansions initially set the pattern for Back Bay development, which is maintained to the present day. The older buildings are continually renovated internally and updated while the distinctive architecture is preserved carefully, as it would be in a historic district setting.

Universities and colleges near the Back Bay are thriving, contributing to the spending in local stores and adding to demand for housing and services. Students and other young Bostonians keep the nightlife lively on the Back Bay's commercial streets. The very positive image of the

Back Bay survives in spite of negatives such as parking shortages, crowded conditions, rush-hour traffic, and overloaded public transportation.

The initial success of the Back Bay in the nineteenth century resulted from the successful sale of house lots to wealthy families. The buyers then engaged architects and planned elegant mansions in the latest French styles. Homes were built over the span of a few decades, and so attractive streetscapes were created along the new, tree-lined streets. Commonwealth Avenue and its leafy mall established the elegance of the Back Bay with its Old-World flavor. This narrow park would later be connected to a string of green spaces stretching out to Franklin Park known as Boston's "Emerald Necklace"; the Back Bay is thus an important link in the park system that starts with Boston Common and the Public Garden.

Prestigious Protestant churches followed their members into the new Back Bay, building solid stone structures in Gothic and Romanesque styles. Key educational and cultural institutions in the Back Bay solidified its image in the first decades: the Massachusetts Institute of Technology, the Museum of Natural History, the Museum of Fine Arts, Harvard Medical School, and more. Early in the twentieth century, Symphony Hall, the Opera House, the New England Conservatory of Music, and the Gardner Museum were located in the nearby Fenway area.

Toward the end of the nineteenth century, the Back Bay established itself as a very successful, wealthy, residential neighborhood. A rich social and cultural life was maintained by the neighborhood's "Proper Bostonian" families. Victorian values and lifestyles thrived in the men's and women's clubs, schools and cultural organizations for children, classical music and theatrical venues, parties, balls, musical evenings in private homes, and rounds of "at home" visiting by women of the higher class.

The Back Bay neighborhood entered a period of decline by 1920, which only deepened after the stock market crash in 1929. Soon after 1910, MIT, the Museum of Fine Arts, and Harvard Medical School moved to new locations where they could have larger facilities and generous acreage that would allow future expansion. In the 1920s the automobile and improved roads serving Boston's suburbs induced many wealthy families to move outside the city, where they could build large homes on expansive lots. The exodus of leading families drained much of the cultural and social vitality out of the neighborhood. This reduced the prestige of the Back Bay and put housing on the market when there was not much demand for homes in the city. Back Bay residential buildings started selling for lower prices, and so began a downward spiral.

For several decades, many of the Back Bay's town houses originally occupied by single families were broken up into small apartments that were rented to clerical workers and young, middle-class workers. The building exteriors and public spaces became shabby, as the owners and the City were less able to maintain them. The Back Bay suffered from the Great Depression of the 1930s as professional and business jobs declined in Boston. The continued movement of families to the suburbs and to middle-class neighborhoods deepened the ongoing deterioration of the neighborhood.

The Back Bay began to rebound in the early 1960s because more professionals valued urban living and convenience to their jobs. At the same time, urban renewal in Boston sparked an interest in the city. The Vault, an organization of business leaders, promoted redevelopment of the city and helped bring in tax breaks for new construction projects.

The Back Bay benefited early and strongly from the growth of the "New Boston" after profits from high-tech industries began to be invested in Boston. In 1965 a new office tower, modern apartments, and a convention center were completed on the site of a large railroad-switching yard that stretched from Boylston Street to Huntington Avenue. This Prudential Center development was followed by construction of the Sheraton Hotel and the John Hancock Tower by the early 1970s. Spurred by these improvements in the Back Bay, gentrification took hold gradually. Most of the elegant Victorian residential buildings have been renovated to very high standards. In recent decades, more and more professionals have moved into the neighborhood and the comeback seems to be complete.

Looking into the future of the Back Bay, there is no end in sight for the high demand and housing prices that have been in effect for some time. Tourism, business travel, and small- to moderate-sized conferences are expected to keep the neighborhood's hotels and restaurants busy. Location is the key to value and success in real estate, and the Back Bay has an ideal location. Since only limited land remains open for development, future construction is likely on air rights over the Massachusetts Turnpike and railroad both east of Copley Place and west of the Prudential Center. Older buildings of lower value will probably be razed from time to time for new construction projects. Nearby universities are expected to continue to thrive and to have positive effects on the Back Bay.

The planning and confidence of the creators of the Back Bay have generally stood the test of time. Attractive streets and architecture continue to shape the image of the neighborhood. The only remaining serious problems lie in the environmental realm. Falling water tables in certain areas threaten the foundations of buildings resting on wooden piles. Corrosive gas from former pollution remains in some places. A severe earthquake near Boston, while not likely, could knock down many older brick and stone buildings on the unstable land of the Back Bay and cause injury and death.

On balance, the future looks very bright for Boston's Back Bay after its first century and a half. People of the twenty-first century owe much to the planners, inventors, contractors, architects, and builders of the Back Bay neighborhood. The most ambitious landfill project and urban development effort of the nineteenth century will long continue to enhance Boston's living conditions and image.

Notes

Preface (pages vii–xiv)

1. Karl Haglund, *Inventing the Charles River* (Cambridge, Mass.: MIT Press, 2003), 95–99; Nancy S. Seasholes, *Gaining Ground: A History of Landmaking in Boston* (Cambridge, Mass.: MIT Press, 2003), 211–232.

1. Prehistory of the Back Bay (pages 1–18)

1. *Uncovering the Past, Northeastern University and Its Environs* (Boston: Northeastern University), 1–4.
2. A terrane is a large area of the earth's crust that shares more or less a common origin and history.
3. *Uncovering the Past*, 1–4.
4. Richard H. Bailey and Benjamin H. Bland, "Recent Developments in the Study of the Boston Bay Group," In *Guidebook for Geological Field Trips in New England, 2001 Annual Meeting of the Geological Society of America, Boston, Massachusetts*, ed. David P. West, Jr., and Richard H. Bailey (Amherst, Mass.: Department of Geography, University of Massachusetts, Amherst, 2001), U4-U8.
5. M. P. Billings, "Bedrock Geology of the Boston Basin," in *Geology of Southeastern New England: A Guidebook for Field Trips to the Boston Area and Vicinity*, ed. Barry Cameron, (Princeton: Science Press, 1976), 38.
6. Lawrence LaForge, "Geology of the Boston Area, Massachusetts," *United States Geological Survey Bulletin* 839 (1932): 8–11; Marland P. Billings, "Bedrock Geology of the Boston Basin," 28; Clifford A. Kaye, "Bedrock and Quaternary Geology of the Boston Area, Massachusetts," *Geological Society of America Reviews in Engineering Geology* 5 (1982): 27–28.
7. W. O. Crosby, "A Study of the Geology of the Charles River Estuary and the Formation of Boston Harbor," in *Appendix No. 7, Geologist Report, Report of the Committee on the Charles River Dam, Appointed under the Resolves of 1901, Chapter 105, to Consider the Advisability and Feasibility of Building a Dam across the Charles River at or Near Craigie Bridge, Boston*, (Boston: Wright and Potter, 1903), 346–347, 355–359.

8. The late Wisconsin substage refers to a time interval between 25,000 and 10,000 years ago.

9. The Laurentide ice sheet at its maximum extent extended from the Rocky Mountains to beyond the east coast of Newfoundland and from the Arctic Ocean to the latitude of New York City. (Michael A. Summerfield, *Global Geomorphology: An Introduction to the Study of Landforms* [New York: John Wiley and Sons, 1991], 351.)

10. D. M. Mickelson, Lee Clayton, D. S. Fullerton, and H. W. Borns, Jr., "The Late Wisconsin Glacial Record of the Laurentide Ice Sheet in the United States," in *Late-Quaternary Environments of the United States I: The Late Pleistocene*, ed. H. E. Wright, Jr., and Stephen C. Porter (Minneapolis: University of Minnesota Press, 1983), 29–30.

11. Harl P. Aldrich, Jr., "Back Bay Boston, Part 1," *Journal of the Boston Society of Civil Engineers* 57, no. 1 (January 1970): 7.

12. Raw radiocarbon measurements are usually reported as years "before present." This is the number of radiocarbon years before 1950; the assumption is that the level of carbon-14 in the atmosphere has always been at the 1950 level. Because this is untrue in practice, radiocarbon years do not correspond exactly to calendar years.

13. D. M. Mickelson, Lee Clayton, D. S. Fullerton, and H. W. Borns, Jr., "The Late Wisconsin Glacial Record of the Laurentide Ice Sheet in the United States," in *Late-Quaternary Environments*, 29.

14. J. L. Fastook, and T. Hughes, "A Numerical Model for Reconstruction and Disintegration of the Late Wisconsin Glaciation in the Gulf of Maine," in *Late Wisconsinan Glaciation of New England*, ed. Grahame J. Larson and Byron D. Stone (Dubuque: Kendall/Hunt, 1982), 236.

15. G. G. Connally, and L. A. Sirkin, "Wisconsinan History of the Hudson-Champlain Lobe," in *The Wisconsinan Stage: Geological Society of America Memoir 136*, ed. R. F. Black, R. P. Goldthwait, and H. B. Willman (Washington, D.C.: Geological Society of America, 1973), 47–69.

16. Arthur L. Bloom, "Sea Level and Coastal Morphology of the United States through the Late Wisconsin Glacial Maximum." In *Late-Quaternary Environments*, 215–218.

17. Robert N. Oldale, "Pleistocene Stratigraphy of Nantucket, Martha's Vineyard, the Elizabeth Islands, and Cape Cod, Massachusetts," in *Late Wisconsinan Glaciation of New England*, Larson and Stone, 4–7; Les Sirkin, "Wisconsinan Glaciation of Long Island, New York, to Block Island, Rhode Island," ibid., 35–59.

18. Byron D. Stone, and John D. Peper, "Topographic Control of the Deglaciation of Eastern Massachusetts: Ice Lobation and the Marine Incursion," ibid., 149–162.

19. Glacial drift is any type of sediment that is transported and deposited by glaciers or glacial meltwater streams.

20. H. W. Borns, Jr., "Late Wisconsin Fluctuations of the Laurentide Ice Sheet in Southern and Eastern New England," in *The Wisconsinan Stage,* ed. Black, Goldthwait, and Willman, 37–45.

21. C. A. Kaye, and E. S. Barghoorn, "Late Quaternary Sea-Level Change and Crustal Rise at Boston, Massachusetts, with Notes on the Autocompaction of Peat," *Geological Society of America Bulletin* 75 (February 1964): 77.

22. Kaye, "Bedrock and Quaternary Geology of the Boston Area," 33.

23. Ibid., 34.

24. Ibid.

25. Ibid., 36.

26. Ibid.

27. Kaye, "Bedrock and Quaternary Geology of the Boston Area," 36; Kaye and Berghorn, "Late Quaternary Sea-Level Change and Crustal Rise at Boston, Massachusetts," 75–79.

28. Ibid., 36. P. S. Rosen, B. M. Brenninkmeyer, and L. M. Maybury, "Holocene Evolution of Boston Inner Harbor, Massachusetts," *Journal of Coastal Research* 9, no. 2 (1993): 363–377.

29. Sheldon Judson, "Figure I-b, Projection of Stream Gradient on the Surface of the Boston Blue Clay," in Frederick Johnson et al., *The Boylston Street Fishweir,* vol. 2, *A Study of the Geology, Paleobotany, and Biology of a Site on Stuart Street in the Back Bay District of Boston, Massachusetts* (Andover, Mass.: Papers of the Robert S. Peabody Foundation of Archaeology, 1949), frontispiece.

30. Kaye, "Bedrock and Quaternary Geology of the Boston Area," 36.

31. Ibid.

32. Rosen, Brenninkmeyer, and Maybury, "Holocene Evolution of Boston Inner Harbor," 371, 375; L. Kaplan, M. B. Smith, and L. Sheddon, "The Boylston Street Fishweir: Revisited," *Economic Botany* 44 (1990): 517; P. E. Newby, and T. Webb III, "Radiocarbon-Dated Pollen and Sediment Records from the Boylston Street Fishweir Site in Boston," *Quaternary Research* 41 (1994): 221–222.

33. H. W. Shimer, "Post-glacial History of Boston," *Proceedings of the American Academy of Arts and Sciences* 53 (1918): 458–459.

34. Rosen, Brenninkmeyer, and Maybury, "Holocene Evolution of Boston Inner Harbor," 375.

35. Kaye, "Bedrock and Quaternary Geology of the Boston Area," 36.

36. Edmund S. Davis, *Nineteenth Annual Report of the Boston Transit Commission for the Year Ending June 30* (Boston: 1913), 44–45.

37. Johnson et al., *The Boylston Street Fishweir,* vol. 2, 4.

38. Charles C. Willoughby, "An Ancient Indian Fish-Weir," *American Anthropologist,* new series, 29 (1927): 107.

39. Davis, *Nineteenth Annual Report of the Boston Transit Commission,* 44–45.

40. Johnson et al., *The Boylston Street Fishweir,* vol. 2, 24, 82–84.

41. Ibid., 24–38.

42. Rosen, Brenninkmeyer, and Maybury, "Holocene Evolution of Boston Inner Harbor," 375; D. F. Dincauze, and Elena Décima, "Small is Beautiful: Tidal Weirs in a Low-Energy Estuary," in *A Lasting Impression—Coastal, Lithic, and Ceramic Research in New England Archaeology,* ed. J. E. Kerber (Westport, Conn.: Praeger, 2002), 78.

43. E. B. Décima, and D. F. Dincauze, "The Boston Back Bay Fish Weirs," in *Hidden Dimensions: The Cultural Significance of Wetland Archaeology,* ed. K. Bernick (Vancouver: University of British Columbia Press, 1998), table 1, 162–163.

44. Dincauze and Décima, "Small Is Beautiful," 1, 74–75.

45. Ibid., 75.

46. Ibid., 78–80.

47. William Wood, *New England Prospect, Being a True, Lively, and Experimental Description of That Part of America, Commonly Called New-England,* 3d ed. (London, 1639), 42–45.

48. Nathaniel B. Shurtleff, *A Topographical and Historical Description of Boston,* (Boston: Published by order Common Council, 1891), 477–480.

49. Wood, *New England Prospect,* 45–46.

50. Nathaniel B. Shurtleff, *A Topographical and Historical Description of Boston,* 140–141.

51. Johnson et al., "Figure I, Map of the Boston Peninsula and Surrounding Regions about 1700," *The Boylston Street Fishweir,* vol. 2.

52. Walter Muir Whitehill, *Boston: A Topographical History,* 2d ed. (Cambridge, Mass.: Belknap Press of Harvard University Press, 1959), 6–7.

53. Ibid.

54. Justin Winsor, *The Memorial History of Boston,* vol. 1 (Boston: James R. Osgood and Company, 1881), 530.

55. Ibid.

2. Why Fill the Back Bay? (pages 19–50)

1. Emerson Ralph, "Boston," in *The Complete Writings of Ralph Waldo Emerson* (New York: Wm. H. Wise and Company, 1878), 896.

2. Nancy Seasholes, *Gaining Ground: A History of Landmaking in Boston* (Cambridge: Mass.: MIT Press, 2003), 154.

3. Ibid., 155.

4. Frederick Gamst, "The Context and Significance of America's First Railroad on Boston's Beacon Hill," *Technology and Culture* (1992): 66–67.

5. Ibid., 92–95.

6. Michael Southworth, and Susan Southworth, *The Boston Society of Architects A.I.A. Guide to Boston,* second edition (Chester, Conn.: Globe Pequot Press, 1984), 163.

7. Allen Chamberlain, *Beacon Hill: Its Ancient Pastures and Early Mansions,* (Boston: Houghton Mifflin, 1925), 79–80.

8. Bainbridge Bunting, *The Houses of Boston's Back Bay* (Cambridge, Mass.: Belknap Press of Harvard University Press, 1967), 47.

9. Seasholes, *Gaining Ground,* 162.

10. Ibid., 173–174.

11. Nathaniel B. Shurtleff, *A Topographical and Historical Description of Boston,* 3d ed. (Boston: City of Boston, 1891), 360.

12. *Boston City Document no. 14* (1863), 41.

13. Bunting, *Houses of Boston's Back Bay,* 45.

14. Whitehill, *Boston: A Topographical History,* 88–89.

15. Isaac P. Davis, and Uriah Cotting, "Tidal Power Proposal" (Boston, 1813).

16. Seasholes, *Gaining Ground,* 155–156.

17. Letter to the Editor, *Boston Daily Advertiser,* June 10, 1814.

18. Uriah Cotting, "Boston and Roxbury Mill Corporation" (pamphlet) (Boston, 1818).

19. Ibid.

20. Whitehill, *Boston: A Topographical History,* 92.

21. E. W. Howe, *Proceedings of the Boston Society of Civil Engineers,* September 1879 to June 1881, 87.

22. Wilbur W. Davis, "The History of Boston as Disclosed in the Digging of the Commonwealth Avenue Underpass and Other Traffic Tunnels," *Proceedings of the Bostonian Society Annual Meeting,* January 18, 1938, 29–31.

23. John Hales, *A Survey of Boston and Its Vicinity* (Boston: Ezra Lincoln, 1821), 25–26.

24. Pervil Meigs, "Boston Tidal Mills," paper presented at the Association of American Geographers meeting in Boston (April 18–21, 1971).

25. Boston and Roxbury Mill Corporation Papers, 1819 file, Massachusetts Historical Society, Boston.

26. Whitehill, *Boston: A Topographical History,* 93.

27. Boston and Roxbury Mill Corporation Papers, 1819 file.

28. Ibid.

29. Boston and Roxbury Mill Corporation Papers, 1821 file.

30. Stephen Salisbury, *The State, the Investor, and the Railroad: The Boston and Albany, 1825–1867* (Cambridge, Mass.: Harvard University Press, 1967), 108.

31. Boston and Roxbury Mill Corporation Papers, 1821 file.

32. Boston and Roxbury Mill Corporation Papers, 1819 file.

33. Boston and Roxbury Mill Corporation Papers, 1822 file, May 22, 1822.

34. Ibid., August 1822.

35. Boston and Roxbury Mill Corporation Papers, 1827 file, March 13, 1824.

36. *Massachusetts Senate Document no. 110,* 1856, 1.

37. Ibid.

38. Salisbury, *The State, the Investor, and the Railroad*, 100–102.

39. Ibid., 101–102.

40. Ibid., 102.

41. Ibid., 102–103.

42. Ibid., 103.

43. Ibid., 103–104.

44. Ibid., 109.

45. *Boston City Document no. 36*, 1849, 1–7.

46. Ibid., 3.

47. Ibid.

48. *Boston City Document no. 14*, 1850, 1–8.

49. Ibid., 12.

50. John Blake, *Public Health in the Town of Boston, 1630–1822* (Cambridge, Mass.: Harvard University Press, 1959), 99–100.

51. *Boston City Document no. 14*, 1850.

52. Jesse Chickering, M.D., "A Comparative View of the Population in Boston in 1850," *Boston City Document no. 60*, 1851, 34.

53. *Boston's Growth: A Bird's-Eye View of Boston's Increased Territory and Population from Its Beginning to Present* (Boston: State Street Trust Company, 1910), 22–23.

54. Chickering, "A Comparative View of the Population in Boston in 1850," *Boston City Document no. 60*, 1851, 34.

55. Boston City Document No. 42, 2–3.

56. Chickering, *Boston City Document no. 60*, 1851, 39.

57. Josiah Curtis, M.D., "Report of the Joint Special Census of Boston," *Boston City Document no. 69*, 1855, 3.

58. Massachusetts Senate Document no. 17, *1857*, 4.

59. Oscar Handlin, *Boston's Immigrants: A Study in Acculturation* (Cambridge, Mass.: Belknap Press of Harvard University Press, 1979), 89.

60. Ibid., 104–106.

61. Otis D. Duncan, "From Social System to Ecosystem," *Sociological Inquiry* V. 31 (Spring, 1961): 140–149.

62. Chickering, "A Comparative View of the Population in Boston in 1851," *Boston City Document no. 60*, 1851, 33.

63. Ibid., 38.

64. Ibid., 36.

65. Ibid., 30.

66. Ibid., 39.

67. Ibid., 14.

68. George Adams, "Population of Boston," *Boston City Document no. 42*, 1851, 14.

69. Curtis, "Report of the Joint Special Census of Boston," *Boston City Document no. 69*, 1855, 9.

70. Ibid., 22.

71. Ibid., 44.

72. Ibid., 23.

73. Ibid., 30.

74. Ibid., 10.

75. Ibid., 19.

76. John Mulkern, *The Know-Nothing Party in Massachusetts: The Rise and Fall of a People's Movement* (Boston: Northeastern University Press, 1990), 70.

77. Ibid., 132.

78. Ibid., 156.

3. Planning and Financing the Back Bay Landfill (pages 51–78)

1. Ino. Apthorpe, *Report of the Committee Chosen by the Inhabitants of the City of Boston, to Take into Consideration the Expedience of Authorizing the City to Make Sale of the Upland and Flats Lying West of Charles Street* (Boston: City of Boston, 1824), 6.

2. Ibid.

3. Robert Gourlay, *Plans for Beautifying New York and for Enlarging and Improving the City of Boston* (Boston: Crocker and Brewster, and Saxton, Pierce, 1844), 14.

4. Ibid., 7–8.

5. Ibid., 8–13.

6. Ibid., 33.

7. Ibid., 31–34.

8. Ibid., 19–21.

9. Ibid., 37–38

10. Ibid., 18.

11. Walter Muir Whitehill, *Boston: A Topographical History,* 2d ed. (Cambridge: Belknap Press of Harvard University Press, 1968), 149–150.

12. David Sears, *Plan for Removing the Nuisance of the Empty Basin and Ornamenting the City of Boston* (Boston: Toppan and Bradford, 1849).

13. Letter to the Editor, David Sears Papers, 1859 file, Massachusetts Historical Society, Boston.

14. *Massachusetts Senate Document no. 45,* 1852, 2–3.

15. Ibid., 3.

16. Ibid., 15–16.

17. Ibid., 17.

18. Ibid., 16–17.

19. *Boston City Document no. 36,* 1849, 6.

20. Justin Winsor, *The Memorial History of Boston,* vol. 4 (Boston: Ticknor and Company, 1880), 36.

21. *Plan Accompanying the Proposal Made to the City of Boston by the Commissioners on the Back Bay* (Boston: Commonwealth of Massachusetts, 1854), 7.

22. *Massachusetts Senate Document no. 17*, 1857, 7.

23. *Massachusetts Public Document no. 12*, 1858, 3.

24. David Sears Papers, 1852 file.

25. *Massachusetts Senate Document no. 62,* 1855, 2.

26. Ibid.

27. David Sears to Gov. John H. Clifford, September 24, 1853, David Sears Papers, 1853 file.

28. John S. Sleeper, "Message of the Mayor of Roxbury, in Relation to the Back Bay Lands" (1857), 5.

29. Jesse Chickering, M.D., *Dr. Chickering's Report, Boston City Document no. 42*, 1850, 59.

30. Sleeper, "Message of the Mayor of Roxbury," 5.

31. Ibid.

32. Horace Gray, Jr., *Reports of the Cases Argued and Determined in the Supreme Judicial Court of Massachusetts*, vol. 9 (Boston: Little, Brown, 1864), 452.

33. *Massachusetts State Laws*, chap. 210, 1859, 917.

34. Ibid.

35. Ibid.

36. Minute Books of the Commissioners on Public Lands, January 23, 1862, vol. 3, Massachusetts State Archives, Boston, 150.

37. *Massachusetts Senate Document no. 16*, 1856, 2–3.

38. *Massachusetts Senate Document no. 173*, 1856, 4–6.

39. *Massachusetts Senate Document no. 16*, 1856, 3.

40. *Massachusetts Senate Document no. 99*, 1856, 1–2.

41. *Massachusetts Senate Document no. 17*, 1857, 3.

42. Ibid., 32.

43. Ibid., 2.

44. Ibid., 4.

45. *Massachusetts Senate Document no. 173*, 1856, 8–9.

46. *Massachusetts Senate Document no. 17*, 1857, 4.

47. Ibid., 5.

48. Ibid., 6.

49. *Massachusetts Senate Document no. 89*, 1856, 1–2.

50. Whitehill, *Boston: A Topographical History*, 151.

51. Mona Domosh, *Invented Cities: The Creation of Landscape in Nineteenth Century New York and Boston* (New Haven: Yale University Press, 1996), 110.

52. *Massachusetts Senate Document no. 17*, 1857, 12.

53. Ibid., 13–14.

54. Ibid., 12.

55. Domosh, *Invented Cities*, 114.

56. Ibid., 115.

57. *Massachusetts Public Document no. 11,* 1884, 1.

58. Karl Haglund, *Inventing the Charles River* (Cambridge, Mass.: MIT Press, 2003), 67.

59. *Massachusetts Legislature Acts and Resolves,* chap. 85, March 21, 1861.

60. *Massachusetts House Document no. 239,* 1861, 2.

61. Horace Gray, Jr., *Reports of the Cases Argued and Determined in the Supreme Judicial Court of Massachusetts,* vol. 9 (Boston: Little Brown, 1864), 452.

62. Minute Books of the Commissioners of Public Lands, November 2, 1865, Massachusetts State Archives, Boston.

63. *Massachusetts Senate Document no. 55,* 1856, 2.

64. *Massachusetts Public Document no. 29,* 1857.

65. Ibid.

66. *Massachusetts House Document no. 62,* 1861, 6.

67. Ibid.

68. Ibid., 6–7.

69. Ibid., 7.

70. Ibid.

71. Commissioners on Public Lands, auction catalogue, December 1, 1860.

72. *Harbor and Land Commissioners' Report, Massachusetts Public Document no. 11,* 1886, 6.

73. Ibid.

74. Commissioners on Public Lands, auction catalogue, October 21, 1862.

75. *Massachusetts House Document no. 16,* 1862, 1.

76. *Massachusetts Public Document no. 11,* 1866, 5.

77. *Massachusetts Public Document no. 11,* 1884, 6.

78. Michael Southworth and Susan Southworth, *Boston Society of Architects A.I.A. Guide to Boston* (Chester, Conn.: Globe Pequot Press, 1984), 256–257.

79. *Massachusetts Public Document no. 11,* 1886, 5.

80. M. D. Ross, *Estimate of the Financial Effect of the Proposed Reservation of Back Bay Lands* (Boston: Committee of Associated Institutions of Science and Art, 1861).

81. Ibid.

82. Minute Books of the Commissioners on Public Lands, vol. 6, December 19, 1867, Massachusetts State Archives, Boston, 95.

4. Locomotives and Steam Shovels (pages 79–92)

1. Natalie McPherson, "Machines and Economic Growth: The Implications for Growth Theory of the History of the Industrial Revolution," in *Contributions in Economics and Economic History,* Number 156, (Westport, Conn.: Greenwood Press, 1994), 12.

2. Ibid.

3. Lance Phillips, *Yonder Comes the Train*, (South Brunswick, N.J.: A. S. Barnes, 1965), 39.

4. The Whyte Wheel Classification System for steam locomotives was devised by Fredric M. Whyte of the New York Central Railroad (*American Engineer and Railroad Journal* [December 1900]: 274) and accepted by the American Locomotive Company in 1903 (John H. White, Jr., *American Locomotives: An Engineering History, 1830–1880* [Baltimore: Johns Hopkins University Press, 1997], 184). Steam locomotives are classified by the number of wheels they have. The first number indicates the number of small front, or leading, wheels. The second number indicates the number of wheels that drive the locomotive. These wheels are larger than either the leading or trailing wheels and support the main weight of the locomotive. The third number gives the number of small wheels that trail the locomotive. They support the weight of the boiler's firebox. A locomotive with four driving wheels only is an 0-4-0 locomotive. The typical American locomotive has four leading wheels, four driving wheels, and no trailing wheels: a 4-4-0.

5. Greg Martin, *Robert Stephenson: Locomotives for North America* <http://www.saxoncourtbooks.co.uk/ontrack/america.htm>, 1–3.

6. White, *American Locomotives*, 33–46.

7. Ibid., 46.

8. Ibid., 66.

9. *The Encyclopedia Americana* vol. 23, s. vv. "Manufacture of rails and structural shapes."

10. White, *History of the American Locomotive*, 184.

11. Ibid.

12. B. B. Adams, Jr., "The Every-Day Life of Railroad Men," *Scribner's Magazine* 4 (New York: Charles Scribner and Sons, Nov. 1888), 557.

13. Charles H. Clark, "The Development of the Semiautomatic Freight-Car Coupler, 1863–1893," *Technology and Culture,* (April 1872): 171.

14. Ibid., 174–175.

15. *Workin' on the Railroad: Reminiscences from the Age of Steam*, ed. Richard Reinhardt (New York: Weathervane Books, 1970) 274.

16. John H. White, Jr., *The American Railroad Freight Car: From the Wood Car Era to the Coming of Steel* (Baltimore: Johns Hopkins University Press, 1993), 490.

17. *Workin' on the Railroad*, 274–275.

18. U.S. Congress, Senate Committee on Interstate Commerce, *Hearings in Relation to Safety Couples and Power Brakes of Freight Trains* (1890), 20–21.

19. Samuel Stueland, "The Otis Steam Excavator," *Technology and Culture* 35 (July 1994), 571.

20. Ibid.

21. Ibid.

22. William S. Otis, Crane-Excavator for Excavating and Removing Earth, patent no. 1,089 (Washington, D.C.: U.S. Patent Office, February 24, 1839).

23. Stueland, "The Otis Steam Excavator," 572.

24. Daniel T. V. Huntoon, *Oliver Smith Chapman*, (Canton, Mass.: Canton Historical Society, 1877), 10–11.

25. Ibid., 11.

26. White, *American Locomotives*, 545.

27. Stueland, "The Otis Steam Excavator," 573–574; John Souther Biographical Files, National Museum of American History, Smithsonian Institution, Division of Engineering and Industry, Washington, D.C.; *Asher and Adams' Pictorial Album of American Industry* (1876; rep. New York: Rutledge Books, 1976), 56.

28. Otis, *Crane-Excavator for Excavating and Removing Earth.*

29. Oliver S. Chapman, Improved Excavator, patent no. 63,857, U.S. Patent Office, April 16, 1867.

30. *Asher and Adams' Pictorial Album of American Industry,* 56.

31. Ibid.

32. Alpheus Nettleton, Dumping-car, patent no. 6,065 (Washington, D.C.: U.S. Patent Office, January 30, 1849).

5. Gravel Trains and Bold Entrepreneurs (pages 93–124)

1. Lyman Abbott, "The American Railroad," *Harper's New Monthly Magazine,* August 1874, 386.

2. Myron A. Munson, *The Munson Record: A Genealogical and Biographical Account of Captain Thomas Munson and His Descendents,* vol. 2 (1895), 916.

3. Ibid., 932.

4. Ibid.

5. Ibid.

6. Ibid.

7. C. A. Brown, "The Charles River Line," *Shoreliner* 13, no. 3 (1982): 29; Ronald Dale Karr, "The Charles River," *The Rail Lines of Southern New England* (Pepperell, Mass.: Branch Line Press, 1995), 288–289.

8. J. E. Alger, Letter to the Editor, *Railway and Locomotive Historical Society Bulletin,* no. 3 (1922): 13.

9. "Plan of Newton Upper Falls," *Atlas of the City of Newton, Massachusetts* (New York: G. M. Hopkins, 1874) pl. K.

10. Susan Abele, Newton Historical Society, personal communication, September 13, 2001.

11. The history of the Boston and Worcester Railroad's management of first the Charles River Branch Railroad and later the merged Charles River Railroad, followed by the New York and Boston Railroad, can be viewed in the annual railroad reports published in the following Massachusetts Senate documents:

19th Annual Report of the Boston and Worcester Railroad Corporation," Senate Document no. 22, February 1851, 29–33; *4th Annual Report of the Charles River Branch Railroad Company, Senate Document no. 3,* January 1853, 40–42; *24th Annual Report of the Boston and Worcester Railroad Corporation, Senate Document no. 2,* January 1856, 41–45; *25th Annual Report of the Boston and Worcester Railroad Corporation, Senate Document no. 2,* January 1857, 42–47.

12. Brown, "The Charles River Line," 29.

13. Karr, *Rail Lines of Southern New England,* 288.

14. *Third Annual Report of the Charles River Branch Railroad Company, Massachusetts Senate Document no. 9,* January 1852, 37–38.

15. Karr, *Rail Lines of Southern New England,* 288–289.

16. *The Fourth Annual Report of the New York and Boston Rail Road Company, Including the Charles River and Charles River Branch Railroads, Being for the Year Ending November 30, 1858,* 2.

17. *Massachusetts Acts and Resolves, 1857,* chapter 70, 688.

18. *Massachusetts House Document no. 33,* 1862, 2–3; Minutes of the Back Bay Commissioners, March 24, 1858; "Ordiorne Assignment," December 1, 1857, case 5, maps, Boston Water Power Company Documents, Baker Library Archives, Harvard University Business School, Boston.

19. Massachusetts, Vol. 73, p. 70, March 27, 1860, R. G. Dun & Co. Collection, Baker Library, Harvard Business School.

20. William D. Edson, "The Hinkley Locomotive Construction Record," *Railway and Locomotive Historical Society Bulletin* 142 (1980): 65.

21. *Boston Traveller,* April 18, 1859, 2.

22. Although George Goss's and Norman C. Munson's names appear together on all the Boston Water Power Company and State landfill contracts, each of their purchases and gravel property leases was done on an individual basis. The same was true of the deeds given individually to George Goss or Norman C. Munson in payment for land filling.

23. *Fourth Annual Report of the New York and Boston Rail Road Company,* 6.

24. *New York and Boston Railroad Report for the Financial Year Ending 30 November 1859,* in Henry V. Poor, *History of the Railroads and Canals of the United States of America* (1860; rep. New York: Augustus M. Kelley, 1970), 140.

25. *Boston Weekly Transcript* June 9, 1858, 1; *Boston Daily Traveller,* April 18, 1859, 2; *New York and Boston Railroad Report for the Financial Year Ending 30 November 1859,* 140.

26. *Boston Daily Traveller,* April 18, 1859, 2.

27. Hiram T. Story et al. to Charles River Branch Railroad, June 12, 1852, Lib. 210, fol. 62, Norfolk County Registry of Deeds, Dedham, Mass.

28. *Boston Daily Traveller,* April 18, 1859, 2.

29. This tooth was probably a mammoth tooth from a preglacial deposit that had been picked up by the glacier during its advance and, later, as the ice

melted, released into a meltwater stream to become incorporated into the esker. Its position twenty feet below the surface is about the position of the two work-men pushing sediment toward the excavator. At the time that the earliest pho-tographs were taken Munson had only one Otis-Chapman steam excavator working in his pits.

30. The Charles River Railroad was consolidated into the New York and New England Railroad in 1856 by an act of the Massachusetts Legislature; George P. Baker, *The Formation of the New England Railroad System,* (Cam-bridge, Mass.: Harvard University Press, 1937), 45.

31. *Engineering News* (July 27, 1905); E. E. Russell Tratman, *Railroad Track and Track Work,* 3rd ed. (New York: Engineering News, 1909), 374–375.

32. Otis Pettee, "Newton Industries and Manufacturers," in *History of Middlesex County, Massachusetts, with Biographical Sketches of Many of Its Pi-oneers and Prominent Men,* ed. D. Hamilton Hurd, vol. 3 (Philadelphia: J. W. Lewis, 1890), 99.

33. Leslie Crumbaker, "James Edwin Chapman, 1838–1912," undated type-script, Needham Public Library Archives, 1.

34. "Plan of Newton Upper Falls," *Atlas of the City of Newton, Massachusetts,* pl. K.

35. George Kuhn Clarke, *History of Needham, Massachusetts, 1711–1911* (Cam-bridge, Mass.: Privately printed at the University Press, 1912), 422.

36. Coburn to Goss lease, October 1, 1858, Lib. 272, fol. 297, Norfolk County Registry of Deeds, Dedham, Mass.

37. *Boston Weekly Transcript,* June 9, 1858, 1.

38. *Boston Daily Traveller,* April 18, 1859, 2.

39. *Boston Weekly Transcript,* June 9, 1858, 2.

40. *Boston Daily Traveller,* April 18, 1859, 2.

41. Ibid.

42. New York, New Haven and Hartford Railroad Company Records, File A-356–53, box 159, Record Group 1, series 2, Archives and Special Collections at the Thomas J. Dodd Research Center, University of Connecticut Libraries, Storrs, Connecticut.

43. Peter Sturley, Access Team Project Leader, National Railway Museum, York, England, personal communication, December 31, 2004; Conrad Jankow-ski, Department of Chemistry, Northeastern University, Boston, personal com-munication.

44. *Second Annual Report, New York and Boston Rail Road Company in Mass-achusetts, Senate Document no. 2,* January 1857.

45. These tracks have been abandoned, but until recently they were used to carry freight to businesses in the area.

46. This section of the former route is now blocked by Route 9, with its high embankment crossing present-day Centre Street.

47. *Boston Daily Traveller,* April 18, 1859, 2.

48. B. B. Adams, Jr., "The Every-Day Life of Railroad Men," *Scribner's Magazine* 4, November 1888, 506.

49. *Boston Herald,* July 26, 1858, 2.

50. *The Boston and Worcester Railroad Annual Report for November 30, 1859,* 8.

51. "Back Bay in 1851," "Back Bay in 1861," "Back Bay in 1871," "Back Bay in 1881," maps compiled by the engineering firm of Fuller and Whitney, Boston.

52. "Back Bay in 1861."

53. "Opinion," *N. C. Munson v. the City of Boston,* case 4, Boston Water Power Company Documents, June 26, 1875.

54. The Boston City Base (BCB) is mean low tide level, that is, 5.65 feet below the National Geodetic Vertical Datum (NGVD), formerly called the U.S. Coast and Geodetic Survey Sea Level datum of 1929. Elevation 0.0 BCB is equal to −5.65 NGVD.

55. Kyle K. Williams Wyatt, Curator of History and Technology, California State Railroad Museum, Sacramento, personal communication.

56. Issac A. Smith, "Rapid Railway Embankment Construction," *Journal of Associated Engineering Societies* (1888–1889): 103–106.

57. Boston Athenaeum photograph collection, Boston.

58. Gow, Charles R., "Boston Foundations Discussion," *Boston Society of Civil Engineers Papers and Discussions* 1, no. 4 (April 1914): 187.

59. "New Land Estimates, 1847–1890," Case 4, Boston Water Power Company Documents.

60. Minute Books of the Commission on the Back Bay, vol. 3, March 8, 1862, 166.

61. Minute Books of the Commission on Public Lands, vol. 2, March 10, 1860, Massachusetts State Archives, Boston, 44.

62. Tratman, *Railroad Track and Track Work,* 40; Frank. W. Hodgdon, "Methods Used in Filling a Portion of South Boston Flats by the Commonwealth of Massachusetts," *Journal of the Association of Engineering Societies* vol. 7, 1888/1889, 7, 9.

63. George L. Vose, *Handbook of Railroad Construction for the Use of American Engineers, Containing the Necessary Rules, Tables, and Formulae for the Location, Construction, Equipment, and Management of Railroads, as Built in the United States* (Boston: James Munroe and Company, 1857), 262–263.

64. "Educators Applaud NEL's Unique Dioramas at May 16th Unveiling," *Wheel* 13, no. 149, *New England Life* (June 1961): 2.

65. Minute Books of the Commissioners on the Back Bay, vol. 2, June 2, 1860, 91.

66. Ibid.

67. Walter Muir Whitehill, *Boston: A Topographical History,* 2d ed. (Cambridge, Mass.: Belknap Press of Harvard University Press, 1968), 138–139.

6. A Shocking Development Fails to Derail the Project (pages 125–154)

1. R. G. Dun & Co. Collection, vol. 73, p. 70, March 27, 1860.

2. "Agreement. Goss et al. and Boston Water Power Company," Lib. 769 fol. 297–300, July 18, 1859, Suffolk County Registry of Deeds, Boston.

3. "Tax Collector's Notice for 1859–1860," Lib. 802 fol. 54, Suffolk County Registry of Deeds, Boston. Goss and Manson [*sic*]—Stores nos. 34, 36, 38, and 40 on eastern Avenue, between stores of Frederick Nickerson and J. W. Converse and Wm. Dillaway, Jr., Tax for 1860. $102.30.

4. R. G. Dun & Co. Collection, vol. 73, p. 70, August 25, 1858, to April 30, 1859.

5. Ibid., April 27, 1859.

6. Ibid., February 8, 1860.

7. Ibid., March 27, 1860.

8. Ibid., November 19, 1860.

9. Power of Atty. Goss to Munson, December 5, 1859, Lib. 825, fol. 173. Suffolk County Registry of Deeds, Boston.

10. Goss to Munson, 136, December 16, 1859, Lib. 813, fol. 45, Suffolk County Registry of Deeds, Boston.

11. Goss to Colburn, October 1, 1858, Lib. 272, Fol. 298, Norfolk County Registry of Deeds, Dedham, Mass.

12. Colburn to Munson, March 21, 1860, Lib. 317, fol. 94, Norfolk County Registry of Deeds, Dedham, Mass.

13. Munson to Dudley, April 8, 1863, Lib. 317, fol. 95, Norfolk County Registry of Deeds, Dedham, Mass.

14. *Free Inhabitants of Upper Placerville, Eldorado County, California, United States Federal Census Records* (June 26, 1860), 883.

15. *Free Inhabitants of Ophir Township, Butte County, California, United States Federal Census Records* (June 26, 1870), 110.

16. *Salt Lake Tribune,* October 30, 1873, November 28, 1874, and October 6, 1875 (from UtahRails.net); Kate B. Carter, "Our Pioneer Heritage" (Salt Lake City: Daughters of Utah Pioneers, 1967), 150–151.

17. Daughters of Utah Pioneers, "News from the Settlements," *An Enduring Legacy,* 10, (Salt Lake City: Daughters of Utah Pioneers, 1987), 26–27.

18. Utah Directory, Salt Lake City, Logan, and Provo, Utah (1910).

19. *Evans & Early Mortuary Records,* September 30, 1904, Salt Lake City Utah; Death certificate, October 3, 1904, File no. 1976, Department of Health. State of Utah.

20. Fuller to Munson, July 27, 1860, Lib. 294, fol. 144, Norfolk County Registry of Deeds, Dedham Mass.

21. Freiermuth et al. to Munson (lease), November 5, 1860, Lib. 294, fol. 144; Kingsbury et al. to Munson, December 1, 1860, Lib. 294, fol. 145; David and Eliz-

abeth Mills to Norman C. Munson, December 8, 1860, all at Norfolk County Registry of Deeds, Dedham, Mass.

22. U.S. Department of the Interior, "Boston South, Massachusetts," 7.5 × 15 minute quadrangle, U.S. Geological Survey topographic map, 42071-C1-TM-025 (1987).

23. "Loading Gravel Trains," *Dollar Monthly Magazine* 19, April 1864, 260.

24. Ledger of the New York, New Haven, and Hartford Railroad, Case 4, vol. 149, Boston Water Power Company Documents, Baker Library Archives, Harvard University Business School, Boston.

25. Ibid. A possible candidate for this partnership is George Whitney, who in 1862 was a senior partner of Whitney, Bridges, and Long, Railroad Supplies, 38 Water Street, in Boston, and who had a house at 4 Billings Court, Newton Upper Falls.

26. *Acts of 1823*, chap. 34, 57–58; *Resolves of 1824*, chap. 26, 444–445.

27. Agreement between Boston and Roxbury Mill Corporation and William Henesy, March 20, 1845, Box 4 (1861–1882), Boston and Roxbury Mill Corporation Collection, Massachusetts Historical Society, Boston.

28. Nancy S. Seasholes, *Gaining Ground: A History of Landmaking in Boston* (Cambridge, Mass.: MIT Press, 2003), 174.

29. "Articles of Agreement made between Timothy Corcoran and John Lynch and the Boston and Roxbury Mill Corporation, Massachusetts Historical Society," Boston and Roxbury Mill Corporation Records, December 13, 1859, Box 3 (1835–1860).

30. Seasholes, *Gaining Ground,* 192.

31. Ibid.

32. Agreement between Norman C. Munson and Boston and Roxbury Mill Corporation, April 28, 1863, Boston and Roxbury Mill Collection.

33. Seasholes, *Gaining Ground,* 192.

34. Agreement between Norman C. Munson and Boston and Roxbury Mill Corporation, April 28, 1863.

35. John Souther file, Massachusetts Historical Society, Boston.

36. N. S. Shaler, "Notes on Glacial Moraines of the Charles River Valley, Near Watertown, April 20, 1870," *Boston Society of Nature History Proceedings* 13, (1869–1870): 278–279.

37. "Estimate of Expenses Moving Gravel from the Banks of Charles River in Brighton to Mill Dam or to a Wharf on the South Side of Main Street in Cambridge," August 10, 1869, Case 4, Boston Water Power Company Documents.

38. Town of Needham Records 7 (1861–1884), 49–50.

39. George Kuhn Clark, *History of Needham, Massachusetts, 1711–1911* (Cambridge, Mass.: Privately printed at the University Press, 1912), 422.

40. Avery to Munson, July 18, 1863, Lib. 316, fol. 63, Norfolk County Registry of Deeds, Dedham, Mass.

41. "Loading Gravel Trains," *The Dollar Monthly Magazine,* 260.

42. Myron A. Munson, *The Munson Record, A Genealogical and Biographical Account of Captain Thomas Munson and his Descendants* 2 (New Haven, Conn.: Munson Association, 1895) 932–933.

43. R. G. Dun and Company Collection 73, April 12, 1864, 319.

44. Ely to Munson, March 21, 1864, Lib. 324, fol. 186, Norfolk County Registry of Deeds, Dedham, Mass.

45. Ronald Dale Karr, *The Rail Lines of Southern New England: A Handbook of Railroad History* (Pepperell, Mass.: Branch Line Press, 1995), 288–289.

46. George Pierce Baker, *The Formation of the New England Railroad Systems* (Cambridge, Mass.: Harvard University Press, 1937), 47.

47. New York, New Haven, and Hartford Railroad case 3; New York and Boston Railroad, 1846–1886, vol. 149, case 3, Baker Library Archives, Harvard University Business School, Boston.

48. R. G. Dun & Co. Collection, vol. 73, p. 319, August 23, 1864; Munson to Crane, August 16, 1864, Lib. 327, fol. 298–299, Norfolk County Registry of Deeds, Dedham, Mass.

49. Crane to Munson, August 16, 1864, Lib. 327, fol. 232, and Crane to American Railroad Construction and Transportation Company, August 16, 1864, Lib. 327, fol. 231 both in Norfolk County Registry of Deeds, Dedham, Mass.; *Acts and Resolves of Massachusetts,* 1866, chap. 105, 68–69.

50. Benjamin G. and Henry C. Kimball of Needham to American Railroad Construction and Transportation Company, November 4, 1865, Lib. 337, fol. 36, Norfolk County Registry of Deeds, Dedham, Mass.

51. Avery to Munson, July 18, 1863, Lib. 316, fol. 63, Norfolk County Registry of Deeds, Dedham, Mass.

52. R. G. Dun & Co. Collection, Suffolk County, vol. 73, May 7, 1870 and May 14, 1870, 319.

53. *Massachusetts Senate Document no. 93,* February 1866; *Acts and Resolves of Massachusetts,* 1866, chap. 105, 68–69.

54. N. C. Munson Accounts, May 1, 1873; "Boston Water Power Company Back Bay Lands, 1852–1872," case 4, N.C. Munson Accounts, 1873–1880, Boston Water Power Company Documents.

55. Seasholes, *Gaining Ground,* 191.

56. Baker, *The Formation of the New England Railroad Systems,* 48; Karr, *The Rail Lines of Southern New England,* 289.

57. Seth Chandler, *History of the Town of Shirley, Massachusetts, from its Early Settlement to A.D. 1882* (Shirley, Mass.: pub. by the author, 1883), 47.

58. R. G. Dun & Co. Collection, vol. 73, p. 319, September 30, 1868.

59. Minute Books of the Commission on Public Lands, May 4, 1865.

60. Ibid., May 30, 1865.

61. Agreement between N. C. Munson and the Boston Water Power Com-

pany, May 1, 1863, case 1: Agreements, 1834–1880, Boston Water Power Company Documents.

62. N. Matthews, Boston Water Power Company, to Messrs Haven and Purdy, Commissioners of Public Lands, June 13, 1865, Boston Water Power Company Documents.

63. The Commissioners of Public Lands to Nathan Matthews, Esq., President of the Boston Water Power Company, June 11, 1865, Massachusetts Historical Society, Boston.

64. January 22, 1866, Boston Water Power Company Documents.

65. Minute Books of the Commission on Public Lands, September 23, 1866.

66. Ibid., June 5, 1867.

67. Ibid., November 7, 1867.

68. M. A. Munson, *The Munson Record,* vol. 2, 932; Karr, *The Rail Lines of Southern New England,* 201–203.

69. Oakman to Munson, November 17, 1868, Lib. 513, fol. 1057; see also Lib. 905, fol. 134 and Lib. 906, fol. 414, Middlesex County Registry of Deeds, Cambridge, Mass.

70. R. G. Dun & Co. Collection, vol. 73, p. 319, May 7, 1867.

71. Ibid., September 30, 1868.

72. *Boston Directory* for 1861, 1865, and 1866.

73. "Memorandum of an Agreement Made and Entered into at Boston, Massachusetts this ___ day of August 1869, by and between Norman C. Munson and Boston, Hartford and Erie Railroad Company," Part C, *Norman C. Munson v. Boston, Hartford and Erie Railroad, Massachusetts,* Reports on Papers and Briefs of the Supreme Judicial Court, vol. 120, Commonwealth of Massachusetts Superior Court, April Term, 1875, 81. (Note: the day's date in August 1869 was left out of the original document.

74. M. A. Munson, *The Munson Record,* vol. 2, 933.

75. "Memorandum of an Agreement Made and Entered into at Boston, Massachusetts the 24th day of October 1867, by and between Norman C. Munson and the Boston, Hartford and Erie Railroad Company," Part A.

76. "Fourth Count," *Norman C. Munson v. Boston, Hartford and Erie Railroads, Massachusetts,* 81.

77. George M. Woodruff, "A Brief History of the New York and New England Railroad," *Railroad and Locomotive Society Bulletin* 22 (May 1930), 57.

78. M. A. Munson, *The Munson Record,* vol. 2, 933.

79. N. C. Munson Accounts, Boston Water Power Company Papers, case 1, May 1, 1873.

80. R. G. Dun & Co. Collection, vol. 73, p. 319, March 12, 1870.

81. Contract between Norman C. Munson and the Boston Water Power Company, November 5, 1870, Lib. 1025, fol. 92, Suffolk County Registry of Deeds, Boston.

82. Seasholes, *Gaining Ground,* 198.

83. Ibid., 196, 198.

84. Boston and Maine Railroad Historical Society, *The Central Mass.,* (Reading, Mass.: Boston and Maine Railroad Historical Society, 1975), 6.

85. R. G. Dun & Co. Collection, vol. 73, p. 319, December 29, 1871.

86. John S. Eldridge to Norman C. Munson and Edward Thompson, Lib. 425, fol. 226, and John S. Eldridge, Jr. to Norman C. Munson and Edward Thompson, June 15, 1872, Lib. 425, fol. 227, both in Norfolk County Registry of Deeds, Dedham, Mass.

87. Edward Thompson to Norman C. Munson, December 13, 1873, Lib. 449, fol. 228, Norfolk County Registry of Deeds, Dedham, Mass.

88. Ezra G. Perkins to Norman C. Munson, May 8, 1876, Lib. 479, fol. 111, Norfolk County Registry of Deeds, Dedham, Mass.

89. U.S. Department of the Interior, "Map of the Norwood, Massachusetts Quadrangle, 1:25,000-scale metric topographic map," U.S. Geological Survey, 42071-B1-TM-025 (1985).

90. D. T. V. Huntoon, "Old Canton Landmarks, Fast Day Walk Continued," *Dedham Transcript,* May 20, 1876, 2.

91. N. C. Munson Accounts, 1873–1880, Boston Water Power Company Documents.

92. Seasholes, *Gaining Ground,* 196.

93. Norman C. Munson's contract with the City of Boston, November 27, 1871, case 4, Boston Water Power Company Documents.

94. Ibid.

95. Seasholes, *Gaining Ground,* 198.

96. Boston and Maine Railroad Historical Society, The Central Mass, 1975, 6.

97. R. G. Dun & Co. Collection, vol. 73, p. 318, June 28, 1873.

98. Seasholes, *Gaining Ground,* 196–197.

99. Agreement between William Woolley and the Mill Corporation, May 1872, box 4 (1861–1882), Papers of the Boston and Roxbury Mill Corporation, Massachusetts Historical Society.

100. February–May 1872, case 5: Reports of cars of gravel 1873–1874, Boston Water Power Company to Norman C. Munson, 1 May 1873, case 4, N. C. Munson Accounts 1873–1880, Boston Water Power Company Documents.

101. *History of Middlesex County, Massachusetts with Biographical Sketches of its Pioneers and Prominent Men,* vol. 3, ed. D. Hamilton Hurd (Philadelphia: J. W. Lewis, 1890), 100.

102. *City Document no. 90,* 1874, 4; *City Document no. 100,* 1875, 4–5; *Haven et al., Huntington Avenue Lands,* 5.

103. Seasholes, *Gaining Ground,* 198.

104. Ibid.

105. Ibid.

106. Haglund, *Inventing the Charles River,* 398.

107. Seasholes, *Gaining Ground,* 202.

108. Harl P. Aldrich & James R. Lambrechts, "Back Bay Boston II: Ground-water Levels," *Civil Engineering Practice* (Fall 1986): 37, 40.

109. Haglund, *Inventing the Charles River,* 394.

110. Seasholes, *Gaining Ground,* 202.

111. Ibid., 202, 206.

112. Karl Haglund, *Inventing the Charles River,* 224; Seasholes, *Gaining Ground,* 206.

113. Seasholes, *Gaining Ground,* 206.

7. Environmental Problems and Zoning (pages 155–186)

1. The water table is a level extending through the loose soil or fractured rock below which all the soil pores and fractures are filled with water and above which the soil pores and fractures are filled primarily with air.

2. Harl P. Aldrich, and James R. Lambrechts, "Back Bay Boston II: Ground-water Levels," *Civil Engineering Practice* (Fall 1986): 33.

3. Clifford A. Kaye, "Engineering Geologic Framework of the Boston Basin," in *Engineering Geology in New England, Session no. 74,* ed. Allen W. Hathaway, paper presented at the American Society Civil Engineers National Convention, Boston, April 2–6, 1979, 16.

4. B. F. Snow, "Tracing Loss of Groundwater," *Engineering News-Record,* (July 2, 1936): 1.

5. F. P. Stearns, "Report of the Engineer," *Report of the Joint Board Upon the Improvement of the Charles River, House Document no. 775,* April 1894, 28.

6. Minute Books of the Commission on the Back Bay, March 23, 1860, vol. 2, Massachusetts State Archives, Boston, 50.

7. E. R. Hoar, June 26, 1875, Boston Water Power Company Documents, Baker Library Archives, Harvard University Business School, Boston.

8. Minute Books of the Commission on the Back Bay, March 10, 1860, vol. 2, 42–44.

9. Minute Books of the Boston Alderman, 1859, City of Boston Archive.

10. Minute Books of the Commission on the Back Bay, August 16, 1859, vol. 2, 10.

11. Ibid., December 14, 1859, vol. 2, 14 and page opposite.

12. Ibid. July 2, 1860, vol. 2, 98.

13. Council Chamber, Boston, September 12, 1861.

14. Commissioners on Boston Harbor and the Back Bay, "Plan Shewing the Size and Structure of Sewers on, and North of, the Mill-dam," August 26, 1854, Lib. 675, fol. 134, Suffolk County Registry of Deeds, Boston, Mass.

15. *Massachusetts Senate Document no. 16, 1856,* 3.

16. *Indenture approved by Governor and Council Setting the Responsibilities of the Commonwealth of Massachusetts, the Boston Water Power Company, and the City of Boston,* February 9, 1865.

17. Harl P. Aldrich, Jr., and James R. Lambrechts, "Back Bay Boston, Part I: Groundwater Levels," *Civil Engineering Practice* (Fall 1986): 39.

18. Snow, "Tracing Loss of Groundwater," 5.

19. Eugene Hultman, "The Charles River Basin," *Proceedings of the Bostonian Society* (1940): 39.

20. Bainbridge Bunting, *The Houses of Boston's Back Bay* (Cambridge, Mass.: Belknap Press of Harvard University Press, 1962) 133–134.

21. Clarke, *Main Drainage Works of the City of Boston* (Boston: Rockwell and Churchville, City Printers, 1885), 13.

22. Ibid., 18–19.

23. Aldrich, and Lambrechts, "Back Bay Boston II: Groundwater Levels," 38.

24. Ibid., 38–39.

25. Clarke, *Main Drainage Works of the City of Boston,* 23–26.

26. Ibid., 79–82.

27. Aldrich and Lambrechts, "Back Bay Boston, Part II," 40.

28. L. B. Manley, "Boston Foundations—Discussion," *Boston Society of Civil Engineers Papers and Discussions* 1, no. 7, (September 1914): 406.

29. Bunting, *Houses of Boston's Back Bay,* figs. 183, 184 (273–274).

30. Ibid., fig. 16, 58.

31. Ibid., 275.

32. "*Encyclopaedia Brittanica,* s. v. Back Bay, Boston," 1896 ed., vol. 4.

33. *Boston City Directory,* 1860.

34. Henry S. Jacoby, and Roland P. Davis, *Foundations of Bridges and Buildings* (New York: McGraw-Hill, 1941), 78.

35. Ibid., 80.

36. Ibid., 84–85.

37. Ibid., 84.

38. Horace J. Howe, "Some Instances of Piles and Pile Driving, New and Old," *Journal of Engineering Societies* 11, no. 4 (April 1898): 303.

39. Rogers Building File, MIT Archives, Cambridge, Mass.

40. Edward F. Stevens, Clerk of Works, "Record of Piles Driven under New Building Boston Public Library, from the plans of McKim Mead & White Architects," Boston Public Library Archives, Boston.

41. "Photos of Works in Progress: August 1888–December 31, 1889," Boston Public Library Archive, Boston.

42. Stearns, "Report of the Engineer," 27.

43. P. K. Taylor and A. F. Brown, *Report on Groundwater Observation Wells for the Inspectional Services Department of the City of Boston and the Ground-*

water Trust, vol. I, (Boston: Stone and Webster Civil and Transportation Services, 1990), 4.

44. J. E. Cotton, and D. F. Delaney, "Groundwater Levels on Boston Peninsula, Massachusetts," *Hydrologic Investigations Atlas HA-513* (Reston, Va.: U.S. Geological Survey, 1975).

45. Aldrich and Lambrechts, "Back Bay Boston II: Groundwater Levels," 35–36.

46. Ibid., 33–34.

47. *U.S. Water News* (February 1986): 11.

48. Ibid.

49. Snow, "Tracing Loss of Groundwater," 4–5.

50. Harl P. Aldrich, Jr., "Preserving the Foundations of Older Buildings: The Importance of Groundwater Levels," *Technology and Conservation Magazine* 4, no. 2 (Summer 1979): 33.

51. Ibid.

52. "Chapter 1," *Introduction to Pile Foundations/Pile Foundation Design: A Student Guide,* 1999 <http://sbe.napier.ac.uk/projects/piledesign/guide/chapter1.htm>, 5.

53. *Franki Pile,* 1994 <http://www.geoforum.com/info/pileinfo/view.asp?ID=15>, 1–3.

54. Clifford A. Kaye, "Bedrock and Quaternary Geology of the Boston Area, Massachusetts," *Geological Society of America Reviews in Engineering Geology* 5, (1982): 37.

55. Ibid.

56. Kaye, "Bedrock and Quaternary Geology of the Boston Area," 37; Donald G. Ball, "Prudential Center Foundations," *Boston Society of Civil Engineers Journal* 49, (1962), 240–241.

57. Kaye, "Engineering Geologic Framework of the Boston Basin," 16.

58. L. B. Manley, *Boston Society of Civil Engineers Papers and Discussions* 1, no. 7 (September 1914): 406.

59. Clifford A. Kaye and Elso S. Barghoorn, "Late Quaternary Sea-Level Change and Crustal Rise at Boston, Massachusetts, with Notes on the Autocompaction of Peat," *Geological Society of America Bulletin* v. 75 (February 1964), 66–67.

60. Michael Southworth, and Susan Southworth, *The Boston Society of Architects A.I.A. Guide to Boston* (Chester Conn.: Globe Pequot Press, 1984), 228.

61. L. B. Manley, *Boston Society of Civil Engineers Papers and Discussions* 1, no. 7 (September 1914) 410–411.

62. John E. Ebel, "Major Historical Earthquakes in Northeastern North America and Their Effects in Boston," Paper presented at the Boston Environmental History Seminar, Massachusetts Historical Society, November 12, 2002, 11.

63. John E. Ebel, "The Seventeenth Century Seismicity of Northeastern North America," *Seismological Research Letters* 67, no. 3, May/June 1996, 54–55.

64. Ebel, "Major Historical Earthquakes," 12.

65. Ibid., 13–14.

66. Ibid., 14.

67. The epicenter is defined as the point on the Earth's surface (ocean in this case) that is located directly above the focus or the point source of an earthquake.

68. Ebel, "Major Historical Earthquakes," 14; Patrick J. Barosh, "The Hazard from Earthquakes in the Boston Area," *Civil Engineering Practice* 4, no. 1 (Spring 1989), 67.

69. "Largest Earthquake in Massachusetts: Cape Ann, Massachusetts, 1755 11 18 09:11:35 UTC, Intensity VIII," *USGS Earthquake Hazards Program* <http://neic.usgs.gov/neis/eq_depot/usa/1755_11_18.html>, 2003.

70. Ebel, "Major Historical Earthquakes," 14–15.

71. Ibid., p. 15.

72. Irving Crosby, *Boston through the Ages: The Geologic Story of Greater Boston* (Boston: Marshall Jones, 1928), 97.

73. John E. Ebel, "Major Historical Earthquakes," 17.

74. John W. Ebel, and Kathleen A. Hart, "Observational Evidence for Amplification of Earthquake Ground Motions in Boston and Vicinity," *Civil Engineering Practice* (Fall/Winter, 2001), 8.

75. Seismic intensity is a way of measuring or rating the effects of a given earthquake in different areas. It is based on the extent of the damage to man-made structures.

76. Ebel and Hart, "Observational Evidence for Amplification of Earthquake Ground Motions," 5–16.

77. Haley and Aldrich, Inc., "Isoseismal/Geologic Condition Maps for Eastern Massachusetts," unpublished report to the Massachusetts Civil Defense Agency, Framingham, Mass., 1983.

78. John E. Coster and Victor R. Baker, *Surficial Geology: Building with the Earth*, (New York: John Wiley 1981), 73.

79. Laurie G. Baise, and Charles M. Brankman, *Final Technical Report: Liquefaction Hazard Mapping in Boston, Massachusetts* (collaborative Research with William Lettis and Associates, and Tufts University), U.S. Geological Survey, National Earthquake Hazard Reduction Program Award Nos. 02HQGR0036 and 02HQGR0040, July 1, 2004, 1–57.

80. Ebel, "Major Historical Earthquakes," 20–21.

81. Massachusetts Emergency Management Agency, "Earthquakes in New England," second edition, 4.

82. Commonwealth of Massachusetts, *Massachusetts State Building Code*, 6th ed. (Boston: Massachusetts State Building Commission, 1998).

83. John E. Ebel, personal communication, August 2005.

84. *Harbor and Land Commissioners' Annual Report, Massachusetts Public Document no. 11*, 1884, 5.

85. Ibid.

86. Bunting, *Houses of Boston's Back Bay*, 250.

87. Ibid., 250–251.

88. *City Document* "Report of the Inspector of Buildings," *no. 12*, 1872, 9–10.

89. Ibid., 11.

90. Minute Books, of the State Commission on Public Lands, April 3, 1860, vol. 2, 58, Massachusetts State Archives, Boston. Emphasis not in original.

91. *Harbor and Land Commissioners' Annual Report, Massachusetts Public Document no. 11*, 1886, 30.

92. Ibid., 32.

93. Ibid., 46–47.

94. "*Harbor and Land Commissioners' Annual Report,*" *Massachusetts Public Document no. 11*, 1893, 21.

95. Ibid.

96. Bunting, *Houses of Boston's Back Bay*, 253.

97. Ibid., 252.

98. "*Harbor and Land Commissioners' Annual Report,*" *Massachusetts Public Document no. 11*, 1893, 21.

99. Ibid.

100. Bunting, *The Houses of Boston's Back Bay*, 253.

101. Ibid.

102. Ibid.

Index

Page references given in *italics* indicate illustrations or their captions.